COACHING IS CHAOS

JOHN KEAR

With Peter Smith

Coaching is Chaos
A Life in Rugby

Scratching Shed Publishing Ltd

First published by Scratching Shed Publishing Ltd in 2012
Registered in England & Wales No. 6588772.
Registered office:
47 Street Lane, Leeds, West Yorkshire. LS8 1AP

www.scratchingshedpublishing.co.uk

Reprinted January 2013

ISBN 978-0956804358

Rugby league photographs © rlphotos.com unless otherwise stated
Family and personal archive photographs © John Kear

A catalogue record for this book is available from the British Library.

Typeset in Warnock Pro Semi Bold and Palatino

Printed and bound in the United Kingdom by
CPI Group (UK) Ltd, Croydon, CR0 4YY

This book is dedicated to all who have influenced me, both in rugby league and also with the lessons of life as we journey through the years.

I am particularly grateful to my parents Herbert and Irene, my brother David and especially my wife, Dawn and my twins Alana and James, who have loved, supported and helped me through the tough times and hopefully enjoyed the good times.

Here's to lots more good times in years to come.

John Kear, October 2012.

Acknowledgements

There are several people I want to thank for their help over the course of my rugby career and during the production of this book.

Firstly I'd like to pay tribute to all the clubs where I've worked and all the people I have come across in the game. Obviously they are too numerous to mention by name, though some crop up in the following pages, but I am grateful to the administrators, all my fellow coaches past and present, members of the media - particularly the BBC and my current colleagues at Sky - and especially the players I have worked with.

Specifically for this book, thanks go to Phil, Tony and Ros at Scratching Shed Publishing Ltd; to the photographers who supplied pictures, particularly Dave Williams; to Andy Farrell for his foreword and to Stuart Martel and Janet Harrison for their valuable assistance. I'd also like to thank the staff at the Carnegie Café Bar at Headingley Stadium, which is a fantastic place to meet for a chat about rugby league.

Finally, thanks to my co-author Peter Smith, even if he did want to leave Chapter 11 out completely!

Contents

*

Foreword

By Andy Farrell OBE

*Former Wigan Warriors, England and
Great Britain rugby league captain.*

*Former Saracens and England rugby
union player; ex-Saracens head coach.*

Member of England RU coaching staff

MY first recollection of John Kear is hating his guts!

I thought I was going to get another Challenge Cup winner's medal in 1998. All we had to do was beat Sheffield Eagles in the final, and nobody gave them a chance against the Cup kings Wigan.

Unfortunately, everyone - us included - had reckoned without the John Kear factor. John was probably the only man in the country who really thought Sheffield were going to win; he came up with the perfect game plan, got his Eagles players fired up and they blew us away.

That was the day that made John famous. It was probably the biggest upset in rugby league history and it took me a while to forgive him for it.

Since then I have played under John at international level

and during his spell as assistant-coach of Wigan and I have nothing but admiration for someone who lives and breathes the sport.

He has developed a thoroughly deserved reputation as someone who is able to pull out fantastic results with limited resources, when it really counts in big games. He is an excellent coach and - just as important - also a very good guy. He has been involved in rugby league coaching for three decades now and you don't have such longevity in a sport like that without a, exceptional knowledge and b, being able to manage people and get the best out of them.

John has both and that is illustrated by how long he has been in the game and the number of clubs he has had. To be able to go from one club to another like he has done, you have to be someone special.

For an ex-winger - they are not noted as the most ferocious of rugby league players - John is an outstanding motivator and I have come to know two sides to him.

One is the calm, authoritative, unflappable character, who is able to get his message across clearly and calmly during team meetings and in front of the TV cameras when he's working for Sky Sports.

But he also has an emotional streak. One thing I remember he would always tell us before games was: 'Go out and bray them' - bray being the Yorkshire word for 'smash'.

John has a real passion for the game of rugby league and his ability to get that across to his players has been one of the secrets of his success.

I was delighted when John asked me to contribute the foreword to this book and I wish him the very best in his new venture as an author.

Andy Farrell, October 2012

Outstanding motivator - John Kear

*

Introduction

YOU know the saying about swans? How they look very serene gliding along on the surface, but underneath they are paddling like mad? Coaching is a bit like that; it might look like everything is plain sailing, but it rarely is.

That's why I've called this book *Coaching is Chaos*, because that is exactly what I do for a living. I manage chaos. When you start your coaching career the first thing you get taught is how to run a training session safely; then you are told about methods of developing techniques and tactics; then team structures, the way each individual has got a role within a team and how to develop that.

It's quite scientific, which is all well and good, but it's not the nitty and gritty, it's not what makes a good coach. That, in my opinion, is being able to think outside the box and to react to what's happening in front of you. Every coach needs to understand and be able to handle the basics I've just outlined. Coaching is about performance - you have to analyse that performance in order to improve, practice and then put everything into action.

It's like a wheel that goes around and that would be fantastic if you were dealing with robots. Maybe in 100 years that's how sport will be played, but at the moment we deal with human beings and when you throw a human element into anything, science and the textbooks can go out of the window. It becomes an art form.

The essence of coaching in my opinion is being able to react to what's happening in front of you and when you are dealing with a group, or a team, the potential for things going wrong is almost limitless. Over three different decades as a rugby league coach I think I have been challenged in almost every way possible; some positive and joyous, others tragic.

A scientific, textbook approach is fine, but you have to have a human element within that. In a nutshell, you need to know how to deal with people. It's the human element which throws all the structures, systems and theory into chaos. That's the most fascinating aspect of coaching for me and it's why not everybody can be a good coach; you have to have an empathy with people and a feel for the group.

Great coaches have to be able to deal with individuals, groups and rapidly changing situations. We all do it differently and no two coaches are the same, but it's the ability to react and adapt that makes the top coaches stand out from the rest.

You'll read a few examples over the forthcoming pages, but here's one from a game I was involved in when I was in charge of Wakefield Trinity Wildcats. We were playing my old team Hull, coached by Richard Agar, in a game at Belle Vue in the summer of 2011.

The first half was close and we went in at the break just 16-12 behind. At that stage I think both Richard and I would have been relatively happy, feeling the game was still there to be won if our players stuck to what we'd talked about and practiced. One of Hull's key players was the centre, Kirk Yeaman. He'd been having some success and had scored a try in the opening 40 minutes, but sometimes things happen which throw the gameplan and all the theory out of the window.

How would you react if, during the half-time break, one of your star players - in this case Kirk Yeaman - had an epileptic fit in the changing rooms, as you were delivering your team talk? Well, that's the situation Richard found himself in that afternoon. He can't, at any stage in his coaching education, have expected something like that to happen. The situation was pretty serious for a while, but fortunately Hull, like all Super League clubs, have a first class medical team and they managed to get Kirk stabilised and out of any danger.

But Richard still had a game to win. There's only 10 minutes between halves and in that time he had to deal with Kirk's illness, get his players settled and focused with their minds back on the job and come up with a way of coping with the loss of one of his main men, plus a substitution he hadn't been bargaining on.

Hull were a left-sided attacking team and they'd lost one of their main strike weapons, in chaotic and deeply disturbing circumstances. You can't learn how to handle that sort of thing from textbooks, it is all about dealing with the here and now. I don't know how exactly Richard dealt with it, but he obviously got things right because Hull went on to win the game 52-18.

Richard and his players coped and we didn't. I was quite close to Kirk from our time working together at Hull and we had a couple of ex-Hull players in our line-up, who were mates of his. What happened knocked us off our stride, we were distracted and we lost the game. Hull used it as a positive - let's go out and win this game for Kirk - and we allowed it to get to us.

That was a lesson learned, though obviously you hope you don't have to deal with situations like that too many times in a career. Fortunately, Kirk made a full recovery and earned a testimonial season in 2013, but that illustrates the sort of unexpected circumstances which can be thrown at any coach at any time. I've had more than my fair share during my career and I've handled some of them better than others.

I don't have many regrets from my lifetime in rugby league, but there are things I would change if I possibly could. Obviously there are bad results and bad performances I'd like to put right, but what happened to Kirk that afternoon illustrated that rugby is, after all, only a game.

Rugby league means the world to me, but when all is said and done there are more important things happening out there and that message was brought home to me and everyone involved in the sport during a tragic few months beginning in the autumn of 2008....

1
✳
Adam and Leon

THE worst day of my career had nothing really to do with rugby. It didn't even happen during the season, but the effects were far more upsetting, devastating even, than any of the many defeats, bad performances or sporting setbacks I have experienced as a player or coach.

On October 13, 2008, I had just returned to the office after a couple of weeks' holiday, following the end of the season. I was coach of Wakefield Trinity Wildcats at the time and things had been going reasonably well. Training wasn't due to resume until the start of November and the players were all away resting and recuperating from a hard eight-month campaign. It is usually a quiet time, chance to catch up on some paperwork and start planning for the new year.

It was completely out of the blue that I received a 'phone call to say Adam Watene, Wildcats prop and senior player, had collapsed during a fitness session at a local gym. And his situation wasn't looking good.

While they are on their off-season break the players are

all given a schedule to complete, to ensure they maintain their fitness levels until official training resumes. Adam was no different, but being the sort of bloke - and professional - he was, he had got a little group sorted. They were going to the gym together rather than training on their own, just to enjoy each other's company and because it is easier to keep motivated when you are with a few of your mates. Then-Wakefield players Dale Ferguson and Sam Obst were part of the group, along with Darrell Griffin, who began his rugby league career with Wakefield before moving on to Huddersfield Giants and later Leeds Rhinos.

That stunning phone call was a total shock and even now I can clearly remember the tension in the office while we waited for more news and an update on Adam's condition. Nigel Wright, an ex-player who was my assistant-coach at the time, had been in the gym when Adam was taken ill and he was the one who contacted me.

It was one of those moments you dread when Nigel told me Adam had stopped breathing. I asked if he had been pronounced dead and Nigel told me not at that point. I felt I had to do something, so I rushed to the hospital where Adam had been taken, along with Richard Tunningley, who was our scholarship manager in those days.

When we arrived we found the players who had been at the gym with Adam sitting in a room, on their own, totally shocked. A doctor then pulled me to one side and told me they had lost him. That is something that will stay with me for the rest of my days.

It was devastating, totally and utterly. The first thing I did was go outside, because I needed a moment on my own. When I went back to where the players were gathered, nobody could speak. There was an eerie silence and an overpowering feeling of shock and disbelief.

The only thing I could think of to ask the specialist was

'why?'. Obviously at that early stage, before all the tests had been carried out, there wasn't much he could say. His reply is something else that has remained with me. He just said: 'Why is the sky blue?'

In a strange way, that was a comfort, because obviously I was wondering about training methods and so on. Straight away, you get that nagging doubt: Was there anything I could have done to prevent this, or is there anything we have been doing that contributed? It was quite reassuring that the doctor didn't think that was the case. Maybe that's a selfish reaction, but I suppose it's human nature.

The next person I saw was Adam's wife Moana. Obviously she was in bits and clearly struggling to come to terms with the news. She was sitting down outside the hospital, utterly stunned and totally distraught. Adam and Moana had two children, Arana, who was 10 at the time, and Ena, four. Unless you have experienced something like that - and I truly hope you haven't - I don't think anyone can fully appreciate how they must have felt.

It was one of the worst days of my life and it is still a very vivid and raw memory. It has taken some coping with and even now, several years afterwards, it is something I still think about and which I struggle to come to terms with. Adam was a young fella, 31 years of age. He was very fit, he looked after himself and he was an absolute gentleman and a family man.

Adam's relatives, many of whom lived on the other side of the world, were the hardest hit, naturally. But to the group of people in the Wakefield changing room, it really did feel like a death in the family. When you are part of a professional sports team, you spend most of your time with the people you work with. You are together every day of the week, you eat together, go away together, do battle together and share each other's hopes, aspirations and disappointments. Inevitably, you do become very close.

Coaching is Chaos

Adam was one of the leaders in our group. He wasn't outspoken or particularly vocal; he led through actions rather than words, but he was a big influence, on his fellow players and the rest of the staff. I always knew I could chat to him and put a point to him and if he said 'sweet, mate' you'd know you were all right. If not, he'd come up with an alternative to the course of action you had planned. He was somebody you could confide in and I liked and respected him a great deal.

Adam had been at Wakefield from day one of my time there in 2006, when the club were in crisis and - it seemed to everyone outside the four walls at least - heading for relegation, which I think would probably have finished them for good as a Super League concern. Adam was instrumental in keeping Wakefield up that year; he was an absolute tower of strength, so the club owes him a lot.

The year after the relegation scare he swept the board at Wakefield's awards night, taking the honours voted for by the players and the coaches' prizes as well. That showed how highly thought of he was. One of my abiding memories of him is after that awards night. His father had flown over from New Zealand and was thrilled to bits by the acclaim his son received. I have got a photograph of them shaking hands and the pride and love on both sides is clear to see. Tragically Adam's dad died midway through the following year.

Adam flew home for the funeral and came back a couple of weeks later, in time for our Millennium Magic game against Castleford in Cardiff. Fittingly, Adam scored one of our tries that day and I remember him pointing upwards to heaven as he celebrated the touchdown. Within months Adam had joined his dad. The mental image I have got is of a proud dad and a loving son and within the space of a year they had both been taken away.

That is what really brings it home to me. It wasn't the loss of a talented, inspirational rugby player, it was the passing of a devoted, much-loved family man and, at such a young age, it all seemed very unfair. Adam's family, his wife and young children, coped admirably and I was very proud to be associated with both the Wakefield club and the sport as a whole in the immediate aftermath and the ensuing year.

There was a memorial service for Adam at Wakefield Cathedral a couple of weeks after his death. That was held on the same day as his funeral, in New Zealand. I spoke at the service, as did the mayor of Wakefield, Jacqui Williams. Adam had been consort to the deputy mayor, Heather Hudson, which I think reflects how highly he was thought of in the area.

Now when Wakefield play Castleford the winners receive the Adam Watene Trophy. That is a really nice touch and means Adam is going to be remembered for years to come, which he deserves to be. Supporters began the Adam Watene Fund, which was backed by the club and raised valuable money for his family, who had lost their main breadwinner.

I thought the club dealt with everything following Adam's passing with a great deal of dignity, respect, sympathy and genuine warmth, which was a fitting tribute to Adam. The first couple of weeks afterwards was a very sombre period, but life has to go on and we were soon back in pre-season training, which obviously was another very difficult time. Normally, it is one of my favourite parts of the year; a rugby league club when the players are away on their annual break is a very quiet place.

Usually when they come back they energise their surroundings and all the other people who work there. It becomes a bouncy, bubbly environment and it is great to be in and around the joint. It's like the *Mary Celeste* when the players are away and it feels as though the club has been reborn when they come back, but it wasn't like that this time.

Though I have vivid memories of the day I received the news about Adam, I can't remember much about the first week the players were back, it was just a blur. It was very difficult to get them into their regular routine; though I tried to create a sense of normality, it was anything but and in fact it was the strangest set of circumstances you could have.

It is a credit to the coaching staff, the club and, probably most of all, the players, how they handled it and managed to come through the other side. We went on to have Wakefield's best Super League season so far and although there's no way I would ever want to use tragedy as an inspiration, I do think it had that sort of effect on the players, especially the ones who had been very close to Adam.

Jason Demetriou typified that. Jason is primarily a centre or loose-forward and the previous year his squad number was 13, reflecting his favoured playing position. After Adam died he asked to wear the number eight jersey, which was Adam's number. Eight is a number normally worn by a front-rower. JD hardly missed a game that season, playing in a lot of pain for much of the time due to various injuries. There were occasions when he should have sat matches out because he was having problems with his knees and other parts of his body, but he insisted on playing on. I know Adam was one of his driving forces. Our half-back/hooker Sam Obst felt the same way, maybe even more so because he was there when Adam died.

None of us at Wakefield expected to be involved in something like that again, but incredibly and tragically, just as everyone was getting back on their feet, we found ourselves in a similar situation only five months later.

Our first game after Adam's death was against Leeds

Rhinos at Headingley Carnegie Stadium on Boxing Day, 2008. We won 22-16 and one of the players who made his first appearance in the senior team that morning was a young back-rower named Leon Walker.

Leon was a Leeds lad who had played youth rugby for Churwell Chiefs before a spell in the Rhinos' highly-respected academy set-up. He then moved on to Salford City Reds and we picked him up from there. He hadn't played a first team game and was not a member of our full-time group, but youth boss Tony Drury was instrumental in bringing him to Wakefield and I remember him saying: 'If you give this kid a chance, he might well force his way into the senior squad.'

On March 22, 2009, we were due to play Celtic Crusaders at Brewery Field, in Bridgend, south Wales, in a Sky-televised Super League game. It started out as a normal match day; we went through our usual pre-game routine, pulled up at the ground and did what we normally do: all the kit was unpacked, the players wandered on to the field and then my phone rang.

The message was that there were problems at the reserve game our under-21s were playing, a few miles away at Maesteg. A player, Leon Walker, had been badly hurt. Initially I tried to keep it away from the first team members, because I didn't know exactly what had happened. It was clear it was something very serious, but at that stage I thought the match was going on and I didn't want anything to interfere with preparations for the Super League game, which was rapidly looming. That changed when I got the news Leon had died.

Here I want to pay tribute to the match referee Steve Ganson, to Neville Smith, who is Sky TV's rugby league producer, and to the RFL. I spoke to Steve and to Nev, to ask 'what are we going to do'? They were both first class. Steve said: 'If you don't feel you can play, the game's off.' Nev made it clear there was no pressure whatsoever from Sky, despite the fact they were due to broadcast two hours of live action that evening and there'd be a huge gap to fill in their schedule if we didn't take to the field. Both Steve and Nev said straight away that what had happened was far more important than a game of rugby league, a television programme or indeed anything else.

Realistically, there was only one course of action. The news filtered through to the players pretty quickly and there is no way they could have gone out there and played. The reserves' game had been abandoned after Leon collapsed and so they came straight over to Brewery Field. We could all see how shocked they were. These were young men remember, most of them were in their teens. You shouldn't have to deal with the death of a mate at that age. One of the few older players in the side, Sam Obst, was particularly badly hit. He had been coming back from injury in the second team and was on the field when Leon passed away. Having been with Adam at the time of his death less than half a year earlier, he was deeply, deeply shocked.

Again, nobody could believe it. Five months ago, we had been devastated, knocked sideways, by what had happened to Adam. We had attempted to come to terms, life was beginning to return to normal and then it happened again. I remember going into the Sky TV van; Eddie Hemmings and Mike 'Stevo' Stephenson, their commentary team, were there and I just broke down in front of them. I had been trying to keep composed, but I couldn't. I am still emotional thinking about it now. It is difficult, because when you lead a group you try to be strong, assured and confident and I felt anything but. It was unbelievable for two tragedies to happen to the same club in such a short space of time.

The game was called off and Sky showed a rerun of the

previous season's Grand Final, after an announcement to say there would be no live match due to circumstances beyond their control. The RFL then faced the job of trying to keep the news under wraps while Leon's poor parents and family were informed. Quite a number of Wakefield fans had made the long trip and Crusaders supporters were arriving at the ground as well, but everyone behaved impeccably.

For us, it was a long coach ride home and I can't remember anyone saying a word the entire time; it was complete silence. Everyone was lost in his own thoughts. I hope this doesn't sound too selfish, but I know we were all thinking the same thing: why us? What followed was another incredibly traumatic, terrible week. Leon's family, who are very nice people, were first class. They remained dignified throughout what must have been an unbearably difficult time and I think and hope the club supported them fully.

It was a slightly different situation this time. When Adam died we had a few months to come to terms with it, but just six days after Leon's death we had another game, at home to St Helens, again in front of the Sky cameras. I love rugby league and I am as enthusiastic about the game now as I was when I was five and six, operating the scoreboard at the Wheldon Road ground, in my home town of Castleford. I will watch any game, anywhere and at any time, but that was one day when I didn't want to be involved in a rugby league match and I certainly didn't want to coach it. The other staff felt the same and the last thing the players wanted to do was put their boots on and play for 80 minutes.

It was the same for St Helens, who must have felt as though they were intruding on private grief. It was without a doubt the most emotional game I have ever attended and the tone was set by a tribute to Leon on the big screen, before the players came out for a minute's silence. Everyone, including me, watched the tribute, which was deeply moving. There was a crowd of 6,038 there that night and you could have heard a pin drop. I am not exaggerating, there wasn't a word spoken for something like 12 minutes. People still tell me it is the most surreal atmosphere they have ever experienced at a sporting event.

That was the major part of the night. We lost the match that followed 42-18, but that was insignificant. Saints didn't want to be there, but they are professionals; they played and got through it and I am sure all they wanted to do then was get away.

When you get something like the death of a player - thankfully very rarely, though there have been a number of tragedies in recent years - it shows the strength of rugby league: the entire sport rallied round. There was a minute's silence, perfectly observed, at all the other games played that weekend, tributes poured in and fund-raising campaigns were started.

There was great support from people concerned with Leon and Adam, the club and their families, but the backing we received from the game in general was deeply moving, from people who didn't know Adam and hadn't really heard of Leon, who hadn't played a competitive first team game. It showed that people really do care, for the ones who have suffered such a sad loss and also for those involved.

The Salford team attended Leon's funeral and there were players present from just about every club in the game, most of whom didn't know the lad. They just wanted to show their solidarity and that is something I will never forget. Crusaders handled a difficult situation very well and their medical staff were first class. One of the people I felt for most was our reserve team physio Claire Spiers. We had to persuade her to carry on in the sport because during the immediate aftermath she said 'that's it, I'm not going on to a rugby league field again', which I can quite understand.

Once all the enquiries had been done and it was clear the on-field procedures had been followed to the letter, I think she managed to come to terms with what had happened. Very bravely, in my opinion, she did carry on, but for a long time, she questioned whether, one, she wanted to be involved in the game, two, she wanted to stay at Wakefield and three, she wanted to set foot on a rugby league pitch.

I can fully appreciate what Claire went through, but I never questioned my own involvement in the game. The two incidents, involving Adam and Leon, were totally separate and neither could have been predicted. It might have been different if they had been impact injuries; then you would have to wonder if the sport at professional level is getting too tough. There would be a case for questioning is it too brutal or physical and do we demand too much from our players? But both players died of heart failure and Adam hadn't been playing a game at the time he collapsed.

Adam was 31, he was full-time and he died in the gym. Leon was 19, part-time and died on the field of play. The circumstances were entirely separate and there was no common thread, other than they were both Wakefield players.

Lessons can be learned though and I know the RFL and individual clubs, including Wakefield, are looking at player screening, to try to detect any heart problems. At Wakefield after the two deaths we put the players through a more rigorous pre-season screening than we had before. I will admit we were a bit jittery and we would do anything to prevent something like that happening again. No good can come out of the deaths of two such young men, but if lives are saved in the future that might be some comfort to Adam's and Leon's families.

Coaching is Chaos

I'm not sure the word cursed is appropriate, but it did feel like there was a shadow over the club around that time. Earlier in 2008, the club lost one of its all-time greats in David Topliss, who had won the Lance Todd Trophy as Wembley man of the match when Trinity lost to Widnes in the 1979 Challenge Cup final. David also played for Hull and Great Britain and was a legend in the game. I never played with David, but I played against him and he was someone I knew very well. He was a big supporter of Wakefield and he had been a spectator at a game a couple of days before he passed away.

He collapsed and died after playing five-a-side football one evening, which was a huge shock to everyone. Whenever anyone organised a touch and pass tournament, David would be there. If you took a hundred 58-year-olds at random and tested their fitness, I am sure he would have been in the top two, at any test you like.

Not only that, but Don Fox, another Wakefield hero and their man of the match in the 1968 Challenge Cup final, also passed away in 2008 and then we discovered that a routine operation on one of then current player Jamie Rooney's knees almost had a fatal outcome.

Jamie went in for minor surgery, a straightforward clean-out, the sort dozens of sportsman undergo every week. For some reason his heart actually stopped beating during the procedure, though thankfully he went on to make a full recovery, with no ill-effects. That was another chilling situation during a terrible year. You had to wonder, what have we done as a club and a group to deserve this?

I hope no club ever has to go through a year like it, but the strength of the club and the sport shone through. Throughout all the heartbreak, I was proud to be associated with both.

2

*

A Cas Kid

I WAS born into rugby league, at 41 Wheldon Road, on the same street as Castleford Tigers' famous old ground. We later moved to 33 Wheldon Road, even nearer to the 'stadium', though that's a pretty grand word for it. We moved from the middle of the terrace to the end, about four houses away from the Early Bath, a famous pub for supporters before and after games.

In those days - I was born on November 25, 1954 - it was called the Bath Inn, but I suppose they changed the name when the BBC commentator Eddie Waring's 'early bath' catch phrase became popular. One of the country's top amateur teams, Lock Lane, were based there for many years, so this was a real rugby league heartland.

You could walk down Wheldon Road from the town centre and on the right there'd be Princess Street and then the ground and then the training field. It hasn't changed much since I was a young lad, though the club are currently hoping to move to a new out-of-town site at Glasshoughton, near the M62 motorway, to ensure they meet the minimum standards for being in Super League.

You could, with a strong wind behind you, literally kick a football from our house to the ground and, not surprisingly, I seemed to spend most of my young life there. In those days rugby league was very much a part-time sport and all the players had jobs, so they trained at night. I used to go along to watch with a group of my mates. If the team were training there would always be practice balls lying around, so we would grab one and have a game on some spare land next to the training pitch. They park cars there on match days now, but when I was young it was gravel and ash and we used to play tig and pass. We'd also watch the players train and hang around them before and afterwards, getting in their way.

It was very exciting for a young kid and it meant I grew up with rugby league in my blood. My brother David was the Wheldon Road scoreboard attendant and he used to take me with him to games, to help out. I have got a programme from Castleford's home derby against Featherstone Rovers on May 1, 1961. That was Cas' last game of the season and it was a re-arranged fixture after the match had been postponed on Easter Tuesday due to snow. I can't say I remember anything about the game itself, but I get a mention in the programme, on the back page. Thanking everyone who helped out at the club over the course of the campaign, the article by Cas secretary Len Garbett adds: 'This includes our scorer, 14-year-old David Kear, who stands on that draughty scoreboard in all weathers. David is helped by his 5-year-old brother John, complete with hot water bottle tucked under his shirt.'

The article got my age wrong - I was actually six - but the bit about my improvised heating system was true. It was a long time before summer rugby came along and winters seemed to be a lot colder in those days, so it was the best method my mum knew of preventing me freezing to death. Working on the scoreboard was my first job in rugby league and it certainly helped with my adding up. I have always been pretty good at maths and I think assisting our David on the scoreboard at Wheldon Road contributed to that. I am certainly very adept at counting in twos (for a goal), threes (a try) or fives (try and a conversion), as it was in those days.

I grew up watching Castleford; I used to go to first team games, 'A' team games - as reserve matches were known - and training nights. It was a marvellous upbringing and my rugby league education didn't just take place at weekends and in the evenings.

I went to Wheldon Lane Junior School, which is where Roger Millward, one of the sport's greatest-ever players, had been a pupil, though he was there well before my time. It was a rugby league school and that meant I played the sport in some organised form from the age of seven upwards.

I was one of the fortunate ones to pass my 11-plus exam, so I went on to Castleford Grammar School. Like at most grammar schools the sport there was rugby union, but there was never any chance of me losing my love of rugby league. I played union at school and then junior rugby league in my spare time. Castleford Grammar was a strong union school and we had some tough battles with our local rivals, Normanton Grammar and King's School, Pontefract. It still seems strange to me that even in the most die-hard rugby league area, the grammar schools played union.

When you live and are brought up in Castleford, a strong dislike of Leeds Rugby League Club (now the Rhinos) is inbuilt. Leeds are regarded as the big city neighbours, a glamour club with a reputation for high-spending and for snatching our - Castleford's - best players.

Cas have other rivalries, with Wakefield and

Coaching is Chaos

Featherstone for example, but if they can beat Leeds it is always regarded as a highlight of the season. Even now, I still like to turn over the Rhinos and not just because over the last few years they have been one of the top teams.

Now, this might shock a few people who understand the rivalry between Cas and Leeds, but for a short time I was actually a Leeds player. It is a bit of a guilty secret. In the early days of my rugby career, when I was playing at under-17 level, I was a half-back and Cas had a good one of those who was keeping me out of the team. So for a while I went over to play for Leeds under-17s.

I sometimes used to travel with Steve Ferres, another Cas boy made good. He played for Bradford Northern - among others - and was a successful coach with Huddersfield and Hunslet. Steve later played a very significant part in one of the biggest moves of my coaching career, when I joined Wakefield Trinity Wildcats and after that he finally landed his 'dream job' as chief executive at the Tigers.

Steve had a Reliant Robin, which a 16-year-old with a provisional licence could drive in those days. The reason for that was they were so under-powered. We used to get overtaken by pushbikes.

Leeds had taken on a few lads I knew, like Les Dyl and Keith Worsley and Keith Voyce, who is my cousin. He was a hooker and ended up at Dewsbury, taking over from Mike Stephenson - now better known as Sky Sports' rugby league pundit Stevo - when he left to play in Australia. But despite the familiar faces at Leeds I only lasted a handful of games. It just wasn't for me; I couldn't settle there and I didn't like it, so I ended up going back home to Castleford and playing for their under-17s.

I used to play rugby union for my school on Saturday mornings and league for the Castleford under-17s the same afternoon. We talk about over-playing now, but in those days I just couldn't get enough, whether it was touch (tig) and pass, union or league. I simply loved being in and around that environment, which is something that has never left me and I hope never will.

I must have watched hundreds of Cas games from the age of five until I left to go to Leicester College at 18. I suppose other communities, like St Helens or Widnes for example, might claim the same thing, but in my opinion there is nowhere in the world that revolves around rugby league quite like Castleford does. It is the lifeblood of the town, even more so since the death of the mining industry; league has done a lot for the area and the area has given a lot back.

One of the great innovations in recent years has been the Champion Schools tournament, which involves hundreds of teams - boys' and girls' - from up and down the country, including the midlands, the south and Wales. It's the biggest rugby league competition in the world, with the finals all being staged on Wembley weekend.

Thousands of children take part, but schools from Castleford regularly dominate, which illustrates perfectly the strength of the sport in the town. Castleford or Airedale High seem to be involved in most of the finals every year. That's something I am very proud of.

In my day Wheldon Lane Junior School would play their matches on Cas' practice pitch, so that shows how closely linked everything was. We used to play Ashton Road, Redhill and Airedale Junior Schools, who all had very strong teams. Unfortunately, even in Castleford, the amount of rugby league being played in schools has declined, but in those days it was central to everything. Junior schools didn't play soccer, they played league. You followed league because you were born in Castleford and that's what everybody else did.

Coaching is Chaos

My dad, Herbert, played half a dozen games for Castleford just after the war, which is something else I am very proud of. I think there has been only about eight father and son dynasties who have played for Cas. Dad was a coal man - delivering rather than mining - and I used to help him on his rounds during the school holidays. I would hold the sacks while he filled them with coal, then I'd sit in the lorry with him while he went out and about delivering. There wasn't much weight training at the time, but that can't have done my upper body strength any harm.

I don't want to sound like an old fogey, but that's how life was in those days. It revolved around the family, playing out with your mates and rugby league. Obviously, we didn't have all the gadgets kids have nowadays and I think we were better for it. There is a plus side to modern technology, I love laptops and Kindles and email, but I don't think it helps develop social skills and community spirit.

Sadly, I think the way lifestyles have changed has had a negative effect on all sports, including rugby league. All the coaching in the world couldn't have developed Roger Millward, he was moulded into a great player by games of tig and pass on the streets in and around Wheldon Lane and on the local recreation ground.

Although he made his name elsewhere, with Hull KR, Roger is one of Castleford's favourite sons. He was catapulted to fame playing in a Sunday afternoon under-16 town competition, which was broadcast live on ITV. Every time Cas were on you could guarantee that Roger would capture the viewers' imagination with his unique skills. He was a great player and it is a shame for Cas that he was coming through at a time when they had two established, world-class half-backs in Alan Hardisty and Keith Hepworth. Without those two in the way he would have gone on to become probably the club's best-ever player.

Instead, the Cas board decided three into two wouldn't go and they sold Roger to Hull KR for £6,000, which must have been the greatest bargain of all time.

Rugby league was and still is my great passion, but I am fortunate I also managed to combine that with my academic work. I liked school; I wasn't one of those kids who had to be kicked out of bed and dragged to lessons. I enjoyed going and I am grateful to the teachers at Wheldon Lane for all their support and encouragement. I remember in particular Mr Belwood, Miss Bullough, Miss Fenton and the head teacher Mr Harrison. They had a massive influence at the infant and junior schools and they helped me pass the 11-plus, which was something only two of us in our year did.

I was proud of that and so were my mum and dad. I don't think I was necessarily brighter than anyone else or I was academically gifted in any way, but I enjoyed the work and I liked the environment and I didn't mind rolling my sleeves up and doing a bit of work. When you enjoy doing something, you become better at it. That applies to rugby as much as schooling.

Sometimes sport and education clashed, like the time Cas played Hull KR in a midweek Challenge Cup replay, in March, 1967. Jack Austin scored the winning try and I'm happy to say I was there to see it, though I paid a painful price.

My dad was adamant I wasn't going to the game, as - at a time before floodlights - it was played during an afternoon and it would have meant missing school. I was equally determined to be there. I went home for lunch in those days and to make sure I went back to school my dad - who was taking the afternoon off to watch the match - drove me back to the entrance in his coal lorry. He dropped me off and watched as I walked through the school gates.

As he drove off I kept on walking, went right the way

through the school grounds, climbed the fence at the far end and then nipped over the railway line and into Wheldon Road. I went into the club secretary Len Garbett's office, took my grammar school tie off and then donned my big coat, so nobody could see I was wearing a school uniform. Len, who knew my parents, was a bit suspicious, but I assured him they had said it was all right, so off I went to do my usual duty on the scoreboard.

There was a huge crowd that day, officially 22,582, but it was reckoned another 8,000 got in for free when some fencing collapsed. At the time the scoreboard was at the Wheldon Road end of the ground, which was uncovered. I remember being amazed by the size of the crowd. Most of the town's population must have been there and you can probably guess who, out of all those people, the first person I clapped eyes on was. I suppose my dad must have known I would find a way to get there, but he wasn't best pleased when he looked up and saw me up on the scoreboard. I got a good hiding later for bunking off from school, but Cas won and it was well worth it.

I finished school with seven 'O' Levels and three 'A' Levels and, after a childhood in Castleford, I went off into the outside world, to Leicester College of Education to study to be a teacher. We had a great lecturer called Will Sharp, who was a big influence on me. He was a Wakefield fella, by a strange coincidence and he instilled old-fashioned Yorkshire values into a teaching philosophy. I've taken those values not only into teaching, but also into life and, of course, my coaching and playing career. Basically, that is so long as you work hard and you are honest with yourself and others around you, you will achieve. I don't think that's a bad philosophy at all.

Leicester isn't a rugby league hot bed; in fact, it is one of rugby union's great strongholds. Naturally when I was at college I played union for them on Wednesday afternoons, which was the time set aside for sport, but whenever I came back home I played league for Castleford under-19s and when I was 20, Castleford offered to sign me on. Malcolm Reilly, another Cas legend, was coach in those days and Len Garbett did the recruiting.

He said they would like me to sign, but my dad said no; he wanted me to finish my degree first. Len was great, he said they'd leave me at college and let me finish my studies, but I could come back up to Yorkshire in holiday time and play for the reserves. Nowadays, clubs have academies and youth set-ups and players are encouraged to base rugby league around their education, but Cas pioneered that 35 years ago. They even gave me the okay to play union on a Wednesday afternoon and this was 20 years before that sort of thing became commonplace, when the 15-a-side game went openly professional. In theory, anyone who played any form of league was deemed to be professional and therefore banned for life from the union code, though I never got any hassle about doing both.

There was never any pressure put on me and that's one of the reasons I still have such affection for Castleford. I grew up there, but also the club really looked after me and treated me right. They respected my wishes and they recognised that education was important to me and my family. I think that's why my dad eventually said it was okay for me to sign for them. It wasn't a case of signing for money, there wasn't a lot of that on offer, and rather it was because we knew they'd look after me and do the right things.

Being born and bred in the town and a life-long supporter, Castleford was the only rugby league team I ever wanted to play for, provided I was good enough. Playing schoolboy rugby I always felt I had the ability to turn professional and it was constantly in the back of my mind that I wanted to follow in my dad's footsteps. Emulating what he had done, by playing for Cas, was a minor goal of mine, but if I hadn't achieved that I think my playing days would have been spent in the other code.

Having tasted union at school and college I knew I could play the game to a reasonable standard and there had been interest expressed in me by some union clubs. In those days, union wasn't a professional game, at least not openly. It was supposed to be strictly amateur, but it's not really a secret that players at some clubs did get paid, their wages being delivered in brown envelopes, hidden in their boots.

Boot money wasn't enough to live on, certainly not for a player of my lowly standard, but it would have supplemented my income as a teacher and to be honest, playing union would have fitted in better with my chosen career in the 1970s. Things have changed, but in those days, teaching wasn't the sort of career professional rugby league players went into, and vice-versa.

In some ways, I was caught between two camps. I was a young kid from a working class background in the rugby league heartland of Castleford, but I was also training to be a teacher in Leicester, one of rugby union's English strongholds.

Although I am a rugby league man, I don't have a problem with union and I would have been happy to play the 15-a-side game, but once Castleford confirmed they were interested in me and Len Garbett offered me terms, there wasn't really a decision to make. It was one of the happiest and proudest days of my life and, after I'd assured him it wouldn't mean neglecting my education, my dad felt the same.

Like a lot of kids with a bit of ability, I played some of my early rugby as a half-back, but basically I was winger/

centre, though I was actually signed as a full-back. That was the position I played for the college in Leicester and I think it's probably the best role for a back in union. When you receive the ball you've got the get-out clause, if you are in trouble, of being able to put boot to ball and play for field position, or hoof it out of bounds. But if there is a bit of broken field you can have a pop at taking on the defence, which is the fun part.

I made my reserve team debut for Cas at full-back, against Batley - a club I was to go on and coach many years later - in a home game at Wheldon Road. From what I can remember we won 10-0 and it wasn't a classic, but it was great to have had a game of professional rugby league and to feel that, to a certain extent, I had lived a dream.

Of course the big one was my first appearance for the senior team, but that turned out to be a painful experience in more ways than one. I spent a fair amount of time in the A-team, which to a degree - pardon the pun - was due to my circumstances. Living in Leicester meant I could not train with Castleford and I only managed to get up for games or during college vacations, so it wouldn't have been fair to select me ahead of someone who attended every training session. The rewards in those days weren't anything like they are now when players at top-flight clubs are full-time. It was nice to get paid, but it wasn't your main occupation.

As things have turned out, I was lucky that the great Malcolm Reilly was first team coach at Castleford throughout my time as a player there and in fact was the only senior team boss I played under. When I started there, John Sheridan was the 'A' team coach, Graham Heptinstall was under-17 coach and Johnny Walker, who has sadly since passed away, was in charge of the under-19s.

Malcolm has been a great influence on me throughout my career. As well as being one of the most successful

Coaching is Chaos

English coaches of the modern era, he was also the best player I ever took the field with. A local Cas lad, he established his reputation as a player with his hometown club before going over and showing the Aussies a thing or two, during a very successful stint with Manly. He probably played his best rugby in Australia and his knee was basically shot to pieces when he came back to finish his playing career with Cas.

He had a stint as player-coach, turning out at loose-forward, second-row and then finally at prop, before hanging up his boots. He also had spells in charge of Halifax and Leeds and then won a Grand Final down under, where he is a legendary figure, with Newcastle Knights. He was also in charge of Great Britain during a time in the late 1980s and early 90s when they came close to winning back the Ashes.

He was a monumental figure in the game and even now I still get a bit star struck when I am in Malcolm's company. Perhaps there have been players with more ability, but for sheer bloody-mindedness and a competitive edge, Malcolm is in a class of his own. He always reminds me of the Dark Knight in *Monty Python and the Holy Grail*. He has both his arms and legs chopped off and then concedes it's a draw. That's the best you'd have ever got off Malcolm.

That is how he trained, played and coached. When we did pre-season training, running up the hills at Kippax, he would run up with the first group, come back down and then go back up with the second and third. If there were half a dozen groups, we would all do one run in six, but he'd do three or four. He was a machine and his conditioning was unbelievable. When we get together now, for past-players' reunions, a bout of arm-wrestling usually breaks out and inevitably Malcolm will be in the thick of it, making sure he wins.

Malcolm obviously thought enough of me to give me a

first go in the senior side, away to St Helens. I would like to think I had really caught his eye with my performances in the reserves, but being honest I think there was also an element of having to pick who was available.

Knowsley Road was never a happy hunting ground for Castleford and it wasn't a game the players used to look forward to. This particular occasion was a mid-week match and our camp was struck down by a bad case of what we used to call Cumbrian flu. In the old part-time days players used to develop all sorts of minor knocks and ailments if they didn't fancy a trip up to the likes of Whitehaven or Workington, or across the Pennines to Saints, where - most likely - it would turn out to be a long 80 minutes, for losing pay.

We went over the M62 that evening with an under-strength team, with me making my debut and another lad, Taylor, getting his first appearance as well, off the subs' bench. I'd like to tell you I played a blinder and we pulled off a shock win, but in fact, Cas got a shellacking and I ended up in hospital.

Putting on a Castleford shirt for the first time in a senior game was a memorable moment, but unfortunately I managed to break my collarbone, which meant I didn't get to repeat the experience for quite some time. Nowadays, there is express physio' service and treatment from top specialists. Back in the 1980s, it was a case of putting it in a sling, resting up for a while and taking painkillers until it healed.

Injuries are part of the game and anyone who played rugby league realised that at some stage or other they would have to take time off from work or their education. In my case, the injury didn't go down too well at Braunstone Frith School in Leicester, where I was working in my first teaching appointment.

The head, Mr Bourner, let me off the last hour of school

on the day of the game. I set off from the midlands in a fraught and nervous state at about 2.30pm, drove up to Wheldon Road, got on the coach there, travelled over to St Helens, played the game, got hurt and ended up in Pontefract Infirmary.

Mr Bourner - in those days it was very formal, all the staff called him Mister and the pupils called him Sir - wasn't best pleased when he got a phone call from me saying I'd be off work for a while.

I loved playing and I was honoured to turn out for Castleford, but being honest, I wasn't any great shakes. I was a journeyman; I was all right, but I wouldn't have got into any of my own teams!

I have no regrets. I think I achieved everything I could with the ability I had, but I will admit I would have liked to have played now, in the modern, Super League era of summer rugby and full-time training.

I feel I would have benefited from that environment, because I was an avid listener and I always wanted to learn and to improve. I think Malcolm liked coaching me for that reason. He appreciated people who tried their best and endeavoured to make themselves better.

During my 12 years on the playing side of things there were people with a lot more ability than me who didn't make as many appearances because they didn't have the right attitude. Ability is sometimes wasted on people because they don't maximise it. I maximised mine and I played as well as I possibly could, with the limited ability I'd got. I don't think you can ask any more than that.

I never won any silverware with Cas, but I did play in some memorable matches. Unfortunately, I played during an era when Hull were the dominant force in the English game and they always seemed to have the Indian sign over us. We could never beat them when it really mattered.

I played in two Challenge Cup semi-finals, in 1982 and 1983, and both times we lost narrowly to the team from the Boulevard. The first time, we were beaten 15-11 at Headingley, in Leeds. We went 11-4 down before mounting a bit of a fightback, but they closed the game out to book their place at Wembley.

A semi-final is probably the worst time to lose a cup tie, but I remember that game as one of the best I had as a player in the Cas first team. I was really pleased with my contribution. We had a pretty decent team in those days, mainly made up of local lads like myself, Gary Hyde, Terry Richardson, Steve Fenton, John Joyner, the Beardmore twins, Barry Johnson and Malcolm, but we didn't have the stars that Hull did.

We had something of an injury crisis and I remember Alan Hardy was at hooker that day, which was a role he didn't occupy very often. Up against a Hull team including 'Knocker' Norton, Dave Topliss, Peter Sterling, Gary Kemble, Dane O'Hara and James Leuluai, we gave a good account of ourselves, but just not quite good enough.

The following year we lost to Hull again, 14-7 at Elland Road. In 1984 we got to the semi-finals again, against guess who, and we lost 22-16 in a replay after a 10-10 draw, though I was injured and didn't play in either of those. We finally managed to win a semi in 1986, beating Oldham. We went on to win the final against Hull KR at Wembley, but I had just started on the coaching side and wasn't in the squad.

I did get to play in a couple of finals, though we lost both of them. The highlight was the 1984 Premiership decider, played on my mum's birthday, May 12. We lost to Hull KR 18-10 at Headingley, but it was a marvellous occasion and at least I had a try to look back on.

It really was a cracking touchdown: John Joyner set it up with a trademark short pass to Steve Robinson, our Aussie stand-off. I supported him and scored between the posts. That was fairly early in the game and at that stage it seemed like it might be our day, but John Dorahy put in a man of the match performance for them and they were more comfortable winners than the scoreline suggests.

My other final was earlier in the same season, when we lost 13-2 to Hull at Elland Road, in the now defunct Yorkshire Cup. That was a poor game, a bit of a non-event. They controlled it throughout, even though we trailed only 4-2 at half-time.

Competing in finals is what you play rugby league for, but I am just as proud to have shared a field with some all-time greats. As I have mentioned, Malcolm Reilly was the best I played with, but there were some terrific players around in the early and mid-1980s.

The best prop-forward I played with, or against, was Kevin Ward, who originally signed for Cas as a centre. He was a big man, but quick with it and immensely strong. He was a very different player to Malcolm, but the only one to rival him as my most-admired team-mate.

As a ball-handler in the forward pack, there were few to compare with Barry Johnson and then we also had John Joyner, at centre, stand-off and loose-forward and the Beardmore twins, Bob and Kevin, who were pretty special players as well. They had an intuition; whatever one did, the other knew about it before it happened. We weren't a particularly successful team, but we were all great friends and we still get together every now and then, for a yarn about the good old days. That's one thing about rugby league, whether playing or coaching, you meet great characters and make true friendships that last for a lifetime.

In terms of people I played against, the best was undoubtedly the Australian Wally Lewis, who had a brief spell with Wakefield in 1983. I played against him at

Wheldon Road, on Boxing Day and it was a privilege just to be on the same pitch. I remember a tackle he made on Steve Fenton, who was playing stand-off and was known for his nifty footwork. He was very quick and elusive, but Lewis got hold of him and nearly knocked him into the car park. I also remember some of his long passes, which had to be seen to be believed. He was light years in front of anyone else; he was playing a year 2000 game in the 1980s, an absolute gem of a player.

I also enjoyed, if that's the right word, playing against the great Aussie scrum-half Peter Sterling and had the misfortune to come up against Eric Grothe, during his spell at Leeds. Known as Rolling Thunder, he was a big, fast and fearsome winger. I had to try and mark him on one occasion and he trampled all over me. Mind you, he is twice my size.

There were also some great English players. One I rate very highly was Des Drummond, a winger who had his best days at Warrington and Leigh. He wasn't the biggest of blokes, but he hit harder than men twice his size. When he tackled you, you knew about it. He was a very good wingman and hard.

Another one was Mike Smith, at Hull KR. I thought he was similar to John Joyner in his guile and his class. Eddie Cunningham was a quality act at Widnes and of course I was around when Ellery Hanley was just coming on to the scene.

When we played Hull in the 1983 semi-final we thought we had a decent chance of getting through and we expected we'd be playing Bradford, who were up against Featherstone in the other last-four tie.

I went with Barry Johnson to watch that game, which was played before our semi-final, at Headingley. Featherstone pulled off a shock win and went on to beat Hull in the final, but Bradford came up with one of rugby league's great moments when Ellery scored a sensational try, beating man after man on a run up the main stand touchline. It was one of the most incredible touchdowns I have ever seen and it marked his emergence as a player to watch out for.

Until 1998, of which more later, Featherstone's win over Hull was regarded as the greatest-ever Cup final shock. They had a wonderful Cup tradition and their triumph that year made a big impression on me. Allan Agar was in charge and I think he deserves a huge amount of credit. You could see the coach's stamp on the way Rovers played, which was unusual in those days. David Hobbs won the Lance Todd Trophy as man of the match, after scoring two tries. For both of them he ran at the small guys on the edges. That was smart coaching and it's something that stayed with me. Funnily enough, I later appointed Allan's son Richard as my assistant-coach when I was in charge of Hull.

3

*

Village People

I CAN remember the exact moment my interest in coaching, or at least the tactics of rugby league, began. It was a game between Castleford and Leigh in the long-defunct BBC2 Floodlit Trophy, way back under the old four-tackle rule and long before my own playing days.

Under the laws at the time if you kicked the ball dead, play would be re-started by the opposition dropping out from their own 25-yard line. I don't know whether it was George Clinton, the trainer, or one of the Cas kickers, Dougie Walton, who came up with the idea, but in this particular match Dougie kept whacking the ball dead and the opposition continually had to drop out, giving possession back. That meant Cas had the ball almost the entire match. I was at junior school, but I found it absolutely fascinating that somebody had come up with a legal tactic which had such a huge bearing on a game. They actually changed the rules because of it; Cas won the game - by a low score - but it was a poor spectacle and it wasn't how the authorities wanted the sport portrayed on television. Nowadays when the ball is kicked dead, the opposition re-start with a 20-metre tap, so they have possession.

That sparked my interest and ever since I have been fascinated by the prospect of out-thinking the opposition. Initially that went hand-in-hand with my love of education; I enjoyed school and liked the notion of learning things, taking new ideas on board and widening my knowledge. I always felt if I could do that for others, it would be a great achievement. That's why I went into teaching and also the key reason for me going down the coaching route. Right from the start I felt teaching effectively was coaching, just not necessarily in a sporting context. In both roles you are trying to educate people and get the best out of them. That has always attracted me; I like the idea of informing, educating and hopefully developing people.

By studying to be a teacher in Leicester I swapped one rugby hotbed for another. That worked out well, because it allowed me to continue playing two different codes, but it came about by coincidence.

As I have mentioned, Leicester is one of the strongholds of the union game in England, but the reason I chose to go there had nothing to do with rugby; it was based on bad advice from the careers expert at Castleford Grammar School. The comprehensive system was just being introduced - my old grammar school was about to become Cas High - and I was told the way forward for English education would be a new three tier set-up of first, middle and upper schools. The careers master assured me there would be a shortage of middle school teachers, so by specialising at that level I would be on the fast-track to promotion and bigger and better things. I took that advice on board and went off to Leicester to study a middle school course at college there.

As things turned out, although that three-tier system was introduced in one or two isolated places it never materialised nationwide, which was what I had been banking on. It all worked out well in the end though and it led me down an unusual and maybe even unique path, into primary school teaching. In those days there were very few male primary school teachers and even today that is a branch of the education system dominated by women, so I wouldn't be surprised if I was the only primary school teacher ever to have played professional rugby league.

There was no great plan; having studied a middle school course, training to teach pupils aged from nine to 14, I had a choice of going into either a primary or secondary school, effectively doubling my options. I applied for jobs in both and it just happened that I got a post in a primary school.

I started off as a class teacher, became a class teacher with overall school responsibility for PE and then a deputy head teacher. I started at Braunstone Frith School in Leicester, from 1977-78, and then did five years at Athelstan, in Sherburn-in-Elmet, near Leeds, before seven years at another Leeds school, South Milford, where I was appointed deputy head teacher.

I thoroughly enjoyed my time learning the trade in Leicester, playing rugby union for the college, as well as the teacher-training side of things and I had 14 great years in the teaching profession. Although the two worlds may seem poles apart my education background has definitely helped my coaching career. I don't think I would have got as far as I have without my schools experience. The principles are the same; in both teaching and coaching you are trying to educate people to get the best out of themselves, make better decisions and to be smarter in different situations.

Playing rugby was a bonus; it was my secondary income and my secondary career. There were times when, for example, a parents' evening might clash with a training night. No question, I had to go to the parents' evening. That always came first and it is why I would have loved to be involved as a player now, when you can devote your whole life to rugby.

For most of my teaching career I was playing rugby as well, but in the mid-1980s I began to turn my attention to coaching, initially as conditioner and assistant team boss at Castleford, then as joint head-coach at Bramley.

I was taking part in coach-education at the same time as my involvement with Bramley and went on several courses run by the Rugby Football League, who eventually offered me a job assisting Phil Larder, then in charge of coaching for the governing body. That was when I came out of teaching, but - while it was definitely the right move for me - I have never regretted one moment of my time in education.

The 14 years I spent as a teacher gave me great respect for the profession and I'll never belittle teachers or the work they do. I know a lot of people seem to think it's an easy life with short working days and long holidays; well, take it from me, it isn't. Like coaching, the devil is in the detail and you can not be an effective teacher without good preparation. Poor preparation leads to poor performance. If you are a good, conscientious teacher you have a lot of work to do outside the classroom.

I love my life as a rugby league coach, but had things worked out just a little differently I could easily have remained in teaching and I would have been happy to do that, though I think it has got much tougher since my day due to all the new government rules and regulations. I am a bit of a fatalist and I think it was fate that I went to college in Leicester, that I went down the primary school route and that I later came across Phil Larder, which led me into full-time coaching. None of that was the plan when I started out.

My teaching career was a source of great amusement for the other players at Castleford, who were more used to getting their hands dirty. In those days a lad from Castleford who became a teacher was seen as someone who had made good and that made me fair game for the changing room jokers. There was no inverted snobbery from people like Keith 'Beefy' England, who worked down the pit; I think they were pleased for me and they thought I had done well for myself. There was plenty of micky-taking, but no negativity. It was a similar story with regard to my team mate and good friend Barry Johnson, who had a job as a personnel officer. There was a diversity in the camp and I think that helped to bond us together. Even the Beardmore brothers had very different occupations: Kev went down the pit and loved that, while Bob went into a white collar occupation, getting on to the managerial ladder at a local plant hire firm. For my part, there was absolutely no question of thinking that because I was a teacher I was in any way better than anyone else in the team. I was a Cas lad, I am proud to have been born and bred there and the values I picked up as a youngster have stayed with me.

Having said that, would I have gone as far as I have in coaching without my education background? Possibly not; I think the education process I went through - studying at school and then college, gaining a degree and later classroom experience - stood me in great stead, both as a player and a coach.

In my playing days I was keen and willing to learn and was able to take on board what Malcolm Reilly and the other coaches were telling me. Being of only limited ability, I had to be. Later, I was trained in how to get an opinion across and in how to make the most of an individual's particular talents, or rather help him do that.

Some of the finest coaches have had an education

Coaching is Chaos

background. Take, for example, Brian Smith, who has had a glittering career in both English and Australian rugby league. It is often said his coaching methods are a bit headmasterish, but they have been very effective. You don't survive as a top level coach in Australia for two decades without doing something right. He has had success at all the clubs he has been with and he is known as a coach who, if there's an ill-disciplined culture in the changing room, will come in and sort it out.

Since the start of my coaching career I have always used methods I picked up in the classroom. There's an old saying in teaching that you can tell, you can show or you can get people to do. The doing part is the most effective way of encouraging anyone to learn and that is a basic teaching philosophy. I also put that into effect when I am trying to educate my players in a match situation, but I am very aware that a learning style which works for one might not be effective for another. You have to be able to present the same situation in several completely different manners; that is something else I learned from teaching.

It works both ways and being a professional rugby player had its advantages when it came to being in the classroom, which was my own coalface. I never got much bother from the pupils because they knew I played for Cas and I think that helped win over some of the parents as well. I certainly wasn't a big celebrity, but I was fairly well-known locally and that got them on my side straight away, especially the ones who supported Cas. There's a scene in the football movie *Fever Pitch* when the main character, who is an Arsenal-obsessed teacher, is speaking to a father at a parent's evening and all the dad wants to do is discuss soccer. It was a bit like that on occasions.

One or two of my pupils have gone on to careers in rugby league. I taught Tim Rumford, who had a spell as player performance manager at Castleford, and Neil Law, who played for Sheffield and York, so I must have been doing something right.

My first practical coaching experience came at Castleford in the mid-1980s and was a direct result of my education background and the fact I had done a physical education degree. Sports science is a huge part of any professional sport nowadays and I suppose I was in on the start of that. Because of my studies I knew about energy systems, good diet and weight-training programmes, things which are taken for granted now but were a novelty in those days. A lot of modern players take sports science degrees and there is a clear pathway from playing into the fitness side of things, but that wasn't the case in my playing days.

I have always been very open-minded about what sports science can offer to the art of coaching. I still believe coaching is an art, but I think you can use the appliance of science to get the best out of players. All that was still some way off when I started and even the top clubs didn't have dedicated conditioners, but Malcolm Reilly recognised that the skills I had learned during my teacher training could be of use, so he asked me if I would like to do some fitness work with the players in the first and second teams.

My entire coaching career developed from that, though I had always felt I had more to offer in that sort of role than I did as a player. I was all right as a player, but nothing special and in some ways that benefited me when I did hang up my boots. Because I wasn't the most talented of individuals I had to think about things a lot more than the natural superstars do. A Garry Schofield or an Alan Hardisty operates on instinct, whereas everything I did on the field was the result of a consciously thought out process. And you can't pass instinct on to others.

My initial role as conditioner also involved assisting the

reserve team coach Dave Sampson. I also did opposition analysis for the 1986 Challenge Cup final, when Cas beat Hull Kingston Rovers, which was a new innovation. Malcolm sent me to watch Hull KR in the lead up to the Wembley game and I produced a dossier on their players' strengths and weaknesses. I know Malcolm found that useful, because he let me take the reserves for a practice game against the Wembley squad. Our job was to play how Hull KR played, obviously to give them an idea of what they would be up against in the final and how they could combat it. That was absolutely revolutionary a quarter of a century ago and it illustrates what a great thinker and innovator Malcolm was. People talk about his competitiveness and his desire for fitness among his players, but tactically he was top class as well. For example, it was Malcolm who introduced the bomb - a high kick aimed at the opposition's full-back or wingers - into British rugby league, among many other things. He thought outside the box and he was creative.

By that stage I was still playing, but mainly in the reserves. I was happy to do that as I was the senior player at that level and Dave Sampson's right-hand man on the field. It was a good way of learning the game from a different perspective. When Malcolm left a year after that Challenge Cup triumph, to coach Great Britain, Dave took over as head coach - with Mick Morgan as his assistant - and I was placed in charge of the reserves. They were good times. I coached the second string - then known as the 'A' team - in 1988 and 1989 and it was a successful period. We did well in the Alliance League, coming fourth and second, and got to the Yorkshire Senior competition final, losing narrowly to Leeds.

More importantly, a couple of the players I coached in the reserves went on to have great careers at first team level. One of them was Tony Smith, or Casper as he is known throughout the game. Ironically, two decades later I took over from Casper as head coach of Wakefield Trinity Wildcats. He was always destined for big things as a player and he fulfilled his potential, playing for Cas, Wigan, Hull and Great Britain. I first met him when he was 16, after Dave Sampson had signed him for Cas. Casper made his debut in the reserves against Wigan and before the game I told him I planned to break him in gently by playing him on the wing. It typified what a cheeky chappy he was when he told me 'I don't want to play on the wing, I'm a stand-off!' I thought for a 16-year-old to say that to his reserve team coach was interesting; it was an indication of his character and I have followed his career ever since with close interest. I am always proud when Cas lads go on to make it at the top level and I hope Casper feels I played some small part in his development.

Within the same team was Dean Sampson, a powerful and hot-headed forward, who just happened to be Dave's son. That was an interesting situation and it gave Dave something of a coaching dilemma. Dean was, in my opinion, the best forward in the reserves and on a number of occasions I suggested to Dave he should be getting a chance in the senior side. Unfortunately, Dave was reluctant to give Dean - or Diesel as everyone calls him - an opportunity, because he thought it would look like nepotism.

It was probably harder for Dean to break into the first team than it would have been for someone else of similar ability, but in the end his dad had no choice, because the lad was playing so well. Dean made his debut against St Helens in the opening game of the 1987-88 campaign and he was more or less a fixture in the team for the next 14 years, eventually making 431 appearances, which is a terrific achievement. Even after he packed in at Cas Diesel carried on playing and as I write this, in 2012, he has just made his debut for the Fryston amateur club in the Yorkshire Men's League competition. I am sure he'll still be playing when he's 60.

For me, coaching the A team and working with people like Malcolm, Dave and Mick - accomplished players and good guys as well - was an ideal grounding. They helped me tremendously, as did David Poulter, who was the Cas chairman. He gave me a great deal of support and is someone I have a huge amount of time for. I would have loved to have stayed at Cas, which I will always feel is 'my' club, but sometimes you have to move on to go forward and that was the situation I found myself in after the Australian Darryl Van de Velde was appointed coach in July, 1988.

I worked with Darryl, who was Cas' first overseas coach, for a year and he was very impressive with some ground-breaking ideas. He brought instant success in terms of winning matches and it seemed they had found someone with a magic wand, a bit like Wigan did when Michael Maguire went there nearly a quarter of a century later and immediately won the Super League title. Cas won 11 and drew the other one of Darryl's first 12 matches in charge and we were all dreaming of the club's first-ever championship crown, but they fell away in the second half of the campaign to finish fifth.

I was happy working under Darryl, but after the way the team performed during his first season it seemed he would be at the club for the long-term, which meant there was no route through to the top job for me. It was a wrench, but leaving Cas appeared to be the only way forward and when an opportunity came along, I felt I had to take it.

In 1989 my mate Barry Johnson joined Bramley, a lower division club in Leeds, as player-coach. He was finding it quite tough, particularly doing both roles, so he asked me to go over and help him. We worked together really well and had a lot of success on the field, taking them up to the dizzy heights of third at one stage in what was a very tough 18-team division, the tier below the top-flight.

At one stage we won seven games out of eight, which was a good-news, bad-news scenario for the club. Players weren't on contracts; they got paid winning money and losing pay and a run of victories really stretched the budget. Eventually we lost to Rochdale - and both sets of directors were equally delighted. The Rochdale board could afford winning pay and ours couldn't. Rochdale had more resources and great ambition as a club, but we also won there - with a depleted team - during my time in charge, when they were top of the league and had Allan Agar as coach and that was one of the highlights of my spell at Bramley.

Bramley was a tough school. They were never one of the glamour clubs, the facilities weren't great, they were constantly in the shadow of their big neighbours Leeds and they weren't well supported, but it was good fun and a valuable learning experience. I will forever be grateful to the three directors Jeff Wine, Ronnie Teeman and Melvyn Levy, along with Barry Johnson, for giving me the opportunity.

We were out of the limelight because we were in a lower division, but as a novice coach that allowed me to make errors and to learn from those mistakes. There was less pressure to get results, because Bramley weren't used to winning and nobody panicked if they lost a few games. I was still teaching at that time so it was a busy period, but you have to put the hard yards in if you want to achieve at anything.

During the time I was at Bramley I wasn't sure how far my coaching career would take me, but I did regard it as an invaluable part of my progression, from conditioner, to reserve team coach, to team boss in a lower division. My ambition was to be a first team coach at the top level, but I didn't take a direct route, I went all the way round the ring road. That certainly didn't do me any harm because if you've got any sense whatsoever you make sure you reflect on and learn from whatever experiences you have, good and bad.

I don't regret any of the time I spent at Bramley and if nothing else, it showed me how lucky players and coaches are at the elite level. At Bramley it was a case of all hands on deck, we had to make do and mend and all that stood me in good stead.

Sadly the McLaren Field ground is a housing estate now, but it certainly had character. Despite being under a new purpose-built stand, the changing rooms were Spartan, small and the showers only worked on a good day. There was also the old-style big bath, which everyone would jump in together.

Behind one set of posts was the Village pub, with a shale bank at the other end. On the opposite side to the main stand was a small shed, for fans to stand under. We trained at McLaren Field and if it was bad weather we had to practice behind the posts, so we didn't cut the pitch up. Nobody thought that was unusual or grumbled about it; it was the way things were in those days.

Thankfully the game has evolved and many clubs now have the use of state of the art facilities, like the Sports Barn at Huddersfield. That's what I feel all Super League clubs should be aspiring towards. I believe upgraded training facilities ought to be a criteria for a Super League licence. When I was at Wakefield we trained all over the area, including at a local public school. The facilities there were top-notch, but they weren't our own. It astonishes me that in the 21st century some full-time clubs are still using school fields to practice on. They should all own their own facilities, with designated team rooms where they can work on game plans and looking at the opposition's strengths and weaknesses. That's as important, if not more so, than other aspects which do feature in the Super League licence process.

There was one occasion when we did train on the pitch in the middle of winter, much to the directors' displeasure. We were drawn at home to mighty St Helens in the first round of the 1989-90 Challenge Cup competition, which was a big deal for a small, cash-strapped club like Bramley.

We were massive underdogs, but we were playing rather well at the time and we fancied our chances of giving Saints a good game, though I didn't really believe we would win. In circumstances like that you have to do anything you can to level the playing field, which is what we did - literally. We were under orders, as usual, to keep off the pitch in training and to prepare behind the posts and that's what we did on the Tuesday evening, the night the directors had their board meeting. But on the Thursday, when we had the place to ourselves, we trained in the middle of the pitch, in a deliberate attempt to churn up the playing surface.

Comparing the strength of the respective teams, we knew if it was a lush, well-grassed pitch they would tear us apart, but we thought a mud bath might bring them down to our level. When the directors turned up on the day of the game they were less than impressed by the state of the field and there were some angry words exchanged. The tactic worked pretty well, however. We lost the game, but only 22-14. To go down by a couple of scores to a Saints side that went on to reach the semi-finals and finished fifth in the Stones Bitter Championship was a really good effort. Ronnie Sharp, in the centres, had an outstanding game for us, as did Steve Carroll. That was one of the most memorable matches of my spell at McLaren Field.

Coaching is Chaos

At one stage, when things weren't going so well, the director Melvyn Levy suggested we came up with a war dance, like the New Zealand haka, to gee the players up. Before the Saints game we also produced a motivational video, to a rock music score, to try and get the boys in the mood for battle.

That was very unusual in those days and we might have been one of the first clubs to do it. We set up a TV/video recorder in the team room and pressed play and the music was blaring out, so much so that the board came along to find out what was happening. We had locked the door and we ignored all the banging and crashing as the players watched the tape. It was quite a funny scene, with the players getting wound up inside the changing room and the directors all banging on the door outside it.

One of Bramley's strengths was their camaraderie and team spirit, but we also had good players. Probably the best was Peter Lister, an accountant who worked for the chairman Jeff Wine. He was a really good footballer, a club record-breaking stand-off who signed for them from Leeds in the early 1980s. He had plenty of talent and I think he could have gone on to a higher stage, but for his laid-back attitude. He was an old-fashioned type of footballer, who liked to have a drink and a smoke and that might have inhibited his progress.

When players are part-time - and earning very little from the game - it is harder to impose rules and restrictions than it is if you're working in a full-time environment. At Bramley, whenever we had an away game in Cumbria we would stop off at a café on the A66 for a pre-match fry-up. That used to irritate me, because I had a PE degree, I had studied diet and nutrition and I was well aware that the last thing the players needed before a game was a full English. But it was the directors' treat and it was something I had to put up with.

Equally, a post-match booze up was all part of the match-day experience. It was a different culture, players worked during the day, they played the game for fun and they liked to let their hair down following a game, win or lose. Although they were paid, they were being paid to do their hobby and if you have a hobby it has got to be enjoyable. That's why you couldn't sling the baby out with the bath water, impose beans on toast or pasta as the pre-match meal and ban boozing. If I had tried to do that at Bramley there would have been a strike, or I'd have been lynched, or both.

Modern-day players aren't saints and obviously some of them like a pint or two, though there are very few who smoke nowadays. Later on in my career I came into conflict with certain players about drinking on the coach home from a game, as I'll reveal elsewhere in this book, but after a Super League match most players would never dream of having a beer; for a start they are too busy doing other things. They take energy drinks to replace what they've lost during the previous 80 minutes, then protein shakes and certain food they need to eat within two hours of the match finishing. There's also the post-match warm-down and re-hab and some teams go swimming straight afterwards, to ease aching limbs. Everything is regulated by the conditioning coach, with advice from nutritionists.

In my Bramley days the lads played, got showered and the first port of call was the bar. Peter Jarvis, a stalwart of rugby league in the city of Leeds who also had a spell as coach at Bramley, ran the Villager pub adjacent to the ground and within an hour of a home match finishing the majority of the side would be in there, all having a good chat, a sing-song and plenty of booze, before heading into Leeds to continue the night out.

Another of the characters in the team was an outside-back, who I am not going to name for reasons which will become obvious in a moment. This kid was an outstanding performer, but we just couldn't get him to turn up for training. He would pop in when he felt like it, which was frustrating for Barry and me as coaches because we could see he had the potential to go a long way in the sport, if only he would apply himself. That led to much conflict between the board of directors and the coaching staff over whether we should pick him in the team. They wanted their star man on the field, but we felt if you didn't train, you shouldn't play.

On one occasion when this lad did come to training, Peter Lister came over to me and Barry and said he needed to show us something. We were already putting the cones out, getting ready to start the session, but Peter said it couldn't wait. Barry and I used to change in the referee's room, for a bit of privacy away from the players. Peter took us in there and said we needed to go and have a look in our star back's bag, because he had brought a gun with him. So we went for a peek and sure enough...We called him over and asked what was going on and he said: 'There's some people after me, so I've got the gun for protection.' We had spent months trying to get him to training and on the one occasion he did turn up we had to send him home! That's the only time I have ever sent a player away from training, but I thought it was a good idea for our safety and that of the other players.

A range of different characters, from varying backgrounds, makes a team. That ethos still exists in the modern game, but it is something which is gradually being lost at Super League level. Now all the players are full-time and there's almost nobody left from the old semi-professional days. Most of the lads running around in the top division have never had a 'proper job' and they don't know anything other than rugby league. Obviously that's a positive in many respects, but I think it is important for players to get a grounding in the real world. Most rugby league people are open and accommodating to fans and the media, but I wonder if that will change in a decade or so, as the sport becomes more insular.

Even now there aren't many coaches who have worked outside the sport. At Wakefield my number two was Paul Broadbent, who had come from a part-time sporting background, but nowadays the majority of coaches take up the reins straight from a playing career. I think it is a good thing to work outside the sport first, because then you appreciate what you have got.

Strangely, I got my big break in coaching as a result of actually giving up the hands-on involvement. I left Bramley early in 1991 and they dropped out of the league a few years later, which was a shame. After leaving McLaren Field the club played for a while at the old Kirkstall Rugby Union Club, which is now Leeds Rhinos' training academy, then had a stint at Headingley itself, as a sort of feeder club for the Rhinos. Great Britain internationals like Barrie McDermott and Terry Newton played for them briefly and Mike Ford, who later joined the England rugby union set-up, was coach, but it didn't work out. Eventually the old club folded and later a new one - the Buffaloes - was formed, playing in the summer national conference. They did very well, but I think it is unlikely Bramley will ever get back into the professional ranks. That's sad from my point of view, because I enjoyed every moment of my time there.

4

*

Vive La France

ADMITTING a brand-new Paris club into the first Super League season, in 1996, was one of the most controversial decisions the RFL (Rugby Football League) has ever made, but it was great for me. It gave me my break back into club coaching after a few years with the governing body. My time at the RFL was away from the spotlight, but it produced one of the proudest accomplishments of my rugby league career.

During my time at Bramley I was also teaching full-time and working as a coach educator for the RFL. I had qualified through their coaching scheme and was passing on my knowledge to other coaches coming through. At that time the RFL coaching department had only one full-time employee, Phil Larder. He had a set of about eight regional coach educators working under him on a part-time basis, me included. We got paid a few quid to cover our expenses, but other than that it was a voluntary thing.

Again, my teaching background helped me make the breakthrough. Phil was aware of my education qualifications and he thought I would be a useful man to have on board. Eventually funding was made available to the RFL to take another full-time employee on and Phil asked if I'd be interested in taking the role.

It meant leaving the teaching profession, which was a hard decision to make, but I was confident I had a long-term future in coaching and had something to offer, so I said yes. In many ways it was the best of both worlds because I was staying in education, but also getting to work full-time in the game I love.

I arrived at the RFL just as the governing body was implementing plans to create an academy system for young players. The original plan was that would be Phil's baby and I was going to head up the coaching scheme. In fact Phil took over as England head coach and that occupied most of his time, so the academy work fell into my lap. Phil left the RFL not long after I arrived, going to Widnes - who he took to the 1993 Challenge Cup final - and then Keighley. Eventually he wound up at Sheffield Eagles and I rejoined him as his assistant, but that's another story.

His appointment with England was a lucky break for me because I went to the RFL as Phil's assistant and got the head job almost immediately; as director of coaching and academy executive. Establishing the academy probably is not something I am going to be remembered for, but I like to think of it as a legacy for the game. It wasn't the most headline-grabbing thing I have done in my career, but I doubt if anything else has been as important for the sport as a whole.

Maurice Lindsay was the chief executive of the RFL and he made it clear the academy was my number one priority. Maurice is one of those Marmite characters, you either love him or hate him, but once he set his mind on achieving something, generally it got done. I think rugby league should be grateful to him for having the vision to implement the academy system, which has been a great success. It's something I am very proud of.

Up until then the professional arm of the game had two levels: first team and 'A' team, as the reserves were known. I was instructed to set up a new under-19 structure, which became the third tier of professional rugby league. Before that there had been a Colts competition for teenage players, but that had disbanded. The academy was far more than a playing competition, it was a whole structure aimed at producing top professionals with access to the best coaching and the best resources.

In a nutshell the idea was to make young players effectively mini-first teamers - so, in theory at least, they could go straight from playing under-19 rugby to the senior side. We were all about creating a clear pathway, which did not exist before. It was an education structure to develop future generations of rugby league players and looking back now, I think it worked.

Nothing in rugby league is ever straightforward. You would imagine that bringing in an academy system with the ultimate aim of producing first team players for top-flight teams and eventually the national set-up would be a no-brainer; it's the sort of thing everybody with the game's best interests at heart should support. Not so, in fact it caused a mini-civil war within the game as BARLA - the British Amateur Rugby League Association - and the RFL took up arms against each other.

There was a massive feeling of resentment at BARLA about under-18s being brought under the professional arm. At one stage it looked as though it would lead to another breakaway, similar to the one which started the whole sport way back in 1895. It was that serious. For one thing, players who aligned themselves with professional clubs were being banned from playing at international level in the amateur game. BARLA offered tours to some exotic locations and many good players were put off joining professional sides because of that. The feeling among some in the amateur ranks was that professional sides were stealing players they had worked very hard to develop, but as far as I am concerned that is just part of a natural process: the cream rises to the top and in rugby league the top is the highest professional division. It should be a source of pride for an amateur club if one of their kids gets signed by Leeds, or Wigan or St Helens. If you were, for example, Danny McGuire's first coach at East Leeds would you be happy he went on to play for Leeds Rhinos and England, or would you rather he stayed in the amateur game?

What is now called the community arm of the game, the grass roots, is all about introducing kids to the sport, getting lots of numbers involved and about player development up to a certain level, but it can only go so far. The clue is in the name - it was the amateur rugby league association; the coaches and everyone involved at the clubs were volunteers. As the professional side of the code the RFL could put more resources into player development and instruct clubs to do the same. That is why the production line really developed from the early 1990s onwards.

Maurice Lindsay was a good man to have at the helm during a dispute like that, because he was prepared to stick to his guns - and if he had an idea worth backing he would throw money at it. He made it clear to me we had to be resolute, stand by what we believed in and make it a success. As far as I am concerned, that is exactly what we did. All this was happening in 1992 and now two decades later the academy is still going strong, it is a vital part of the sport at Super League level and the England academy team are up there among the best in the world at their age group, beating the Aussies and the Kiwis on a reasonably regular basis. Being able to do that is the true measure of success in rugby league.

I feel I was instrumental in the formation and development of the academy system in this country. I know I keep mentioning the word 'proud', but I reckon that really is something to be proud of. If you aren't convinced have a look at the squad list of a Super League club and check out how many first team players came through the academy ranks.

Along with Wigan Warriors, the best examples are Leeds Rhinos and St Helens, the two most successful sides in the game over recent years. When they played each other in the 2011 Super League Grand Final Rhinos had nine academy products in their winning team and there were 11 on the Saints side. Would players like Wigan's Sam Tomkins, Rob Burrow and Danny McGuire at Leeds or Saints' Jonny Lomax and Lee Gaskell have come through without the academy system? I doubt it and the game would be far poorer if they hadn't.

While I was at the RFL I was fortunate to coach the national academy side and in that team we had people like Jason Robinson, Phil Clarke and Andy Farrell, who were the first to emerge from the new system. They all went on to become superstars in the game and there are so many others who have followed them through. I would say the academy team at Leeds which included the likes of Burrow and McGuire was probably the best there has ever been at that level and Rhinos reaped the benefits by winning six Grand Finals in nine years once those youngsters had become established at senior level. Players who are now regarded as rugby league greats came through a system I was very much involved in formulating and establishing.

Since my day the academy system has continued to

develop, but changes at the end of 2012 are a major concern to me. The RFL - prompted by clubs who don't want the cost of running two lower grade teams - have decided to scrap the under-18 and under-20 competitions and replace them with one under-19 set-up.

I'm not in favour of that. It worries me where the next generation of players are going to come from. I predict that we'll soon be seeing a new influx of overseas players, not top-notch NRL stars, but Tongans, Samoans and Papua New Guineans who come over here, play in the 2013 World Cup and catch the eye of Super League clubs.

I think the RFL should have kept the under-20s, or perhaps made it under-23s. Super League clubs have had to axe players aged over 19 who are not in the first-team squad and that is very early to be thrown on the scrapheap.

Championship clubs are picking up a lot of the discarded youngsters, but it is very difficult for a lad of 20 to go from an age-group competition to playing in a good standard like the second tier every week. You've got people like Makali Aizue running around in the Championship and he's a pretty tough cookie. A 20-year-old stepping up and playing against the likes of him is going to get knocked about a bit.

I worry we have lost our way in terms of talent identification and the development pathway, which is something that needs addressing. Money has been put before development and that upsets me, considering all the hard work that was put into establishing the academy in the 1990s.

As I have mentioned, though I did a lot of the hands-on work, Maurice Lindsay was the driving force behind the academy set-up and he deserves a lot of credit for that. He was also involved in my return to club coaching, under what were very bizarre circumstances.

The early 1990s were a revolutionary time in rugby

league and that culminated in 1996 in the switch from the old winter season - which ran roughly from August/ September until April/May - to a new summer timetable, beginning in the spring and ending in early autumn. As part of that Super League was introduced, funded by Rupert Murdoch's Sky TV.

The initial plan was for certain clubs to merge, for example Castleford, Featherstone and Wakefield would become Calder, Hull and Hull KR would join forces and there would be one Cumbrian super-club. Those proposals were quickly dropped because of opposition from fans, but one new club was created: Paris St Germain.

This was going to be rugby league's big breakthrough, away from the heartlands in the north of England on to a new international stage, based in one of the world's greatest cities. But anyone who knows anything about rugby league - or sport in general - would have had major concerns about its viability and those fears were quickly realised.

Rugby league is well-established in the south of France, but virtually unknown in the capital. At the time there weren't enough French players to supply a Super League team, so imports had to be brought over from Australia and New Zealand and simply planting a club in new territory, without years of work preparing the ground, proved to be a recipe for disaster.

Initially Paris was a success, their first game - against Sheffield Eagles - drew a crowd of nearly 18,000 and they pulled off a great win to give them a flying start. They won two and drew one of their opening four games, but after that the wheels fell off and they had only one more victory all season.

Only the bottom team was relegated in 1996 so that one win, over London in July, was enough to keep them up, finishing two points above Workington Town - and I was coach at the time. I had been doing some hands-on coaching with the national academy team and assisting Malcolm Reilly and then Phil Larder with Great Britain and England. I was flown out to assist with the 1992 GB tour to Australia, which makes me a Lion, something else I am very proud of. I was also involved with Great Britain in the 1992 World Cup final, under Malcolm, and England in the 1995 World Cup, when Phil was in charge.

All that had allowed me to keep my eye in and I must have been doing something right, because when Paris ran into serious problems and they needed someone to go over there and try and sort things out, Maurice turned to me. We had a meeting and he told me: 'I am going to second you to Paris, it'll be great for your development.' That was the carrot, the stick was: 'Your job is to keep them in Super League!'

Michel Mazare was the Paris coach and he had appealed to the RFL to send someone over to give him a hand. I was available and, being on the RFL pay roll, there was no added cost, which obviously was a massive bonus. I was a bit like the Magnificent Seven riding to the rescue, except there was only one of me! I spent 14 weeks in France and while it wasn't the most successful period of my career in terms of results, we got the job done. That epic victory over London kept us in the competition, by the skin of our teeth. We finished with seven points, two ahead of Workington who were relegated. Naturally I would have liked to pick up more victories, but performances improved during my time at the club and that is something else I look back on with a great deal of satisfaction.

As coaching assignments go, it was a tough one. Before taking charge I watched Paris play at home to Castleford (lost 54-22) and away at Sheffield (lost 52-18). It was evident the players had very little technique and there was no structure in defence. They could play in patches, for 20 minutes or so, but were very naïve and struggled against better-organised English teams.

Part of the reason for that was the difference in standard between Super League and the French competition. Also, unbelievably, some of the French lads were still playing for their original clubs, alongside their involvement with Paris - so until the domestic league finished they could be taking part in two games in one week.

The win over London was obviously the highlight of my time in France, but there were some other memorable matches. We lost 26-24 at home to Warrington in my first game as coach, 14-10 away to Workington - in what was billed as le Crunch, a relegation decider - and 24-20 to visitors Wigan. For me the most poignant game was at Cas two weeks before the end of the season. We gave a great account of ourselves and only lost 22-18. Considering the score when Cas had visited Paris a couple of months earlier, that represented a massive improvement.

One of the amazing things about that first Super League season was Leeds' form, or lack of it. They won only six matches all year and finished third from bottom. They were locked in a desperate relegation battle when we went there in July, so much so that their coach Dean Bell came out of retirement to play in that one game, which we lost 34-12.

By the end of the year we had become very competitive. I would like to think some of that was down to my coaching - and that's definitely what I tell everybody - but also the French season had finished and the homegrown players were able to go full-time with Paris, so that helped. Vincent Wulf who was one of my better players also played for Villeneuve, for example. You don't have to be a brain surgeon to realise that performances will improve if your troops are only playing one game a week, rather than two.

The French season ended around the time I arrived, so the cards were dealt in my favour and I took advantage of that good hand. It turned out to be a fantastic move for me because I began to develop a reputation as a good coach and someone who could turn an ailing side around. I was also prepared to make the best of a difficult situation, because coaching Paris wasn't like being in charge of any other Super League team. Surreal is the word that best sums it up.

For a start, we weren't actually based in the French capital, other than for matches. We trained in Toulouse at a place called Crepes. That's a bit like Loughborough University over here; it is the premier physical education institution in the south of France. The facilities were excellent, but it was a long way away from the Charlety Stadium, where we played our home matches.

If we had a game over the Channel we flew from Toulouse to England; when we were at 'home' we would jet up to Paris on the day before the match and stay in an Ibis hotel next to the ground. We tended to play home fixtures on a Saturday evening, so we would arrive in Paris on the Friday night, have a team meeting and evening meal at the hotel and then train at the ground in the morning before the game. That was the only time we spent in Paris, maybe two days per fortnight.

That illustrates how logistically awkward it was and for that team to stay in Super League, given the difficulties of doubling up in the French Elite competition and training in the south of France, was a terrific achievement for all concerned. I enjoyed the whole experience, though it wasn't easy. I was staying in a hotel and living out of a suitcase and I had to pick up the language as I went along. I had a bit of schoolboy French and I was surprised how quickly that came back to me, though I had to use a lot of sign language as well. It was a great life experience and working with Michel Mazare was an absolute pleasure.

In fact I have a lot of time for anyone involved in French rugby league because they have had to go through so much to keep the sport alive over there. The code was introduced to France in the 1930s and ever since its enemies have been trying to kill it off. Rugby league was actually banned by the Vichy government during the Second World War and had all its assets seized, at a time when it was making real inroads and had the potential to become the dominant form of rugby across the Channel. It has never really recovered from that and French rugby union has done everything in its power to kill the 13-a-side code off. Even now we are all supposed to be friends there is a lot of resentment and hostility in powerful French union circles towards league, but great people like Michel Mazare have kept the 13-a-side code going and they deserve enormous credit for that.

Michel is a lovely fella and he really looked after me during my stint with Paris. When I arrived he took a step back from coaching and became the team manager, but he was a great host and made me feel welcome. I also had good support from Dave Ellis, another Cas lad, who helped out on the backroom staff. Dave had spent time with Villeneuve and some rugby union teams over there and was fluent in the language, so he was a huge asset. Dave went on to be part of the coaching set-up with the French national union team. Another big help to me was Yvan Grésèque, whose son Max was a talented little half-back who later played for the French Test side and had a spell on trial under me at Wakefield.

We had some good players too; people like the New Zealander Vincent Wulf, who later became a naturalised Frenchman, the French lads Patrick Entat, Pascal Bomati and Pierre Chamorin and the Aussies Deon Bird and Todd

Brown. It may not have been the most talented side ever to play in Super League, but you couldn't knock their enthusiasm and the post-season party is one I will always remember. The club hired a boat on the Seine, a trip which almost ended in disaster. In fact, it was an in-Seine escapade.

A few drinks were taken to celebrate our survival in the competition and Vincent Wulf decided it would be a good time to take a swim. He was first into the cold waters, followed by the prop forward Vea Bloomfield and then rest of the team, bar me and Pat Entat, who were both far too sensible to take part in such silliness. It was a huge relief when we managed to get them all back safely on board. Maurice Lindsay was happy with the job I did there and I think he felt I justified his faith in me, but he would have been less pleased if I had managed to drown half the team.

There was an opportunity for me to stay on with Paris after 1996. When we played in Yorkshire we tended to stay at a hotel in Bramhope, near Leeds and train at the local West Park rugby union club. That was where the new England rugby union coach Stuart Lancaster held a pre-Six Nations training camp many years later.

The weekend we faced Leeds in that crucial bottom of the table clash the directors approached me in the hotel and offered me the coaching job for the following season. I was tempted, but I didn't believe the club was sustainable. I could see that money was going out, but there was nothing coming in and that was the reason I said no.

I would have loved PSG to be successful, but that was never realistic. Paris is a long way from rugby league's French strongholds and the people in the capital city just weren't interested. After the euphoria of that first night and the win over Sheffield the crowds declined rapidly and - despite the official attendance figures - gates were down to the hundreds by the end of the campaign. There was no development work in place, nothing to make people aware of the existence of a club and nothing to encourage them to watch or play the sport. The logistics of training in the south of the country and flying to games were also unworkable on a long-term basis. When we were training in Toulouse the interest in the game and the Paris team was phenomenal, but as soon as we decamped for the capital nobody knew or cared who we were. Even at the start, when they played in front of decent crowds, all the tickets were give-aways.

Paris finished second from bottom again in Super League II, but that proved to be their final season and the club was wound-up. The initial idea was they would take a year out and return to the competition in 1999, but nobody really expected their comeback to happen and so it proved. I was sad about that, but not surprised. Fortunately lessons were learned and I was delighted when Perpignan-based Catalan Dragons entered Super League a decade after Paris. Being in the south of France that was a case of right place, right time and Paris definitely wasn't, but I wouldn't have swapped my time there for anything.

5

*

Shuddering at the Memories

WORKING for the RFL was a good experience, but being in charge of Paris made me realise how much I had missed the hands-on, day-to-day aspect of coaching, so when I was offered a chance to get back into the club game I jumped at it.

In October of 1996, after finishing with Paris, I took Great Britain academy to New Zealand, at the same time as the senior side - coached by Phil Larder - were away on their autumn tour, against Papua New Guinea, Fiji and the Kiwis.

The academy campaign was a tremendous adventure. We played a total of seven matches, beating Auckland under-19s, Maori Colts and Canterbury under-19s and losing to Central Districts, plus all three Tests against the Junior Kiwis. Results-wise it could have gone better, but we were competitive in every match and I felt it was a successful tour. We got a bit of a touch-up in the first Test, which we lost 35-14, but it was only 27-24 in the second and the final game saw us edged out 37-36 - and we would have had a draw if Ian Watson's late drop-goal attempt had been on target.

Coaching is Chaos

The Junior Kiwis had a powerful squad, including future Super League stars of the quality of Lesley Vainikolo and Kylie Leuluai, so losing to them was no disgrace. Our group was also very strong: we had Gary Broadbent at full-back, Terry Newton at hooker, Nick Fozzard at prop and Ian Knott in the second-row, plus the likes of Marvin Golden, Daryl Cardiss, Paul Johnson, Nathan McAvoy, Jamie Field and Jon Clarke, who all went on to make an impact in Super League.

Jim Hartley managed the academy tour and I was helped by my assistant-coach Ray Unsworth, who was Wigan academy coach at the time. It was good to work with people like that and also to test myself - and see the players challenged - in a tough environment. The opposition were huge and very physical, but our lads stood up to them and a few of them came back from that tour as men.

While we were in New Zealand I went for a coffee with Phil Larder and he told me he was moving from Keighley Cougars to Sheffield Eagles. He asked me if I would go with him as his assistant and I took up the offer, which meant leaving the RFL and returning to the club game on a full-time basis. Working at Sheffield particularly appealed to me because I liked the idea of being involved at a club outside the heartlands of the sport where it was a bit of a backs to the wall scenario, as it had been in Paris. The Eagles were established in the top-flight by then, but were also in transition.

Gary Hetherington, who founded the club in 1984, was in the process of leaving to become chief executive at Leeds. One of the last things he did - alongside the chairman Terry Sharman - was appoint Phil and me. Gary took us both to the Flying Pizza restaurant in Leeds and offered us the job. I knew he really wanted us, because he paid for the food. That was a remarkable event as he is one of the tightest men in the sport.

To be honest, my expectations about Sheffield exceeded the reality. Initially Phil didn't really have to sell Sheffield to me because I was keen to get back into club coaching and I saw it as a great opportunity. But I was assured the Eagles were a sleeping giant and that if they performed well in Super League and had some success they would get huge crowds. I think people associated with the club really believed that, but as events proved, it was a long way from the truth.

There were certainly good intentions at Sheffield and some ideas which were ahead of their time. Under the new owner, Paul Thompson, Eagles became the first Super League club to be floated on the Stock Exchange. Two and a half million shares were made available and to my mind that indicated how forward-thinking the club was. Unfortunately, the flotation ran aground and Eagles could not capitalise on the on-field success which was just around the corner.

Phil's reign as coach lasted just 12 games. We lost all but four of those and one of the victories was our opening fixture against lower division Leigh in the Challenge Cup. By the middle of May Phil was on his bike and I found myself, unexpectedly, appointed as the new head coach.

Phil had been up against it right from the start when only 12 players turned up to our first training session, held at a school in Sheffield. With the change of leadership things like recruitment had been neglected. That made it a tough situation for the new coach because he came in without having a full squad to work with. He had to go back to Keighley for some players he had worked with there and was also forced into taking a chance on one or two others who were unproven at that level. The lack of recruitment before we came in put us behind the eight ball and that was reflected in the start we made to the 1997 Super League season, which cost Phil his job.

Coaching is Chaos

Phil was unlucky; I thought he was a very gifted coach and he had enjoyed success with Widnes, Keighley and - relatively - Great Britain, but things just didn't work out for him at Sheffield. Sometimes it happens like that; it didn't mean he was a poor coach, because what works for one group of players may not with another.

I think Phil probably went into the job - as I did - thinking the club was in a better state than proved to be the case and after we had made a poor start he wasn't able to turn the tide. Technically, he was very good, one of the best I have come across, but I think he tried to implement too many changes, too quickly.

Crucially, he lost the changing room. An example was our second Super League game of the season away to Halifax, which we lost 18-16. Speaking to the media after the match he described the players as 'one of the thickest teams ever'. Not surprisingly that upset quite a number of them, particularly the senior and most influential players, Paul Carr among them. It is always a bad sign when a coach starts blaming his players in public.

The outburst after the Halifax game drove a wedge between Phil and his players and the gulf got wider and wider as the season went on. On one occasion Phil blew up at Paul Carr during a training session at Don Valley Stadium. Paul ran the wrong line and Phil really ripped into him. Phil was very demanding and he wouldn't tolerate mistakes, even in training. Paul was highly upset and the two of them almost came to blows. I had to hold Paul back and then walk him a few times around the running track, talking quietly to him, to calm him down. Sometimes that happens in professional sport and usually it blows over, but unfortunately this time the rift grew so serious it couldn't be mended. In situations like that the board of a club have two choices: sack the coach or change the players - and it is easier to do the former.

I respected Phil, enjoyed working with him and we had a good relationship, though we did fall out a bit towards the end of his time at Sheffield. The disagreement was over recruitment: I wanted to sign Andy Hay from Castleford - which is what eventually happened - and Phil felt his son Dave Larder was a better bet. Dave had a great career, but I think Andy, who is now assistant-coach at Hull after a similar stint with Cas, was a better player. Funnily enough, Dave is now assistant to coach Mark Aston at Sheffield, which shows how the wheel turns.

That dispute meant we didn't part on the best of terms, though things could not have worked out much better for Phil and I am sure he now regards leaving Eagles as a blessing in disguise. By the end of the year he was part of the England rugby union set-up and he was a key member of Clive Woodward's backroom staff when they won the World Cup in 2003, earning an MBE in the process. He is now living in Spain for half the year, in semi-retirement, so I doubt he has many regrets.

I wasn't surprised by Phil's switch to rugby union. When we were working together he told me all the big money would soon be in the 15-a-side code. It wouldn't be for everyone, but the path he followed after Sheffield suited him down to the ground and I was pleased for him.

I was appointed Eagles' coach the day after Phil left. There was nothing untoward, I didn't play any part in his exit and I wasn't aware of it until it was officially announced. The Eagles' management obviously saw some plus points in the work I had been doing as Phil's assistant and with us dangerously close to the relegation zone and half the season gone, they didn't want to be mucking about trying to find a successor.

Terry Sharman rang and arranged to meet me, we had a chat and he offered me the job. I was proud and privileged to accept because - despite the poor results so far - I could see there was real potential in the team. They hadn't responded to Phil's methods and man-management, but there were some good players at the club and I felt I could bring the best out of them.

My first game was at home to Halifax, which we lost 49-24, but things settled down pretty well after that. We were eighth when I took over and that's where we finished, but performances did improve. I got my first victory in my second match, 38-12 at Warrington, and there was a memorable game against Perth Reds in June, in the World Club Championship. We were losing 22-4, but stormed back to win 26-22.

After losing seven of the first 11 games after I took over, we came home with a wet sail and won five of the last eight. With a bit more luck, we might even have reached the Premiership final. That season it was a 12-team Super League and they all took part in the end-of-year play-offs.

In our first game we were at home to ninth-placed Warrington and we won that one 26-16. Next we went to London Broncos; they'd had a great year and were runners-up on the league table - and we thrashed them 58-16. That is still one of the best team displays I have been involved with.

When I went into the Press conference afterwards and I was asked 'what did you think of that?' I told the startled media: 'I think I've had an 80-minute orgasm.' Keith Senior had a sensational game and looked every bit an international centre and every player in the team played to the best of his ability.

That was the first time I thought I had a team capable of winning a major trophy. I'd suspected they could be a good side if and when they put it all together and the display that day proved it. We went to Wigan in the semi-finals and lost 22-10, but the game could have gone either way.

The Premiership wasn't a well-loved competition and it has since been replaced by the Grand Final play-offs, but our run that year was hugely significant. It gave the players an injection of confidence and as far as I was concerned, the seed of an idea was planted. Nobody considered Sheffield to be serious contenders for silverware, but I was convinced that - given a bit of good fortune and a favourable draw - we could have a real crack at the Challenge Cup in 1998.

Looking back on the performances and especially the wins we'd had since May, I felt we had a pretty decent rugby league team, but the players hadn't believed in their own ability. There were players, Nick Pinkney and Martin Wood, who had been brought in from Keighley and were still coming to grips with the top division, there was an old Sheffield clique - Mark Aston and Paul Broadbent - and a gaggle of overseas players, led by Rod Doyle and Paul Carr. It was a talented mix, but they needed moulding into a unit, so they could all sing off the same hymn sheet. That's what we worked on over the second half of the season and when they won at London I think they suddenly started to think 'we might have something here'.

What I had seen in the Premiership competition gave me an indication of what the team could do and where we needed to strengthen. We didn't need wholesale changes; it was just a case of adding some quality in the right areas. Dave Watson, a multi-talented Kiwi, fitted the bill perfectly. He was high maintenance off the pitch, but a superstar on it. We also added a strong-running back-rower in the shape of Michael Jackson and come the spring of 1998 I felt the pieces of the jigsaw were at least all in the box, if not yet put together.

It's not often in rugby league - or any other walk of life - that things go exactly according to plan, but our 1998 Challenge Cup campaign did. Everything was geared around reaching Wembley and winning the final and - as I'll explain in the next chapter - we did just that.

The Wembley victory over red-hot favourites Wigan Warriors was the greatest day in Sheffield Eagles' history, but sadly it also marked the beginning of the end and within 18 months, the club - as it had been - no longer existed. The theory that success would turn the Sheffield people on to rugby league proved to be a myth.

A week after the final we played Wigan again, in the league at Don Valley Stadium and 7,365 turned up to see us lose 36-6, not that anybody in our camp was too bothered about the result, but that proved to be the biggest attendance of the season and the rest of our home games attracted about half of that.

In other words the die-hards remained, but winning the Cup didn't pull in any new supporters. For a while we were heroes to the national public, thanks to the BBC's coverage of the game and everybody in rugby league loved us. They could see what we had done with a young club based outside the established heartlands and lacking the resources other clubs had, but in our home city nobody really cared. It was the biggest shock in Challenge Cup history, but that wasn't understood in Sheffield as a whole.

Within the sport, what we had achieved got me noticed and it did the same for Dale Laughton, Mark Aston and especially Keith Senior, who had Leeds and Wigan chasing him for a year before he finally signed on at Headingley. But we remained unknown in Sheffield itself. Open top bus rides are a tradition after a Challenge Cup win. I did one with Castleford in 1986 and the town was packed. It was the same later on when I was a member of the coaching staff at Wigan and we won the trophy. After Hull's triumph in 2005, when I was head coach, we got off the bus at the Town Hall and all you could see was a mass of black and white.

When we had our open top tour of Sheffield, four men and a dog turned up - and I think the dog went home early. There was no civic reception arranged and Terry Sharman had to convince the council our achievement was worth celebrating. Eventually we had a bit of a do, the mayor turned up and a few curled up sandwiches were provided, but we got the distinct impression it was all a big inconvenience.

That was really sad, after we had made history. In January 2000, less than two years after the Wembley victory, the re-formed Sheffield Eagles were beaten at home by amateurs Thornhill Trojans in the Challenge Cup, which illustrates how far and fast the decline was.

I don't blame the club, they did everything they could to kick on from Wembley, but they were fighting a losing battle. It took me a while to realise that and so I made a naïve decision which I have regretted ever since: I turned down an offer to coach St Helens.

After the Cup win my stock was extremely high and I was a man in demand. Tim Adams, who succeeded Terry Sharman as Sheffield's chairman, told me he was determined to make Eagles an elite club and he made it clear I was an integral part of his plans. I wasn't ruthless enough, I showed loyalty to the club and it didn't work out.

We talked to some quality players, including Henry Paul and Fereti Tuilagi, about joining us, but we simply couldn't match their wage demands. They weren't being greedy or asking for more than they were worth, but they wanted the going rate for players of their ability. When Henry mentioned a figure to Tim and the owner Paul Thompson, you could see the colour drain from their faces.

We had just won the Challenge Cup with a wage bill of £780,000 and they suddenly realised how much it was going to cost if we were to join the elite in Super League. After that I don't think we were ever really in with a shout.

Coaching is Chaos

We didn't handle winning the Cup very well once we returned to Super League action. We played 19 games after the final and won seven of them, with two draws. We had a good spell from late-June to early August, when we won five out of six, but there was only one victory in our final seven and the season culminated in an embarrassing 50-0 hammering at St Helens.

Wigan, incidentally, lost only twice in the league all year, home and away to Leeds Rhinos. They finished top of the table and beat Leeds in the first Super League Grand Final. We were walloped 44-6 at Central Park in August so the two league games against them after Wembley saw us score 12 points and concede 80.

Mid-way through the season Shaun McRae confirmed he would be leaving his job as Saints coach at the end of the year and they targeted me as his successor. Eric Hughes was in charge of the football side of things over there and Alan Rowley, whose son Paul now coaches Leigh and played in Super League for them, Huddersfield and Halifax, was also involved.

They invited me over to the ground, we had a chat and they offered me the job for the 1999 season. I was impressed by Saints' set-up and the playing staff and the money was better than I was on at Sheffield. I think you have to do these things right, so I had told Tim Adams I was interested in speaking to Saints and he said he wouldn't stand in my way, which is credit to him, but he also asked me to talk to him after they had made an offer.

I did that and I was blown away by what Sheffield offered to keep me. It was obvious they wanted me at the helm and Tim painted a bright picture of where the club would be going in the next few years. In fact where they were going was Huddersfield, but none of us knew that at the time.

I was sold on Eagles' glowing prospects and I turned Saints down, which in hindsight was the wrong thing to do. Saints are a genuinely big club with a track record of success. They attract a good following, boast an excellent youth system and have always had a board who've been prepared to back ambition with hard cash when it comes to recruitment and putting structures in place.

Ellery Hanley got the job instead and he guided them to the Super League title in 1999. When he left mid-way through the 2000 season Ian Millward took over and they won the Grand Final again, going on to achieve the feat for the third time in 2002. They also won the Challenge Cup in 2001, so that was four trophies in three years after I had said no. I watched those successes with envious eyes. I regret turning Saints down and if I had my time again I would make a different decision.

The 1999 campaign at Sheffield was disappointing. We finished 10th in a 14-team league, winning 10 and drawing one of our 30 matches and failing to qualify for the end-of-season play-offs. We also went out of the Challenge Cup at the first attempt, losing away to Salford.

It was a bit like a rehearsal for what I was to go through 12 years later at Wakefield: we spent the entire year with the sword of Damocles hanging over us. Rumours began to surface that the Eagles would be merging with Huddersfield Giants at the end of the year, with the new outfit playing over in West Yorkshire.

It was all done and dusted before we had the details confirmed, but I knew there was something drastically wrong when I was told we had 11 players contracted for the year after and they were the only full-time players we would have. A Super League club couldn't operate like that, with 11 full-timers and the rest part-time, so it was obvious things were afoot. The financial situation at the club meant they had to do something, Paul Thompson was keeping Eagles afloat on his own, but that wasn't sustainable in the long-term.

The demise of the old Eagles club was sad, but a phoenix did rise from the ashes in the shape of a new outfit, still based at Don Valley but playing in the semi-professional Northern Ford Premiership. Mark Aston founded the club and has remained there, as coach and chief executive, ever since. He doesn't know this, but at the time the merger talks were taking place I was keen on the idea of Eagles being relaunched as a lower division feeder club, with Tubby as coach.

He is a great reader of the game and that is why he has done so well with Sheffield, despite very limited resources. Keeping the club alive has been a feat in itself, but now they are a top-end Championship side and I was delighted when they won the 2012 Grand Final, from fourth on the table.

Mark has done a fantastic job, still based on the old Eagles ethos of hard work and enthusiasm. I have a great fondness for Sheffield, I always look for their results and the club will forever have a place in my heart, despite the way things there ended for me.

When we joined forces with Huddersfield it was billed as a merger, but in reality it was a take-over. They - Huddersfield - had a benefactor in Ken Davy who was willing to bankroll them, but we didn't have those sorts of resources. Huddersfield had finished bottom in 1999, for the second successive year and the 'merger' meant they retained their Super League status, but they were the dominant partner in every respect, as illustrated by the name: Huddersfield-Sheffield Giants.

They had a superb facility and a wealthy backer, but their team wasn't good enough. We had the better players and confirmed Super League status. We were sold it as an equal partnership, with the plan being to play seven home games at Bramall Lane and a similar number in Huddersfield, at McAlpine Stadium as it was then. Half the training was going to be in Sheffield and half in Huddersfield. When it came to it, all the training was in Huddersfield and the plan to share games between the two venues was quickly dropped. In August they played Castleford at Bramall Lane and only 2,102 fans turned up. It was announced after that there would be no more matches in Sheffield, which I am sure was the plan all along. I say 'they' because I had moved on by then.

The 'merger' was confirmed on September 30, 1999 and I left the club on July 13 the following year. It was a very unhappy time and one of the lowest periods of my coaching career. I wasn't able to appoint my own staff, both Steve Deakin and Simon Worsnop were released and I was told I had to take the Huddersfield assistant Phil Veivers - now coach at Salford - and their conditioner Trevor Commons.

When the merger was announced I should have walked away. I stayed put and lived to regret it. The cultures at the Eagles and Giants were very different. Gary Hetherington is a tough task master and very careful with his cash. His legacy was that players at Sheffield tended to be over-worked and under-paid, whereas it was the opposite at Huddersfield.

An example: In my first choice team I had Darren Turner on the bench, with Johnny Lawless as my starting hooker. The third rake in the organisation was Danny Russell, who was retained from Giants' previous squad. Johnny and Rocky's payments combined were less than what Danny Russell was on. Johnny, who is someone I like a lot, pulled me to one side about that and made it clear he wasn't happy. I had every sympathy for him.

The squad was divided into a number of cliques, there

were the ex-Sheffield and ex-Huddersfield players, plus an overseas group and another who travelled over together from St Helens. Getting everybody to mix was really difficult and the gulf in wages among some of the players only added to the problems. I did try to put structures and systems in place and I think that was a minor success. After I left Tony Smith came over from Australia to take the post and he complimented me on the job I had done there.

In league and Cup, I was in charge of Shuddersfield for 19 games and we lost all but three of them, including a run of 10 straight defeats at one stage. They lost eight out of 10 after my departure. Huddersfield lost their first 16 Super League games the following year, finished bottom and were relegated. Eventually Tony Smith - who is a superb coach - managed to bring his own players in and impose the sort of culture he wanted there, but it took a spell in the lower division before he could do that.

You live and learn and I think the tough experiences I had at Shuddersfield made me a better coach. What doesn't kill you makes you stronger and I am a firm believer that reflective learning - learning from experience - is the best method of education.

Having said that if I knew then what I know now, I would first of all have taken the Saints job and secondly, would have quit when the merger was announced. I think I could have gone from there into a head coaching role at another, bigger, club. As it turned out, I had to serve two spells as an assistant before I got back into a Super League hot seat.

6

*

When Eagles Dared

AT Sheffield Eagles' very first training session ahead of the 1998 campaign I told the players: 'We are going to win the Challenge Cup this year!' I don't recall anybody laughing, but they looked at me as if I was barmy. It took a while for them to buy into the idea, but everything fell into place as we went along.

It wasn't just the players who were told that. I said the same thing to the media - and got a similar response. I wanted to show I had faith in the players; it was mind games, I was trying to brainwash them into believing what I was saying, that we could win the sport's oldest and most famous trophy.

Pre-season was structured so we would come out all guns blazing. Those were the days when the Challenge Cup was staged as a pre- and early-season competition, with the first four rounds played before the league matches began and the final in May. I appointed Steve Deakin as my assistant-coach with Simon Worsnop as conditioner and they did a great job. We did a lot of technical work on defence, a lot on speed and agility and even more on individual skills, so while some teams were still finding their feet, we were at our peak right at the start of the campaign.

We also had the luck of the draw, which is crucial to a successful Cup run. For the second successive year we were drawn away to Leigh in our first match and we cruised through that one, winning 66-11. Next up were an amateur side, Egremont, at home and we thumped them 84-8. Rob Purdham, who later went on to play with great distinction for London/Harlequins and England, starred for the Cumbrians that day and had a top game. I actually asked about him afterwards, though nothing came of it.

While we were easing through against lesser opposition, the leading lights were beating each other, which was a major bonus. Leeds lost at home to Castleford in the opening round and Cas then beat the Super League champions Bradford Bulls next up, so two of the big guns were already out of the competition.

Then Wigan drew St Helens in the quarter-finals, so we knew if we got through our last-eight tie - away to Castleford - we would have a real chance of going all the way to Wembley. The players hadn't really believed it was possible at the start of the year, but everything seemed to be going in our favour and all their initial scepticism vanished.

Getting past Cas wasn't going to be easy. After beating Leeds and Bradford they thought it was going to be their year and with them having home advantage we had it all to do. But by that stage everyone at our club was beginning to buy into the idea that we could win this thing - even the board of directors. They gave us a big vote of confidence by agreeing to fund an overnight stay before the game, despite the fact it's only about 25 miles from Sheffield to Castleford. We stayed at the very nice Village Hotel, in Headingley, which added the finishing touch to our excellent preparation.

There was one scare when Johnny Lawless went down ill and we had to bring Gareth Stephens into the team, but he had a cracking game and set up a couple of tries, so that piece of misfortune worked out in our favour. Gareth was instrumental in taking us a step further and the way we turned a setback into a positive added to the growing confidence in the camp.

It was Eagles' first Cup quarter-final and their debut on the BBC and we went into the game as massive underdogs, but battled through to win 32-22. The game will best be remembered for Keith Senior flattening the Cas centre Barrie-Jon Mather early in the second half, getting away with it and then going on to score two crucial tries. BJ had been having a great game and had scored a brace of touchdowns himself, but he had to go off after being poleaxed and we took control following his departure.

BJ had just scored when there was a flare-up and the pushing and shoving ended with Keith laying him out. At the end of the game the Cas coach, Stuart Raper, said they should have had an eight-point try - that's a try, conversion and a penalty for the foul - and Keith should have walked. I'm not sure about the eight-point try, but he was right about the rest of it. It was as obvious a red card incident as you will ever see: poor BJ happened to be in the wrong place at the wrong time and found himself on the end of a Senior haymaker.

I tried to play it down after the game, but once I'd had a look at the footage I knew Keith would get called before the RFL disciplinary and was facing a long ban. That said, I don't think it was Keith's fault; Dean Sampson was to blame. Diesel ran in at Darren 'Rocky' Turner, who reacted and then Keith banjoed the nearest Cas player, who happened to be BJ, who got one full on the jaw. That made Keith a hate figure in Castleford, where he is still blamed for them not getting to

Wembley that year. He gets abuse when he goes back to the town even now.

Anyway, when things like that go in your favour you have to take advantage and we did. We were the better team over the course of the game and we deserved to go through. And yes, the fact we had beaten Cas in probably the biggest game in Eagles' history did make it extra special for me.

I will always be a Cas fan, but when my teams come up against them I'll do everything possible to make sure we are the ones celebrating at the end. I've faced Castleford in some big games - including possibly the most crucial game in Super League history, which I will talk about later - and there has never been any divided loyalty on my part. After we had dumped them out of the Cup and shattered their dreams I definitely wasn't feeling sorry for my old club. Beforehand they seemed to think all they had to do to grab a place in the semi-finals was turn up; even my Auntie Kath was telling me they were going to win the Cup. Everyone in the town felt the same and it was great to prove them wrong - and to do it in style. Cas didn't play poorly, but we were very good.

That win ticked all the boxes: afterwards it wasn't just me thinking we could get to Wembley and win the Cup, the whole squad now felt the same way. To add to the celebrations, we avoided Wigan in the semi-finals. We drew Salford and Wigan took on London. That was pleasing, but I also wanted Wigan to win and to get to the final. I told Kath Sharman - Terry's wife, who worked in the offices at Sheffield - that if we were to win the Cup I didn't want anybody saying we had done it the easy way. I wanted us to beat the best team in the competition, which Wigan were, even if they no longer enjoyed the dominance they did in the late 1980s and early 90s.

There has probably never been a less glamorous semi-final than our clash with Salford. The team from the Willows have not won the Cup since 1938, we had never reached the last four before and neither club was well-supported. Only 6,961 fans turned up to the Headingley showdown, which is really poor for a Cup semi-final, but the game meant everything to the players and coaches involved.

We had to manage without Keith Senior, who got a four-match ban for his assault on BJ and in truth we didn't play well, but that was one of those occasions when only the result matters. If it had been a boxing match Salford would have won on points, but the scoreboard is what counts and at the end of the game it read Eagles 22, Reds 18.

It was my biggest game as coach and the most important match most of the players - on either side - had been involved in. For a long time it looked like we might come up short: we went 18-10 down with 15 minutes to go and two scores is a mountain to climb in a Cup semi-final. In situations like that you need players to do something special and our key men came up with the goods. First Nick Pinkney put a chip through and Mark Aston - who will admit he was never blessed with blistering pace - read it perfectly, the ball popped into his hands and he scored a reviving try.

He kicked the goal to leave us only two points behind and then Dale Laughton came up with the winning touchdown. That had nothing to do with me, it was all Dale's own work; an on-line move against three defenders with sheer strength and determination taking him over. I'll be grateful to him for that for the rest of my life.

The belief gained in the Cas game shone through in those final 15 minutes against Salford and it was that which saw us home. Salford were slightly the better team overall and they threw everything at us in the closing stages, but we hung in there, we believed in ourselves and we held on.

Without Keith we put Bright Sodje on the wing and Matty Crowther was in the centres. He did a high-quality job and saved the day on the final play of the match. The hooter went and half our players stopped, but you should play to the whistle and Salford did just that, almost to match-winning effect. Steve Blakeley made a break and Matty hit him with a great cover tackle. The Salford man tried to offload, spilled the ball in the tackle and knocked-on, the referee, Stuart Cummings, blew the whistle and we had done it.

The feeling then was unbelievable, not just for me but also for the players, the staff, the directors and the supporters. Our fans weren't the greatest in number, but they made up for that with their enthusiasm. Many of them had followed the club right from the start, through more thin times than thick and we were all delighted for them. They were real supporters in the true sense of the word. Non-critical, they didn't moan and groan however poor the performance might have been, they were always behind us and they thoroughly deserved to enjoy a win like that one.

There was crowd trouble after the game, which perhaps took some of the gloss off it. A Salford follower ran on to the field and had a go at Stuart Cummings, who ended up with neck, back and ankle injuries. It might have been worse, but Bright Sodje came in and rescued the official. We were tackling everything that moved that day, including pitch invaders.

There was more than a month - and four Super League games - between the semi and final. We lost three of them and didn't play well at all. We were at Wembley so half the job was done, but being in a final was a leap in the dark. We had focused on getting there, but none of us was exactly sure what to do now we had.

We had a chat after the Salford game and I told my assistant Steve Deakin: 'You're in charge of the team for the next four matches and I'll concentrate on getting ready for the final.' I was still there, keeping an eye on things, but Steve did all the planning and preparation for the league campaign while I tried to come up with a plan to beat Wigan, who had thrashed London 38-8 in the other semi-final.

Analysing the opposition is a part of coaching I really enjoy and I have always been keen on doing my homework. By the time I had finished I felt I knew Wigan pretty well, so it was simply a case of making our players aware of their troops' strengths and weaknesses, areas we had to work on in our own game and ones we could exploit in theirs.

Wigan won their four matches before Wembley, running in 120 points and conceding 38. They were bang in form and, to be honest, they had a better team than we did. Everybody outside our club thought we were going to Wembley just to make up the numbers and we used that to our advantage.

We were a good team and all the pundits lost sight of that, because they were focusing so much on Wigan. There were a few media events in the lead up to the final which our captain Paul Broadbent - known as Beans - and I had to attend. We would turn up and then spend the whole time tucking into the sandwiches and talking among ourselves while all the press boys chatted to the Wigan contingent. Nobody wanted to speak to us.

I was angry about that at the time, because it was disrespectful, but it gave us a bit of added motivation, to go out and prove all the so-called experts wrong. Beans (Broadbent, broad beans) is a pretty intense character at the best of times, the sort who would argue with himself in solitary confinement, and I spent the week leading into the final whispering in his ear about the way we were being ignored. The media did a great job stoking the embers, so there were a few blazing fires when we did finally get out on to the pitch.

When I looked at my Wembley line-up, I knew the players out there had what it takes to win big games. The side was: Waisale Sovatabua at full-back; Nick Pinkney and Matty Crowther on the wings; Whetu Taewa and Keith Senior in the centres; half-backs of Dave Watson and Mark Aston; Paul Broadbent and Dale Laughton in the front-row either side of Johnny Lawless; Paul Carr and Darren Shaw in the second-row and Rod Doyle at loose-forward. On the bench we had Michael Jackson, Darren Turner, Martin Wood and Lynton Stott.

I'm not going to bore you with a match report, but a lifelong bond was forged during the Cup run and sealed at Wembley and I will forever be thankful to those players - and the ones who appeared earlier on but didn't feature in the final - for their efforts.

I didn't feel we deserved to be written-off in the manner we were, but it is fair to say Wigan were in far better form. I wasn't too concerned about the results in the build-up to Wembley, but I was pleased and at least a bit relieved when we got our act together away to Huddersfield the week before the final.

Huddersfield weren't the best opposition and it was a game we went into knowing we should win, which we duly did 48-18. What made it such a gratifying performance was the fact Was Sovatabua was sent-off just before half-time and we still managed to out-play them with only 12 men. I had the feeling after the game that perhaps we had got our timing right - and when Was got away without a ban that was just a little extra fuel on the fire.

Going into the final I had some help from my old mate and coaching partner at Bramley, Barry Johnson. He had been in Castleford's Wembley winning team in the 1986 final and, fortunately for us, had kept a diary. He had noted everything they did in the week before the final and he came in and passed some tips on to the Sheffield players. Barry is a smart bloke and he painted a vivid picture of what it was like to walk out at Wembley. He even showed us a video with footage of David Watkinson - the Hull KR hooker - with his head down after the final whistle, while all the Cas players celebrated. The message was clear: There are two experiences in every final, which one do you want?

The players mentally rehearsed what it was going to be like walking out for the final and when we had a look around the stadium on the day before the game, I made them climb the famous steps to the Royal Box so they could imagine getting their hands on the Cup.

We were told we wouldn't be allowed to warm-up on the pitch, so we would have to get ready in the changing rooms. During the pre-match visit we measured those out, marked some concrete to the exact dimensions and warmed-up in that area before our last training session, to replicate the conditions we'd face the following afternoon. We made sure every base was covered and I honestly don't think our preparations could have been any better. I wanted the players to know what to expect come the big day.

I do not believe in treating semi-finals or finals as just another game, for the simple reason they aren't. They are special, emotional occasions. I wanted the players to embrace the occasion and to get emotional, but I knew they needed to control those emotions. I told the players to use their senses, make sure they smelled and heard and saw what it was like, so they could store those memories for the rest of their lives.

It might have been past its sell-by date, but I loved the old Wembley. The walk from the changing rooms to the pitch was sensational. It was up a long, dark tunnel and you emerged into the bright light and noise as you reached pitch level - rather like being born.

The mind games continued in the tunnel as we were waiting to take to the field. We had a call, '98' to signify it was going to be our year. As we were lining up alongside Wigan,

Coaching is Chaos

Johnny Lawless was screaming '98' at their players. They must have been wondering 'what's this demented little bloke doing'?

It wound all our lads up and showed Wigan we weren't scared of them and we were prepared to stand toe to toe and eye to eye with them, which was how we played. We knew we'd have to be at the very top of our game and would need Wigan to be a bit below their best, which is how it turned out.

Mark Aston won the Lance Todd Trophy as man of the match, and deservedly so. He carried out our planned kicking game to perfection. Wigan's right winger was Mark Bell, a tall, rangy fella who wasn't the most agile when turning to collect the ball. On the other flank was Jason Robinson, one of the most effective wingers in the world, so you don't need to be a master coach to figure out you are better kicking to Bell when you are kicking from distance. That's what Tubby - Mark Aston's nickname - did, time after time.

Then when we got in their 20 the plan was to grubber into the in-goal if we were kicking to our left, which was Bell's side. If we were kicking to Robinson we would try and sit it on his head. Four minutes into the game we were camped in their 20, Tubby kicked to our right and Nick Pinkney timed his run to perfection, plucking the ball out of the air and touching down.

It was like a switch had been flicked: that successful move showed the players - and coaching staff - that our game plan would work and we did have what it would take to win the game. The performance over the full game was sensational; it was 33 minutes before we made an error, which is incredible in a Challenge Cup final, especially the players' first one.

With about seven minutes left Henry Paul lost possession. He came out from dummy-half, looked one way and tried to pass the other, but knocked-on. We were 17-8 up at the time and they had thrown everything except the kitchen sink at us. They'd scored one try and then Andy Farrell had got over the line for what might have been another, but Tubby got underneath and held him up, preventing him grounding the ball. It was one of the best defensive plays I have ever seen.

When Henry lost the ball, Johnny Lawless was really smart. He didn't dive on it; he was happy to waste some time and let the Wigan man pick the ball up. Henry reacted quite angrily, along the lines of 'what are you doing, you upstarts'? Johnny told him: 'We've got you,' and that was the moment I knew the game was in the bag. The players just weren't going to give it up; they were so tenacious in everything they did. If someone had fired a gun at them, they'd have caught the bullet before it hit them that day, it was a 10 out of 10 performance.

The feeling afterwards was euphoric, but there was no sense of relief. We had achieved what we'd set out to do, but there had been no pressure on us because nobody had thought we could win. We just enjoyed the day.

The lap of honour afterwards was a fantastic experience and the party at our hotel in the evening was even better. I can still remember every incident of the game and the immediate aftermath, even if some of the celebrations are a bit hazy, not because I've re-watched it, but because I was determined to take it all in. I didn't know if I'd ever get to another final, so I was determined to make the most of it.

The CD on the coach on the way home was The Pogues and we sang all the way back from London to Sheffield. I keep a copy in the car and if ever I need cheering up, that's the music I turn to because it will always remind me of what we achieved on that remarkable May afternoon.

Perhaps the only person involved with Sheffield who

couldn't fully enjoy the day and the aftermath was Lynton Stott, who was an unused substitute in the final. I wouldn't blame him if he still held that against me, though he has shown no sign of a grudge and he behaved with total professionalism throughout.

I have sometimes been asked why I didn't give him a run in the final, so now is an opportunity to explain that. When I was a schoolboy and throughout my playing days my dream was to play at Wembley. It must have been agonising for Lynton to get so close and then ultimately miss out. I know he was itching to get on, because Steve Deakin kept telling me so over the radio.

I do feel bad about that, but my main job was to win the game and I felt the best way to use my substitutes was by rotating the forwards. Lynton was a winger or full-back. I wasn't coaching the under-10s, when you give everybody a run, this was the Cup final and I had to utilise my players to the team's best advantage.

In those days you could name four substitutes and make six changes, so there wasn't a lot of margin for error. Under the 12 interchanges rule, which was introduced later, I am sure he would have got on, but I couldn't make a change for the sake of it, because we were playing so well and the result was in the balance until the closing stages. If I could have done I would have given him a run with a few minutes to go when the game was won, but I had used all my changes by then. Lynton is a smashing lad, I apologised to him straight after the game and he said there were no hard feelings. He has got a Cup winner's medal, he knows he was a valuable part of our run to Wembley and what we did that afternoon and he still attends all the reunions, which is credit to him.

One thing happened in the build-up to the Cup final which I have never spoken about before and which I am pretty sure the players, to this day, are unaware of. I almost missed the game after being taken ill two days before, at our London hotel.

We travelled to the capital on the Thursday and went out tenpin bowling and then for a Chinese meal in the evening. I had an allergic reaction to something I ate and at one stage I was quite seriously poorly. I was in real discomfort and could hardly see. We went back to the hotel after the meal and by the time I got to my room I was beginning to itch. I came out in hives, all over my body. I got into a cold shower, as I thought that would help, but it made no difference.

I rang the team doctor, Janet Hornbuckle. She rushed to my room and fortunately she had some Piriton, which is an allergy cure, with her. That settled everything down, but at one stage my eyes had swollen up so much they were starting to close and she was on the point of taking me to a hospital. We kept it from the players and the only people who knew were me, the physio and the doctor

The medicine cured the problem, but before that kicked in I was beginning to panic because I was convinced I was going to miss the biggest game of my life. I was desperate to be there and to be part of it and it looked like it might be taken away from me. I will always be grateful to the Doc for getting me through.

7

*

World Cup Woes

IT'S never nice getting sacked, in any walk of life. Sadly, the way things are these days, I don't think anybody has a job for life any more. There has never been any real job security in sport and going into coaching you know are going to get the Spanish fiddler (elbow) at some point, so it is a matter of making the best of a bad situation when it does happen.

I have been sacked twice in my coaching career. We'll come to the second occasion a little later, but the first time was when I left Huddersfield in the year after the so-called merger with the Eagles. I would have liked to have made a success of the Shuddersfield venture, but the odds were stacked against me and in all honesty I don't think anyone could have kept them off the foot of the table in 2000.

It was an impossible situation and it came almost as a relief when I was eventually put out of my misery and, looking on the bright side, at least it gave me an opportunity to concentrate full-time on the next big challenge, that year's World Cup.

I'd already had some Test experience, coaching France for one game, at home to Russia, in 1998. I had stayed in touch with Michel Mazare from my Paris days, he was involved with the French Federation and asked if I would go over and coach the national team.

Joe Lydon, who was on the backroom staff at the RFL, had indicated that I was in line for the England job in 1999 and probably the World Cup as well, so helping France out seemed like a good way of dipping my toe in the water and gaining some international experience.

We beat Russia comfortably and it was a good way for me to wind down after the 1998 season. I did it for expenses because I didn't want to sign a contract and possibly harm my chances of getting the England post the following year.

I like the French people and those involved in the game over there. We went into camp at Crepes, which I was very familiar with and then we played the game, which went as well as expected. It was all pretty low key and I saw it mainly as helping a mate out.

As I had hoped, I was appointed England coach against France the following year, 1999, when Great Britain - under Andy Goodway - were away in Tri-Nations action against Australia and New Zealand. We won 28-20 in Carcassonne after being 14-10 down at half-time and then thrashed France 50-20 at the Boulevard, in Hull, 10 days later. Leon Pryce, who went on to have a superb career with club and country, made his international debut that day. He now plays in France for Catalan Dragons.

After that series I flew out to join up with Great Britain as one of Andy Goodway's assistants. Great Britain had an awful time on that tour. They scraped past the Queensland Cup champions Burleigh Bears - the Aussie equivalent of a team like Featherstone Rovers or Leigh Centurions - 10-6 in a warm-up game, but got hammered 42-6 by Australia and

Coaching is Chaos

26-4 against the Kiwis. Embarrassingly, Great Britain then had to take on Aotearoa Maori in a curtain-raiser to the final between the Aussies and Kiwis, though they managed to save a bit of face by winning 22-12.

After that disastrous tour - which included GB's worst-ever defeat by New Zealand and second-heaviest loss to Australia - it was all doom and gloom for the international game. The crowds were poor, just 12,511 for the clash with Australia, and all the pundits were again writing off the British game, claiming we were years behind the Aussies and now the Kiwis as well. That was the background to the 2000 World Cup, which effectively had the credibility of Test rugby league riding on it. It was a 16-team competition with Great Britain split into separate English, Welsh, Scottish and Irish teams - and I was in charge of England.

Looking back everybody regards the tournament as another fiasco and a terrible failure on and off the field. To be honest, I can see where they are coming from on that score, but it is also widely believed that England were poor throughout. I disagree completely with that and I think it is an insult to the players and staff involved. In fact, we did pretty well in very difficult circumstances and it was a tournament I really enjoyed.

Dave Howes, who later became my agent, was the England team manager. He was the RFL's public relations chief in the 1970s and 80s and then had spells running St Helens and Leeds, before becoming a player manager. He did a great job with England and he ensured we had the best possible preparation.

The tournament and the England team were sponsored by an American company, Lincoln Financial Group. They paid for us to have a warm-weather training camp in Florida before the competition began and we were treated very well indeed over there. Dave's organisation was first class, we had a superb camp, there were lots of activities for the players to do so they weren't bored and we developed a really good team spirit.

Even with such good preparation we were up against it during the tournament itself. For one thing, we had to cope without some star players. The world's best winger, Jason Robinson, turned us down because he was on the point of going to rugby union and three key forwards, Barrie McDermott, Terry O'Connor and Chris Joynt, all opted to play for Ireland.

We also had plenty of injuries so we had to choose a squad full of kids, but they gave a great account of themselves and that experience set some of them up for outstanding Super League careers. And as ever, we were up against a sceptical media. Before the quarter-final against Ireland I remember Ian Millward, the St Helens coach, saying they were the favourites to win that one, which was the sort of thing that always comes in handy for motivation purposes.

They certainly had a decent team, including three good Aussies in Danny Williams, Luke Ricketson and Kevin Campion and a host of established Super League stars, for example Steve Prescott, Brian Carney, Michael Withers and Tommy Martyn. In terms of experience they probably did have the edge, but we beat them 26-16 in a cracking game at Headingley and that was a fantastic result for England. In fact, of the five matches we played, we only had one off day, which sadly was the semi-final against New Zealand.

We opened up against Australia in the first rugby league match played at Twickenham and lost 22-2, which was a creditable effort. We conceded four tries, but posed them some problems with a very young and inexperienced team. We also had to cope with a bizarre situation on the morning of the game when one of our players was arrested over an allegation of rape and two others - who were due to play that evening - had to go to a police station to give statements in his defence. He was later cleared of the charges, but you can imagine the unsettling effect that had.

After that we came up against two of the minnows, Russia and Fiji. We beat Russia 76-4 and Fiji 66-10 and even then we picked up injuries to key people, like Leon Pryce, so others had to play out of position. Kris Radlinski was one of the best full-backs of modern times, but he played as a centre against Fiji.

By the time the quarter-finals came along I was under pressure personally because I had David Waite looking over my shoulder. He was an Australian coach who had been brought over as the RFL's technical director. I had been told the governing body would interview me for the Great Britain job, along with Malcolm Reilly and David Waite, but you could have got long odds on either me or Malcolm being appointed. As it turned out we were interviewed and David did get the role, the first time it had gone overseas.

Under the circumstances it was a good effort for England just to reach the last four, though it would have been considered a catastrophe if we hadn't. From my point of view I quickly realised being in charge of the national team in those days was a huge honour, as it is now, but it was fraught with difficulties.

There is always a club versus country scenario, because a player's club pays his wages and he is their asset, so they don't want him damaged or worn out. When I was in charge of England, clubs were less committed to the international game than they are now and on a number of occasions I know players were told by their club coach to cry off, supposedly due to injury. Fortunately in the years since there has been a growing awareness among clubs that, for the sake of the game in this country, we do need to have a strong international team. That's why clubs have been prepared to release players to go into camp mid-season and why they haven't made too much of a fuss when England have played a stand-alone mid-week fixture in high summer, as preparation for the autumn internationals.

In 2011 the England coach Steve McNamara named an elite squad and a second-string Knights group at the start of the year and they got together on a regular basis, at Loughborough University, throughout the year. They still do so. I would have loved to have preparation like that. There were no programmes in place in my day; it was a matter of having a look at videos of players in action or watching them live, selecting what you thought was the right squad, getting them together a few weeks before the tournament began and then doing the best you could. That's why the camp in America was such a bonus and I believe that time spent together contributed to our largely positive performances. We played some very good rugby in four out of five matches, but unfortunately for us the game that mattered the most - the semi-final against New Zealand, at Bolton - was the one we under-performed in.

I will hold my hands up and take a large amount of responsibility for that. I picked Paul Sculthorpe in the second-row and in hindsight - that word again - it was a mistake. Paul was a great player, but he hadn't trained all week because of an injury. I risked him and just as the team didn't have the best of nights, Scully didn't either. He wasn't fit and he should not have played. If I had my time over again I would leave him on the sidelines for that game, though to be fair, you can't blame one player or one selection decision for a 49-6 shellacking.

I valued my time as England coach and I have no regrets, though I do feel it came a little too early for me. If I had been given the opportunity around 2004 or 2005, that's when I would have been ready. I still feel as if I could contribute now and I would have taken the post if it had been offered to me in 2010 after Tony Smith departed and when I was being strongly linked with it in the media.

My then agent David Howes let it be known that I was interested and at first the signs were pretty positive. I was happy at Wakefield and would have had to take the post on a part-time basis initially, but nothing came of it and I wasn't interviewed for the role - despite what some newspapers said.

Coaching a national side is different to coaching a club team and I am certain I could handle it even now. Steve McNamara, who was Tony Smith's assistant, got the gig and after a tough first campaign in 2010 he did a decent job in the 2011 Four Nations. England got to the final and were some people's favourites for the title, but were well beaten by Australia in the final at Elland Road. I was genuinely pleased for him when England got through to the decider, beating the world champions and Four Nations trophy holders New Zealand in the process and I wish him well in the 2013 World Cup. Up against the Kiwis and mighty Australia, he will certainly need it. The 2013 event will be the first World Cup in Britain since 2000 and I hope lessons have been learned, both on and off the field, because it will be a painful experience if they haven't.

As of 2012, the last time England/Great Britain beat Australia in a home series of any sort was more than half a century ago, in the 1959 Ashes. The most recent Test series win over the Kangaroos was in Australia in 1970 and though Great Britain won the World Cup two years later that was on a count-back to the group matches after they drew with Australia in the final. Since then, nothing: there has been a number of World Cup and Three/Four Nations finals and several deciding Tests, but Australia have won the lot.

That shows how good the Aussies are, especially in pressure situations, but as a proud Englishman and a lover of rugby league it really hurts. Going so long without a major international success is embarrassing, but I also think the game over here has to get real. Every time we lose to the Aussies, we go through a huge amount of soul-searching about why they are so much better than us, but the fact is we aren't comparing like with like.

Rugby league people in this country need to realise that in Australia they tend to have the first choice of the best athletes in the Sydney and Brisbane areas. Rugby league over here is strong in Yorkshire, Lancashire and Cumbria and growing in other areas, but we don't have first pick anywhere. Football has always been ahead of us in the queue and that's never going to change.

I'll give you the Manchester City and England player Micah Richards as an example. He went to school with my lad and was a top rugby union player. He would have been equally good in league because he was so fast, strong and powerful, but he went to play football and you can understand why when you look at the wages even fringe Premiership players earn. Players in the lower divisions take home as much as good Super League professionals do.

Australia has a much stronger sporting culture than we do and rugby league is a far bigger game over there than in England, even in our heartlands. In England our culture is to watch and comment, but down in Australia it is to play and do. We have loads of armchair critics and keyboard warriors, but not enough participants. Until we raise the number of people, particularly young kids, playing the game, we are always going to struggle.

Can we ever beat the Aussies? Yes, I think we can, once in a blue moon. We haven't done in any Test match since 2006, but there's always a chance we may have a good day and they could be off their game. Perhaps at some stage we'll even overcome them in a match that matters, a final or a deciding Test, should they bring Ashes rugby back on to the agenda. But our national team is a reflection of the standard of the competition over here and that is not as good as Australia's NRL. They have a higher standard which produces better quality players. People say State of Origin, a three-game mid-season series between New South Wales and Queensland, is what makes the Aussie national team so good. That's a major factor, but it is also the strength of their domestic competition which gives them the edge over us.

Over recent years we have fallen behind the Kiwis as well. Australia didn't lose any international competition from 1972 to 2005, but New Zealand won the Tri Nations final that year, the World Cup in 2008 and the Four Nations two years after that. It is no coincidence the Kiwis' national team has risen to new heights since Auckland - later New Zealand - Warriors joined the NRL. The vast majority of New Zealand's top stars play in the NRL and they are exposed to a more intense competition every week. That is bound to improve them as players. If we had a team in the NRL performances by our national side would improve. Logistically, I don't see how that could happen, but maybe a Champions League-type format might work.

We had the World Club Championship in 1997, when all the Super League sides were involved in a tournament against the whole of the NRL. Out of 60 matches Super League clubs won eight, including my Eagles team's comeback victory over Perth Reds. That's why it hasn't been tried since, though the Super League Grand Final winners take on the NRL champions in a one-off game at the start of every season and don't have a bad record in that.

I would welcome an extended World Club Challenge, for example the top four Aussie sides against Europe's best quartet. I say Europe because Catalan Dragons are now on the verge of becoming a top-four side. Super League has improved since 1997 and I am confident we would fare much better and I also think it would create interest and raise standards, as it has done in other sports. Rugby union has a great format in the Heineken Cup and the Champions League is soccer's leading club competition, slowly taking over from the FA Premiership as the thing everybody wants to compete in and win.

If we can expose English players to the very best opposition more regularly, they would get better. A lot of thought would have to go into how the competition could be structured; maybe the top-four would have to withdraw from the Challenge Cup, but I certainly believe it would be a success. There would be some disruption to the current calendar, but it would be worth it. The question is do we want to produce international players capable of beating the Aussies or Kiwis? If we do, we have to be prepared to make radical decisions.

The England coach Steve McNamara rattled a few cages with his selection policy for the 2011 Four Nations, but I applaud him for that. The most controversial pick was Castleford Tigers stand-off Rangi Chase, who was born in New Zealand. He played for the Maori against England the year before and for the other nationalities Exiles team in the mid-season warm-up fixture, but qualified for this country through residency after being here three years.

There was an outcry about his selection and I agree it is sad Steve Mac didn't feel we had enough high-quality, home-grown half-backs. Personally I would have selected Danny Brough - who played under me at Wakefield - ahead of Chase. But I have no issue with the principle of picking players on residency grounds. The qualification period should probably be longer, but Steve didn't break the rules, he took advantage of them. The Aussies and Kiwis do it all the time and nobody bats an eyelid.

Steve also selected the Brisbane Broncos centre Jack Reed, who was born in Silsden, near Keighley, and the West Tigers forward Chris Heighington, whose parents are English. They both have an Aussie accent, but also a legitimate claim to play for England and, along with Gareth Ellis and Gareth Widdop who are based over there, they brought an NRL ethic to the team. That can only be a good thing in my opinion. You have to use the best players who are available. If Chase had scored the winning try in the Four Nations final from a pass by Reed, everyone would have said it was a selection masterstroke. Though actually, this being rugby league, the keyboard warriors would probably still have complained.

The Aussies have realised we do have some quality young players in this country, which is why Gareth Ellis, Sam Burgess and James Graham have all signed big money deals with NRL sides. It is not ideal for Super League to be losing its best stars, but the experience they gain down under will benefit the national team. For a start, by playing with and against them every week they will realise the Aussies are not unbeatable supermen and are human, just like everybody else. Also, if they return to clubs here - as Ellis has gone on to do with Hull - they will come back as better players, because they will be steeped in good habits. You have to have good habits to play in the NRL. You have got to kick-chase well and I think that's the main facet of the game in which they are better than us. Every time it really matters in a big game, they kick us to death. However, I don't think there will be a flood of British players going to play in the NRL, simply because that competition has a deeper talent pool and they don't need to rely on imports.

In 2011, Steve McNamara gave quite a number of young

kids an opportunity in his Four Nations squad, if not the team itself, and that was a positive step towards the 2013 World Cup. I am sure that tournament will be a success financially and hopefully it'll be the same for England on the pitch, which realistically means at least reaching the final.

We have a chance; I think the England back division is looking very strong, with Sam Tomkins and Ryan Hall now both established as world class talents. Jack Reed could make one of the centre berths his own over the next few years, Ryan Atkins has a lot of potential and Tom Briscoe, Ben Jones-Bishop and Zak Hardaker are players with a big future. We've not yet seen what Jonny Lomax and Lee Gaskell - among others - can do at international level and they should be knocking on the door; an encouraging prospect.

My main concern is with the forwards. Do we have players coming through to replace the likes of Jamie Peacock, Adrian Morley, Garreth Carvell, Jamie Jones-Buchanan and Kevin Sinfield, who are all 30-plus? Some of those are still being picked for the national side but whether they can still do a job in 2013 remains to be seen.

The area where the Aussies and Kiwis have the edge over us now is at one, six, seven and nine - or full-back, stand-off, scrum-half and hooker for those of you brought up on squad numbers. I am a big fan of Sam Tomkins, but Australia did a fine job of containing him in the 2011 Four Nations and they have got someone even better in Billy Slater, who is the best full-back in the world, at either code of rugby.

If you look at what has happened in Australia's State of Origin over the last few years, it illustrates why we haven't been able to beat the Kangaroos since 2006. New South Wales have lost the last seven series and the reason for that is Queensland have been able to field Slater at full-back,

Coaching is Chaos

Darren Lockyer at stand-off, Johnathan Thurston at scrum-half and Cameron Smith as hooker, with Cooper Cronk snapping at their heels. Put those players together in any team, rugby league or union, and they would be very hard to beat. Lockyer has hung up his boots now, which is good news for England and New South Wales but a loss to the sport, but the others will be there in 2013 and even now that must make them strong favourites.

The signs are the tournament organisers have learned from the experience of 2000. There will be fewer teams this time and hopefully not as many mismatches. The RFL have also been cleverer with the venues, with most games due to be played in the heartlands and one or two in expansion areas like Bristol and Ireland. Playing most of the matches in the north will make it more parochial, but it will guarantee bigger and more enthusiastic crowds. That said, I do think it is a strange decision to play England's biggest group game, against Australia, in Cardiff, as part of a double-header also involving Wales. South Wales isn't particularly easy to get to from the north of England, so that could be a hard sell.

I am looking forward to seeing how some of the emerging rugby league nations, for example the United States and Italy, fare. Paul Broadbent, my captain at Sheffield and assistant-coach with Wakefield, has been part of the Italian backroom team and he did a great job helping them qualify for the tournament. Their star man will be Anthony Minichiello, who played 18 Tests for Australia when he was at the peak of his powers. Recruiting a player of his quality is a big coup and he will certainly add some interest to the tournament. That is something the developing nations need to do, seek out players who are qualified and get them involved. It's what Ireland did in 2000 and that policy took them to the quarter-finals.

I would love to see England established as the best team

in the world, but I'd also be delighted if we could be challenged by more than a couple of other teams. At the moment we know if England play anybody other than Australia or New Zealand, they are probably going to win.

It would be great for the sport if Wales, France, Ireland, Italy, Russia, America, Jamaica, Lebanon and all the others who are now dipping their toes in the waters could get to a standard where they can also compete at the highest level. That is a long, long way off, but I applaud everyone who is involved in development work in those countries.

8

*

Part of the Union

I AM not sure if full-time, professional rugby league will exist in 100 years' time. Coming from a Castleford lad who is steeped in the game that is a big statement to make, but I worry that the threat from rugby union has put the sport's long-term future in real doubt.

It is not a major regret, it certainly doesn't compare with turning down the St Helens job, but I do sometimes wonder if I made a mistake when I opted not to take up a full-time coaching role in the 15-a-side code. I look at the success league stalwarts Phil Larder, Shaun Edwards and Andy Farrell have had - and the money they've made - and it is hard not to wonder what if....

Castleford is a die-hard hotbed of rugby league, but - strangely - growing up there did give me a background in union. I was one of only two pupils in my year at Wheldon Lane Junior and Infant School - myself and Sharon Clegg out of a class of 31 - to pass the 11-plus exam, which meant I went on to Castleford Grammar School.

It says a lot about the tradition, history and background of the two codes that even in Castleford the grammar school played rugby union. It's Cas High now and they are one of the best rugby league schools in England, but back then no grammar school in the country would have contemplated playing league. Fortunately that is now beginning to change.

I played union for Cas Grammar from 11 to 18, as well as league. I played union on a Saturday morning, then league for Leeds under-17s, Cas under-17s and eventually Cas under-19s in the afternoon. Doing my teacher training in Leicester I was also involved in union there so I have never had a problem with the other code, unlike some in our game.

There is some snobbery in rugby union towards league, which is still perceived as being a northern-based working class sport. I get quite angry about that, but respect has to go both ways and I admit there are many league people who look down their nose at union, which is known as 'rah-rah' or 'kick and clap'. You can work out the origin of those nicknames for yourself. I don't like that attitude either; I am not an inverted snob and I don't regard rugby union as any less of a game than rugby league - they both have their own merits, but they are different sports with different qualities.

It doesn't appeal to me as much as league does, but I can see the merits in union and I understand why its supporters love it so much. I would never say league is superior to union or vice versa, though there are things which each code does better.

There are good people in union just as there are in league and if I had taken a different path in 2001 I might have thrown my lot in with the 15-a-side game on a permanent basis. I had a spell out of rugby league after the 2000 World Cup, during which time I did some work as a consultant for Cardiff Blues. They were coached by Lynn Howells, who was also on the Welsh coaching staff and became head coach of Wales after that. Dai Young, who is now at Wasps, was also at Cardiff. He had been one of the final generation of Welsh union players to go north, in the early 1990s, before the 15-a-side game went openly professional. He played for Leeds and Salford before heading back to his homeland and returning to union.

It was Dai's influence which got me actively involved in union coaching. Lynn and Dai came to Huddersfield when I was coaching the Giants in 2000, to have a look round and see what ideas they could pick up from rugby league. We got on well, kept in touch and after I had left Huddersfield and finished with England Lynn asked if I would be interested in going down there and helping out at Cardiff. It was a good opportunity for me to broaden my horizons - plus I was out of work at the time - so I jumped at the chance. While I was with Cardiff I would spend two days a week in Wales for training and also go down there on match days. It was an enjoyable time and it gave me a healthy respect for rugby union, on top of the experience I'd had as a youngster.

Officially I was a consultant, but I mainly did defensive work. I must have done a decent job because I was offered an opportunity to join one of Cardiff's rivals, Newport, as full-time defence coach. I chose not to do it and instead went back to rugby league, initially with Wigan and then Hull.

I was involved in a Challenge Cup-winning campaign with both so things worked out well for me back in the north, but even so I often sit back and wonder if I made the right decision. I am realistic enough to admit rugby union offers greater possibilities; it is much higher profile and is very highly paid, in comparison to rugby league.

The reason I decided to go back to league was that I felt I still had a point to prove after getting the bullet at Shuddersfield and also in light of how the media perceived

England had performed at the World Cup. I did not want to be seen to be running away from a challenge.

The relationship between league and union has changed completely in my lifetime. Up until union went openly professional in 1995, there was outright hostility between the two codes and someone like me, who had played and enjoyed both from an early age, was very much a rarity.

League clubs saw rugby union, particularly in Wales, as a rich source of playing talent and that caused a great deal of resentment. Many of Wales' top stars went north and were therefore lost to the national team because anyone who had any involvement in league was effectively banned from union for the rest of his life.

Officially, they were deemed to have made themselves professional and there was no going back from that. I still think it is amazing that apartheid in South Africa was overthrown before union players were allowed to give league a try without facing life-long sanctions. Once union went openly professional - I say openly because obviously some of the top players did get paid either in kind or via envelopes left in their boots - a pathway opened up between the two codes and players are now free to play either or both if they want to. Ironically, union has begun raiding league's best talent and the tide is all flowing the opposite way to how it did for the 100 years before 1995.

There is still some resentment, both ways, especially among the older generation, but I think for anyone who has been brought up in rugby over the past couple of decades, the barriers are well and truly down and so they should be.

When the Welsh international superstar Jonathan Davies signed for Widnes in 1989 he was told not to bother going back to the club where he had played all his junior rugby union. It was the same with John Bevan, who played on the wing for Warrington and who I came into contact with down in Cardiff. That was wrong. In the south of England union was - and perhaps still is - perceived as a middle-class sport for public schoolboys, but rugby is very much a working class game in Wales and I don't think any talented player could be blamed for wanting to cash in on his ability. He couldn't do that in supposedly strictly amateur rugby union, so if he wanted to get away from the mines and factories and make some good money, he had to go north. It was often an economic decision, not a case of betraying his roots - and it is the same now with league players who are lured to union by the offer of massive wages.

Soon after union went professional, Leeds Rhinos took the city's union club under their wing. They now both play at Headingley and share facilities and ideas. The players mix freely and that would have been unimaginable just two decades ago.

At amateur level clubs from the rival codes often share facilities and community (the new politically correct name for amateur) rugby league sides have sprung up all over the country in previously virgin territory, because they can now use union pitches and players during the summer when the 15-a-side game is on its off-season.

So league has benefited in that regard and we have picked up some good players from that direction. The prop Darrell Griffin - who has played for Wakefield, Huddersfield and Leeds, as well as England - began his league career with Oxford Cavaliers for example. But I think it is union which has gained the most from the new closer relationship between the sports; not just through a new source of players, but also coaches and ideas.

When I went to Cardiff, close ties between the two codes were in their infancy, but there was no resentment towards my league background. As I have mentioned, Dai Young was heavily involved in getting me down there and Lynn

Howells became a good friend of mine. Funnily enough he later found himself in the heart of league territory, coaching second-tier union outfit Doncaster Knights. I found Welsh rugby union people in general very welcoming and open to fresh ideas, which is what you want as a coach.

The flow of ideas at the moment is largely one-way, but that's mainly due to union's superior resources. I strongly believe there are things league can learn from union, as it can from any sport. Nobody has got a monopoly on ideas, no sport, team or individual. If you ever think you know it all and you close your mind, you stop developing and progressing. One example is how to kick a ball. Perhaps we have caught up a bit now and I reckon kickers like Kevin Sinfield or Jamie Foster could match anyone in union, but at the time I was down there, their kickers were technically far superior to anyone in league.

The reason we have closed the gap in that particular skill is because we have taken on board union's way of doing things. When I was at Hull one of the most influential things we did in the build-up to the 2005 season was bring in Jon Callard - the former England union international - to work with our kickers. Jon had a spell at Leeds Tykes, Rhinos' union sister club, and I believe he did some work with Kevin Sinfield as well. We got him over to Hull and he made an outstanding contribution. He spent a lot of time with our two main kickers, Paul Cooke and Danny Brough, and he overhauled their technique. He analysed how they kicked out of hand and off the floor - place kicking - and they both became more accurate with the boot because of that, which was one of the reasons we did so well in 2005.

I have always felt that to win anything you need to have a goalkicker with a success rate of 80 per cent or more. In 2004, Paul Cooke's strike rate was about 69.5 per cent, which simply isn't good enough. The following year, when we won the Challenge Cup, came fifth in the league and won a play-off tie, both our kickers were over 80 per cent. A lot of that improvement was due to Jon Callard.

League coaches tend to concentrate on defence when they go to union, which is what I did at Cardiff. The management down there thought they could learn a lot from the way league teams defended. I spent a lot of time looking at one-on-one defence and systems and structures around the breakdown of the ruck. It wasn't as much about what was actually happening at the ruck, more where the main defenders should be positioned and what the three-quarters and the edge defenders - the ones a little further away from the breakdown - should be doing.

In rugby union at the time it was all about a drift defence; at Cardiff we didn't feel that was the best approach so we used what became known as the blitz, based on intense, aggressive line speed. That worked very successfully for us. I did a lot of work looking at individual techniques and also two or three-man tackles, to see how we could control the ruck area, as well as the area around the ruck and the edge defence.

Having studied both codes, I think rugby league players have better attacking ability. They are more schooled in what I would consider to be the basics: how to grip a ball, catch, pass and tackle. In rugby league we major massively on those, because they are the core skills, but we hardly ever do work on other aspects of the game which are central to union, such as scrummaging. In union they spend a huge amount of time on scrummaging, lineout plays and kicking. When you do that other techniques have to take a back seat and it tends to be passing, catching and one-on-one defence which gets neglected.

I do believe union has taken strides forward over the past few years and one of the reasons for that is the influence of league coaches, though obviously full-time training has also played a big part. Union is now an added career option for league coaches because the demand is there and better resources are on offer. Die-hard leaguies, like Shaun Edwards and Graham Steadman, have gone over to union and done very well at the highest level. I still see Graham at Super League games. I know he is still a massive league fan, but why would he want to come back when the rewards - financially and in terms of profile - are so much greater?

At Wakefield my full-time coaching staff consisted of me, my assistant Paul Broadbent and our conditioner Colin Sanctuary. A top union club will have a head coach, kicking coach, skills/attack coach, forwards coach and defence coach, plus people working on performance analysis and elite players' individual development.

I have always been very keen on performance analysis and that is something done much better in union than league. They have more access to technology and can employ people specifically dedicated to that aspect of match preparation. In league we have player performance managers for the scholarship system, but not the senior team. Toby Booth, at London Irish, told me they have an elite player performance manager whose job is to study player performance analysis, go through it with each individual and then draw up programmes for everybody in the squad.

We tried to do something similar at Wakefield, but we just didn't have the time because we were doing everything else as well and also we didn't have the financial resources. That said, I think because of the nature of our game we produce better running rugby players, which stems from that focus on gripping the ball, catching and passing.

All the skills that are basic to both games, we do better. The perception is that union scrums are superior, but I think that is a bit of a red herring. We don't have contested scrums any more in league; the half-back feeds the ball to his second-row and it comes straight back out again. Scrums are now just a way of breaking up play, rather than a method of contesting possession. Contested scrums are supposedly a big feature of union, but still nine times out of 10 the team that feeds the scrum wins the ball. Lineouts - which league abolished in 1906 - are more evenly-contested, but that comes down to the ability of the hooker or whoever's throwing the ball from the sidelines.

I think that restricts the type of athletes who can make the grade in rugby union. In Wales there are some very good rugby players who fall by the wayside because they can't play second-row, flanker, or No 8 simply because they aren't big enough for lineout work, despite their other abilities.

The league clubs based in Wales have picked up one or two good players because of that and I think it is an area we should do more to tap into. Wigan have developed links with the lower division South Wales side and they are throwing resources at rugby league development in the Valleys. That is a smart move and I wouldn't be surprised if they picked up some quality players through that. Leeds also see south Wales as an area they can recruit from and had a couple of promising youngsters Jack Pring and Ollie Olds on their books until they were released at the end of 2012 when the under-20s competition was scrapped. I haven't seen enough to them to know if those two will ever make it in Super League, but having come through the Rhinos' system they will have got a good grounding and that can only be good for the Welsh national side in the future.

Union people will tell you their game is more technical than league and that our game is too predictable because of the five plays and a kick element. Again, I would dispute that. As coaches we look at how players catch the ball, grip it and carry it and there's a real technique to that. It sounds very basic, but try a little experiment: hold a rugby ball in both hands and then get someone to attempt to knock it out. You will be surprised how hard it is not to let go.

Union is more technical with regard to static play, but not when it comes to running rugby or to making tackles. In rugby league a greater number of tackling styles are required: front-foot tackles, side tackles, rear tackles, gang tackles, back-foot tackle; there just isn't that variety in rugby union.

In my opinion union is more predictable and it is easier to defend, simply because the ball is not in play as often. Some union supporters will claim league is a stop-start game, because there's a play-the-ball after every tackle. In fact league is faster and more continuous. In some union games a team may make between 80 and 100 tackles over the course of 80 minutes. Glenn Morrison, the Australian forward who was my captain at Wakefield and is now coach of Dewsbury, made 40-plus tackles per game, every week. That was expected of him. In the 27-game 2011 regular Super League season three players, Danny Houghton (1,060), James Roby (1,032) and Ian Henderson (1,019), made more than 1,000 tackles.

There are more tries in league and a greater variety of ways to score them. In union there are often tries when you don't see the ball, because the touchdown comes from a push-over or a maul. In league you get the occasional try from dummy-half, close to the line, but most of them are very well created. Again in 2011, Warrington scored 33 tries from inside their own half. Even Crusaders, who were bottom of the table, did that on 17 occasions.

These factors are a big part of why I prefer league to union, but as I mentioned at the start of this chapter I am not confident about the code's long-term prospects as an elite, full-time sport. People have been writing rugby league off ever since it split from rugby union in 1895, but I believe the threats to the game now are greater than ever, leading me to question whether in the long-term future there will be rugby league at professional level.

The sport will survive in some shape or form, I have no doubt about that. There will always be rugby league played in places like Cumbria, Featherstone/Castleford and Wigan/St Helens, but in a few generations' time it might be amateur, or at best a semi-professional, part-time game.

The dangers are two-fold: union will swallow league or there will be a hybrid game, combining the two sports as they are now. Union is now actively targeting league's best players and that must be a worry. It is not a concern if players nearing the end of their career opt to cross codes for one final pay-day, but what is more of an issue from league's point of view is the exodus of some of our best youngsters. Sam Tomkins is probably the finest young player in either code running around in this country at the moment, but he has already made an appearance in union for the Barbarians - when he stood out in what was his first ever 15-a-side game - and Premiership clubs are queuing up to poach him when his Wigan contract expires. His brother, Joel, has already crossed the great divide.

I don't blame any league player who decides to go to union for more money. If you work at the local corner shop in Yorkshire or Lancashire and a supermarket in London offers to double your pay, you would probably take the cash, especially if you were young and ambitious. We are all free, willing and able to make our own decisions and if someone offers an opportunity to a young man from the north, I don't think it is right to bad mouth him if he takes it.

Perhaps people brought up in league do owe the code some loyalty, but unfortunately that doesn't pay the bills or put food on the table. As well as being able to offer greater financial rewards, union is less physically demanding than league and its profile is far higher. I also don't think the negative attitude of some of those supposedly involved in league helps.

Chris Ashton was one good young player among many when he played for Wigan. He went to union and became a household name and a nationally recognisable star. The sort of tries which have made his name in union are scored every week in Super League, but largely go unnoticed to a wider audience.

It is a sad fact that union can offer more to an ambitious young man. At international level, union's crowds are fantastic, seven or eight times what we get for some Test matches and they are growing very rapidly in the club game. Club union used to be watched by two men and a very bored dog; now they are selling out good-sized stadiums. Clubs like Leeds, Wigan and Hull can match union's crowds, but at the bottom end of Super League we have fallen behind. That is one reason I would like to see Super League split into two divisions of 10, because we need to create greater interest and more close and meaningful matches, to keep our sport alive.

The crowds Chris Ashton plays in front of every week aren't any bigger than Wigan attracted during his time there, but since he swapped codes he has become an England regular and he has already played in a World Cup. The best players want to represent their country and in league, those opportunities don't come along often enough.

In 2011, England played a one-off mid-season game against Exiles, a warm-up Test in France, three Four Nations group games and the final. Every season union has autumn internationals against the southern hemisphere, the Six Nations in February and summer tours, plus regular World Cups and a British Lions tour every four years.

We have lost that, which was our choice as a game. We used to have Ashes tours every four years, but we married our season with the Aussie one and went down the England/Wales/Scotland/Ireland route, rather than Great Britain. That's a decision made by the sport and, unless there's a will to change it back, we have to live with it.

Not every good league player will move to union, even if he gets an offer. The sports are different and not everybody can adapt. It is easier for backs than forwards, but there have been as many failed converts as successes. Chris Ashton and World Cup winner Jason Robinson have both been a huge hit, but others - Lee Smith and Chev Walker to name just two - weren't able to make the transition and came back. Neither of them, I think it is fair to say, has made the impact he had before he crossed to union.

It was exactly the same when the flow was from union to league. For every Jonathan Davies, there was also a John Gallagher. Davies was a fantastic rugby player and he was equally effective in either code. When Leeds signed the All Blacks full-back John Gallagher, he was rated as the best union player in the world, but he couldn't hack it in rugby league. He was a union player, not a league one. Leeds could have gone to most amateur rugby league clubs and developed a full-back who was just as good, at a fraction of the cost. Union clubs can afford to splash big money on untried - in union that is - league players, but that is not exactly a vote of confidence in their own youth systems.

I don't think anybody in league should lose sleep worrying about the sport's future in relation to the 15-a-side game; it's more a case of accepting the union threat as a way of life. I really don't see there's much we can do about it, but the biggest hope we have got is that the media want to maintain two separate codes.

I can see the attraction to a TV company of Leeds against Bath or St Helens versus Saracens - either in union or a hybrid game - but at the moment they have the best of both worlds; league in summer and union during the winter months.

Since 1995, there has been talk of a merger between league and union. I believe a hybrid game combining rules from both is now a real possibility. Some rules have been drawn up and it's an interesting prospect. Chris Anderson from rugby league and union's Bob Dwyer have given the idea their backing and I reckon there is some mileage in that. Leeds Rhinos have already been approached about the idea and they say they are keen to take part in a hybrid game against one of union's leading Premiership sides.

Hybrid has been trialled at schoolboy level in Australia. The rules have been designed so union or league players can compete without being disadvantaged. Games are 13-a-side and are played under league rules (with play-the-balls) when a team have the ball at their own end, but union laws (rucks and maul) apply when they cross the half-way line.

The people behind Hybrid Code, as they call it, say they aren't interested in their game taking over from league and/or union. What they want to do is resolve the arguments which have always raged between codes - such as who would win if the Kangaroos took on the Wallabies.

No union team would be able to live with a league outfit under 13-a-side laws and the reverse applies. League players aren't the right shape to play union and they wouldn't be able to get hold of the ball, at scrums or in the lineout. There have been cross-code matches, 40 minutes of league followed by a second half of union, but they tend to be 40-0 at half-time and finish 40-all. In 1996 Wigan played Bath at league and then union and each side won their own game quite comfortably. Because Hybrid combines elements of both games it should be more of an even playing field and the best athletes ought to come out on top. Of course the driving force is money. Fans and TV companies would pay top dollar for a showdown between leading teams from each form of the game, though whether anyone sees it as more than a once a year type venture I am not too sure.

At the moment Leeds Rhinos share their facilities with a rugby union club because they want to maximise their revenue all year round. Having both codes at Headingley means they double the number of matches played at the stadium and it is in use during the winter months, when there's no Super League.

Union in Leeds is not well-supported, so there could come a time when Leeds Rugby drop the union side of their business and adopt a club playing the hybrid game - and the same could apply in reverse to Harlequins Rugby Union, where London Broncos are currently tenants.

I realise this is going to seem like a bleak scenario for die-hard league people, but I am a firm believer in having an open mind. Whether you perceive something as a threat or an opportunity depends on where you're coming from, but you have to be willing to take new ideas on board.

I care about rugby league, but I also care about sport in general. I would love to see league thrive and develop and I am encouraged by the steps the code is taking in new countries and other areas of the UK, but until we find a way of retaining our best players, rewarding them and raising their profile on a level that union can, the future will be uncertain. And how we do that, against far richer opposition, I simply don't know.

9

*

Maurice Dancing

HE wouldn't win many popularity contests in rugby league, but I owe Maurice Lindsay a lot. He has had a major influence on my career and was partly responsible for my return to the sport with probably the biggest club of all.

I got most of my early breaks due to Maurice. In his role as chief executive of the RFL, when I worked there, he sent me to Paris St Germain and played a part in me being given an opportunity at international level, both with the academy and full national teams.

Then when he returned to Wigan - where he had so much success in the 1980s and 1990s - as chairman, he employed me as an assistant to their Australian head coach Stuart Raper. Stuart saved Castleford from relegation in 1997 and turned them into title contenders over the following couple of years, gaining a big reputation as a smart operator in the process.

When Frank Endacott was axed as Warriors boss mid-way through the 2001 season, Stuart was first choice to take over. Joining Wigan was a big move for him and I had to pinch myself a few times when I arrived there as his right-hand man. Having been sacked by Huddersfield and also missed out on the Great Britain job, going to Wigan - even if it wasn't as head coach - was a golden opportunity to rebuild my career.

I'd already enjoyed some success as a head coach, but I had no problem with the idea of getting back into the game as an assistant. Believe it or not, I didn't regard it as a step back - just as I didn't 10 years later when I left Super League to join Batley Bulldogs in the Championship. The fact is I like coaching, at any level. I enjoy helping players become better and I am fascinated by group dynamics, trying to read individuals and bind them together into a cohesive unit. As long as I am coaching I am happy, whether that is as the head honcho or one of his helpers. Anyway, I was joining a great club and was delighted to have an input. Assistant-coach at Wigan isn't a bad job; it's something a lot of people in my profession would give their right arm to do.

The thing I am most proud of is the way my move to Wigan came about. Maurice obviously rated me, but it was the players who really made it happen. Stuart spoke to several of Wigan's key men, who I had worked with at international level, and Andy Farrell recommended me for the job. Stuart Raper went to Maurice and he rubber-stamped what Andy had said, so at the start of the 2001 campaign I found myself back in rugby league, working on the biggest stage in the British game.

Even non-sports fans, who know nothing about rugby league, have heard of Wigan Warriors. It is one of the biggest clubs in the world - alongside Brisbane Broncos and several of the Sydney outfits - and the greatest in this country. Leeds would be up there as well among the two biggest clubs in the northern hemisphere with regard to resources, fan-base and facilities, but Wigan has the edge.

I didn't realise what a big club it was until I found myself on the staff there. No exaggeration, it is like working for a Premiership football side. The facilities are first-class, everything is done to the highest-possible standards and the interest in the club, both locally and at national and international level, is phenomenal.

It was a major shock going from clubs which were massively under-resourced, as Sheffield and Huddersfield had been, to a wealthy club like Wigan. They had a world class gym under one of the stands at JJB Stadium, as it was then known, as well as their own running track. There were specific areas to work on tackle-technique and we could use the 3G pitches at the neighbouring Soccer Dome if we wanted or needed to, which is a huge bonus when most of your pre-season is in winter. We also trained at the nearby Robin Park complex, which is also used by Wigan Athletic.

When I walked through the door on my starting day the first people I saw were the Great Britain captain Andy Farrell, fellow international Denis Betts and overseas duo Adrian Lam and Dave Furner, all world-class players. And they weren't the only ones of that calibre at Wigan; also in the squad were Gary Connolly, Craig Smith, Julian O'Neill and Jamie Ainscough - players who would be superstars at any club in the game. I was like a little boy at Christmas, every day I worked there.

For a small-ish town, Wigan is a sporting mecca. Not only does it boast a Super League rugby team, there's also a Premiership football side. And uniquely, in Wigan it's the rugby team which is the major force. Owner Dave Whelan's cash took Wigan Athletic from the lower divisions to the Premiership and they have managed to hold their own against some giants of the world game, but rugby remains the heartbeat of the town and always will.

When what is now the DW Stadium stages Premiership

football the away end is always full, but there are big gaps in the home fans' three stands. For Super League games there's very few spare seats anywhere. The only time they get a small crowd is when the opposition aren't well supported; if Huddersfield, London or Catalan are the visitors. When the likes of St Helens, Leeds or Warrington come to town the place is packed out and - in my opinion - the atmosphere is unrivalled.

That brings its own pressure, because as far as rugby is concerned Wigan people won't accept anything other than success. Second best is a long way short of good enough. Right from the start it was made clear to Stuart he had to deliver silverware, so there was very little margin for error.

That can sometimes bring the best out in people, but to be honest during the time I was there the expectations were too high. The era of Wigan's total dominance of the British game was over, but still fresh in everyone's memories. For a decade or so from the mid-1980s Wigan were unstoppable; they won eight successive Challenge Cup finals and numerous other trophies and everyone else was simply making up the numbers.

That was because Wigan were the only club with a full-time professional structure. All their rivals were still part-time, with players working through the day and training at night. Wigan were able to cherry-pick the biggest names in the game and nobody else could compete.

Super League, funded by money from Sky TV, changed all that. Every top-flight club went full-time, a salary cap was introduced and it became more of a level playing field. When I joined Wigan they had not won a trophy since the 1998 Grand Final and the natives were getting restless.

Wigan still set very high standards, but other clubs had begun to match that. Everybody within Wigan - the directors, spectators and even the players themselves -

found it hard coming to terms with that. They still expected to win everything, but that was no longer the reality. Since Super League began in 1996, Bradford, St Helens and Leeds Rhinos have all had the edge over Wigan at some time, despite the Cherry and Whites winning the first Grand Final in 1998. After almost getting relegated in 2006, Brian Noble began a revival which really took off when Michael Maguire was appointed coach in 2009.

They finished top of the table and won the Grand Final in Maguire's first season in charge, were Challenge Cup champions the following year and returned to top spot in 2012 under Shaun Wane, re-establishing themselves as one of the top clubs - if not *the* top club - in the game. But success was a long way behind and in front of them when I joined and after you have been at the top for so long it is difficult to adjust to being back in the pack. That was the situation Wigan found themselves in at the turn of the millennium. Not being top dogs any more hurt everyone associated with the club. However, I think in the two years I spent there we began to turn things around. In 2001 we got to the Grand Final, but that was a painful experience as we were hammered by Bradford Bulls in one of their finest performances of the summer era.

The following season we reached the Challenge Cup final as massive underdogs against St Helens and pulled off a victory which ranks among the best of my career, so it was a mixed bag. Apart from the title decider, 2001 was a decent season for us. We finished second to Bradford in the league on points difference and then beat Hull 27-24 in the opening round of the play-offs. After that we went to Valley Parade, Bradford's temporary home, for a qualifying semi-final and pushed them all the way - outscoring them three tries to two - before losing 24-18. That sent us into a final eliminator against St Helens and we hammered the arch rivals 44-10 to qualify for Old Trafford.

Coaching is Chaos

We entered the Grand Final with a strong game plan and full of confidence, but it was a disastrous night from start to finish. Remarkably, considering the experienced players we had in the team, Wigan froze. Defences in Grand Finals are ferocious, especially at the start. Our plan was that if Bradford kicked-off we would work the ball to Andy Farrell, he would whack it downfield, everyone would chase and we'd pin them near their line and hunt a mistake. We would be very physical and really give them some punishment in that early set.

The first part of the plan worked all right, we got the ball to Faz - as Andy Farrell is known - and he hammered it downfield, but Harvey Howard charged up and tackled the full-back from an offside position. Rather than giving them some aggressive defence near their own line, we conceded a penalty and found ourselves tackling close to ours.

From that moment on we were like rabbits caught in the headlights. We totally failed to handle the occasion and I think that was because of the expectation which had been heaped on us. Bradford had a reputation for failing to perform in big games: after losing the 1996, 1997 and 2001 Challenge Cup finals and the 1999 Grand Final and after we had pushed them so close in the semi-final people thought we were going to blow them off the park at Old Trafford.

The game was over by half-time, when we trailed 26-0. It was slightly more even in the second half, thank goodness, but the final score was an embarrassing 37-6. We were awful and never got into the contest. Their Australian full-back Michael Withers was magnificent and picked up the man of the match award, Henry Paul and James Lowes had big games and everyone in their team played well, whereas as a unit we all under-performed.

It was a different story in the 2002 Challenge Cup. We beat Hull, the French side UTC, Leigh and then Castleford in the last four to reach the final - Wigan's first since the loss to Sheffield four years earlier - but went into the decider as distant outsiders against a Saints team who were the holders and in red hot form. They destroyed Leeds 42-16 in the semi-final and everybody thought, a bit like Wigan in 1998, all they had to do to collect the trophy was make sure they turned up at the game on time.

I still regard Wigan's victory that year as one of the competition's biggest shocks, if Wigan winning anything can be considered a surprise. The final was played at Murrayfield in Edinburgh and Wigan fans stayed away in droves. The club couldn't sell its allocation of tickets and our supporters were massively out-numbered on the day.

Strangely, most of the neutral fans that afternoon were supporting Wigan, which was almost unheard of. During the run of eight successive Wembley victories the whole game had been desperate to see Wigan's stranglehold prised loose. Now because Saints were perceived as the big-time Charlies and we were the underdogs, the non-committed fans all got behind us.

We definitely learned lessons from the previous year's Grand Final debacle. We coped with the Murrayfield experience a lot better than Saints did and I'd like to think I played a part in that. Stuart had never coached in a Challenge Cup final before and he was happy to make use of my experience from 1998.

I've got a DVD of the final and there's a moment near the end when it looks like we are going to win the game. As the camera focuses on Stuart he gets up and punches the air, but I pull him back down into his seat. I was telling him 'settle down, let's celebrate when the time comes'. Stuart is a good guy and he turned to me a lot in the build-up to the final, though he very much remained the man in charge. He was a very good head coach and very innovative. He revived

Coaching is Chaos

Castleford and I think he did a fine job during his tenure at Wigan, so I was pleased for him, probably more than anyone else, when the final hooter went.

Ahead of the final we spoke about the way Sheffield had done things in the run-up to their big game against Wigan, but it wasn't a very similar situation. Whereas Sheffield were a small club with a team full of journeyman players - albeit some very good ones - Wigan had a gaggle of superstars in their side. There wasn't much I could tell the likes of Andy Farrell or Jamie Ainscough, who had a brilliant match, about playing in big games. They didn't need a picture painting about what it was going to be like and I couldn't tell them how to approach it, but there were certain things I could highlight and obviously our game plan worked, because we were on top throughout.

Wigan's medic, Dr Zaman, should have won the man of the match award. He did an incredible job getting Kris Radlinski - who did take home the Lance Todd Trophy - on to the field. Rads' recovery from an infected foot and his performance that afternoon are among the most amazing things I have ever seen and have entered Wigan club legend.

The day before the final there was genuinely no chance of Rads playing. We ran with Gary Connolly at full-back in training because Rads was hobbling about with a slipper on his foot, but the doctor worked a miracle during the 24 hours leading up to the game. Rads had been in hospital prior to travelling to Edinburgh and we had all given up hope of having him in the team. Doc Zaman worked a miracle, he took a huge amount of fluid out of the foot - which wasn't pretty to observe, but was effective - and with the help of pain-killing injections, he was got ready to play and Kris went out and had the game of his life. I don't know where he pulled that from, because he must have been feeling terrible. Having an infection runs you down at the best of times and if it had been any other game he wouldn't have played, but Stuart took a chance and Kris wrote one of the great Challenge Cup stories.

We did have contingency plans in case Kris either dropped out at the last minute or couldn't last the pace, but he played the full game and I don't think anybody has been more deserving of a winner's medal. In my eyes, Rads is one of the modern greats. He was an outstanding player and would be up there among the top-10 full-backs to have competed in Super League. Maybe even the top two or three. Defensively, he was sensational; he was superb under the high ball and he could read a game, which is so important when going into a tackle. His decision-making with regard to which tackle to make - whether to allow the ball-carrier space or to close his space down - was second to none. He had a magnificent ability to use the touchline and there weren't many better one-on-one defenders.

Nowadays full-backs - Brent Webb, who has just moved from Leeds to Catalan Dragons, is a good example - play as an extra pivot and that's the one thing Rads lacked. He wasn't a naturally gifted ball-player, but he made up for that with his support play down the middle channel. He was a regular try scorer and for many of his touchdowns he didn't have to beat a man, he simply got on a team-mate's shoulder, waited for the last pass and then ran between the posts. That sounds straight-forward, but it is an instinctive skill not many players have.

He is a good guy as well and a one-club man and everyone at Wigan was chuffed to bits when he grabbed the glory that afternoon at Murrayfield. That is why the Challenge Cup is so magical, because there's a story thrown up every year. Kris Radlinski literally climbing out of his sick bed to help Wigan pull off an unexpected victory over the hot favourites and their arch-rivals is one of those tales which will be talked about for as long as rugby league is played and I am very proud to have been associated with it.

It was a great final, a really high quality game of rugby league. Both teams scored three tries, but we got the glory 21-12 thanks to Faz's kicking and Adrian Lam's drop goal. When we got back to Wigan, the reception we received was overwhelming, it seemed like the whole town turned out to cheer us. People were packed nine or ten deep along the open top bus route and when we got to the town hall the area outside was absolutely packed. It was quite a contrast to the scenes in Sheffield after the Eagles' Cup win. It was a special day and I think it was the perfect illustration of how much rugby league means to the people of Wigan.

Andy Farrell was the Cup-winning captain and he is someone else I have a huge amount of time for. Before our time together at Wigan I worked with him during the 2000 World Cup when he was the England captain and I gained a huge amount of respect for him then. I still have a letter he wrote after that campaign thanking me for the whole World Cup experience. That's a mark of the man, but he underlined what a class act he is by apologising for the team's performance. He said he felt the players had let the management down; I don't think that was the case at all - they gave their all and came up short in the semi-final - but I can't think of too many players who would take the time to write a letter like that. Faz is a true gent, a good bloke and I think he was actually under-rated as a player; he played stand-off, second-row, loose-forward and even prop to a very high standard.

There aren't many players who could do that and the fact Faz could was a credit to his skill level and ability, but also his fitness, toughness and aggression. He was also a world-class goal-kicker and an inspirational leader and he is the sort of player any coach would want in his team.

Towards the end of his playing days he left Wigan and rugby league to join Saracens in the other code. I know people will say he wasn't as good a player in union as league, but that wasn't anything to do with lack of ability or not being able to handle the transition. It was because he had played more than a decade of top-level rugby league before he made the switch, with barely any rest periods. He played in tough positions and he carried the Wigan team on his shoulders at a time when expectations were high, but other sides were beginning to catch up. I like Faz as a person and respected him as an athlete and in my opinion, he was a true rugby league great.

After arriving in union he became a dual international, went on to coach Saracens and was part of the England back-room team. That was no surprise, I was always sure Faz would make a top-class coach, though I would have liked it to have been in rugby league. He is the sort of person who would be successful at whatever he decided to do. He has chosen rugby union, but he remains a rugby league man at heart and it would be nice to see him back in our game one day. He is technically very clever and he is a good man-manager, who inspires respect. One story from his Wigan days sums that up perfectly.

The coaching staff - Stuart, Billy McGinty, Nigel Ashley-Jones and I - were having a cup of coffee in Stuart's office, mulling a few things over before training, when Andy came in and told us he had sent a player home! We asked what he meant and he said the player had come in smelling of booze; Faz had spoken to Denis Betts and they had decided to throw him out of training. He said: 'That's not what we do at Wigan, it's not acceptable at this club so I've told him to f-off and come back when he has sobered up and he is ready to go to work.'

That was an example of the standards they had at Wigan,

which were very much policed by the players themselves. The captain took the decision and he knew we would back him. Others might have looked after the player, maybe said he wasn't well, because he would have faced even tougher action if Stuart or I had seen him in that state. But it was the culture at Wigan, the senior players set the standards and if you fell below them, you were on your bike.

I would have been happy to stay on at Wigan after 2002 and, as far as I know, they were keen to keep me. Instead, I took the option to move back to Yorkshire, to join Hull, but I want to stress now that it was my decision, despite a newspaper rumour that something untoward had gone on. I wondered about whether to comment on this at all, because I didn't want to give any credence to a baseless rumour, but have decided to so I can set the record straight. The fact is I left Wigan because I had a great opportunity at Hull. There was no other reason. A newspaper reported that I had got into trouble with Wigan over my expenses, but there was no truth in that whatsoever. That came about because of a mis-understanding, but there was no issue between myself, Stuart, Maurice Lindsay or the club.

I was away on tour with England 'A', in the south Pacific, when my wife rang me to say a paper was running a story about my expenses. That was the first I had heard of it. There was no foundation whatsoever in what had been written; a mountain had been made out of not even a molehill, it was at worst a divot in the ground. I have got a good name - especially in rugby league - and it was a shock to find myself the victim of what was basically a piece of muck-raking. But I'm not the first person that has happened to and I won't be the last.

It was hurtful at the time, but there is no way that was involved in me leaving. I left because of the opportunity at Hull - and it wasn't a case of me approaching them, they sought me out. I spoke to both Stuart and Maurice and they both told me I should do what I felt was right. There was no 'thank God for that, let's get shut of him'.

I knew there was nothing in it and so did everyone at Wigan, but what annoyed me was the impact the story had on my family. I knew it wasn't true so I wasn't overly worried, but my wife Dawn and my two kids James and Alana took it hard. I was on the other side of the world when they were reading negative coverage about me in the newspaper. They were upset and concerned and they were desperate to know what was happening and was I about to lose my job? That's the thing that angered me the most.

I have no problem with journalists, most of them. I'd consider some of them to be friends of mine and I do a lot of work in the broadcast media, but I think they need to realise what impact their words can have on people on the receiving end, especially when there's no substance in it.

The job on offer at Hull was first team coach, working under head coach/director of coaching Shaun McRae. I have known Shaun since 1992 when he was conditioner for the Australian national team and I was the Great Britain assistant-coach. We bumped into each other at an international game in Wigan where I was working for the BBC and he was on media duty with Sky. We had a chat and he asked if I was interested in going to Hull. There was a vacancy because Tony Anderson had left his role as assistant-coach to take charge at Halifax, who were then a Super League club.

For me it was a new opportunity and, arguably, a more senior post and there was a bit more money involved. That wasn't the major issue, but it did show that Hull meant business. The club had recently 'merged' with Gateshead - which was in fact a take-over, in a similar fashion to when Huddersfield swallowed up Sheffield - and the directors were willing to make resources available, with regard to salaries, to get Hull on the up.

When I first joined Wigan the club put me up in a hotel over there. Later I got a house in the area, but my wife has a good job as a Personal Adviser for Looked after Children and Children who have left Local Authority Care for Barnsley Council, so moving over to the other side of the Pennines had not been an option. When we had been due to make an early-morning start I always went over to Wigan the night before, to make sure I was there in good time. I was splitting myself between Yorkshire and Wigan and the prospect of less travelling and the fact I would be able to live at home full-time also played a part in my decision to take up Hull's offer.

I also had to think about my future prospects. I could see a clear path to becoming the main man at Hull, but the road was a little more rocky at Wigan, which is one of the most coveted coaching jobs in sport. The late Mike Gregory was coming through at the time and he took over the reins when Stuart eventually left the club, but in 2002 we'd had a good season and won the Challenge Cup and it seemed to me that Stuart's star was in the ascendancy. I thought he would be there for a number of years and I really believed Wigan would go from strength to strength following the Cup triumph.

Hull were very much an up and coming club at the time and I felt there would be opportunities to further myself there. Shaun had told me right from the start he did not envisage being at Hull in the long term and when he did leave he would put me forward as the man to take over. Shaun was big friends with the South Sydney chief executive Shane Richardson from their time together at Gateshead. I reckoned if Shane got the opportunity he would make an effort to get Shaun over to Sydney with him. Shaun is an Aussie and obviously coaching in the NRL would be a dream come true, if the chance came along.

I was confident I could add something to the club as first team coach and believed I could take Hull forward if the hot seat came my way, which seemed quite possible. Leaving a massive club like Wigan wasn't an easy decision to make, but I weighed everything up and it seemed like the right thing to do.

It turned out I was right about Hull and the prospects there, but wrong as far as Wigan were concerned. Actually things at Wigan got much worse, very quickly, so it turned out to be a good time to leave. They did reach the Grand Final again in 2003 and Challenge Cup showpiece the following year - losing both - but the club was at the top of a slippery slope. Looking back perhaps there were signs of that: it was an ageing team on the point of breaking up. They did have some good youngsters coming through, most notably Sean O'Loughlin and Gareth Hock, but they were very inexperienced.

Mike Gregory was taken ill - and, tragically, later died - and some wrong decisions were made behind the scenes. Wigan ran into financial problems which led to them almost being relegated in 2006 and they would have gone down instead of Castleford if they hadn't brought in Brian Noble as coach and spent big to sign a couple of match-winning players.

Wigan struggled for a good many years, but I am pleased the club has now got back on its feet because I really believe a strong Wigan is good for the game of rugby league. It is an international brand with a huge fan base. A powerful Wigan means a strong British game; it is still one of the best player-producing areas in the country and the potential to draw in crowds is huge. Brian Noble steadied the ship in Super League terms, keeping them in the competition and taking them to the verge of a Grand Final on a number of occasions, but they made the breakthrough when Australian Michael

Coaching is Chaos

Maguire - assistant coach of the NRL champions Melbourne Storm - was appointed boss for the 2010 season.

He toughened Wigan up and brought in a new ruthless style of play, which saw them finish top of the table and beat St Helens in the Grand Final. The following year they were Challenge Cup winners and finished second in the league, though they didn't get as far as Old Trafford. Maguire's team were effective and I was pleased to see them get back on the horse, but I wasn't a fan of the way they played the game and I wouldn't like to see those methods become widespread in our competition.

I think rugby league is a gladiatorial sport, a tough game that is hard enough as it is. Melbourne used some dubious tactics in the NRL - which led to the introduction of a two referees system over there - and Wigan played to a similar style. They made it very unpleasant for the ball carrier, through wrestling techniques and pressure applied to the joints of the man in possession. I would not say they were deliberately told to do that, but they seemed to have a tendency to put three or four men in a tackle, taking the ball-carrier's mind off getting the ball back into play. I remember Jeff Lima attacking - and I don't think that is too strong a word - the leg of Leeds Rhinos forward Chris Clarkson during a game at Headingley, which I was commentating on for the BBC. He was suspended for one game, but I felt he should have got a six-match ban. I really don't believe there's room for tactics like that in our game.

Maguire concentrated on introducing a take-no-prisoners edge to Wigan's defence, but once they had got that they began to play some excellent rugby on the back of it. Their 2011 Challenge Cup final win over Leeds was a classic and it showcased everything that is good about our sport. Leeds contributed with a stirring fightback, but the first half an hour or so, when Wigan swept into a 16-0 lead, was a masterclass. They weren't just defensively awesome, they played some terrific stuff with the ball in hand. That final was a bit like the 2002 one, in reverse. Tickets were like gold dust in Wigan, but Leeds failed to sell out their allocation.

Having said I'm pleased to see the Warriors back among the big guns and that I believe a strong Wigan team is good for the game, I was delighted they didn't retain the Super League title in 2011, Michael Maguire's second and last in charge. After adding three top-quality Aussies to the side which won the 2010 Grand Final it looked like Wigan were on the verge of a new era of dominance and that would not have been positive for the sport.

Fortunately we are no longer in the 1980s, when Wigan had resources other clubs didn't. Warrington have won three Challenge Cup finals in four years, which is a remarkable achievement. I think Huddersfield will win a trophy at some stage soon, both Hull clubs are on the up, Catalan Dragons are making strides and of course Leeds and St Helens both remain a major force. That's what any vibrant competition needs, a number of teams capable of winning things, rather than just one side sweeping up all the silverware.

Everyone expected it to be a Warrington v Wigan final in 2011, but instead Leeds played Saints for the fourth time in five years. I think that made it one of the best Super League competitions there has been. Leeds, under a new coach Brian McDermott, had a pretty miserable year and in mid-season it looked like they might miss out on the top-eight. They eventually finished fifth, won through to Old Trafford by playing sudden-death rugby every week and beat Saints in an absolute classic. And in 2012, when everyone again expected a Warrington-Wigan showdown, they repeated the feat! I think that has breathed new life into Super League; every club who qualifies for the play-offs will now believe they have a realistic chance of winning it.

Coaching is Chaos

Before Leeds' twin triumphs, Bradford Bulls - who came third in 2005 - were the only team to win the Grand Final from outside the top-two. Wigan reached the final from third in 2003, but lost to Bradford - and every other final since 1998 had been first versus second.

To come from fifth once was a fine achievement - to do it twice was awesome. In the 2011 play-offs, Leeds only had one home game, when they beat Hull and then they had to go away to two teams who had finished above them on the table, Huddersfield and Warrington. And after that they had a final against a team who had finished higher than them on the ladder. A year later, they beat in-form Wakefield at home, vanquished Catalan Dragons in France and then turned minor premiers Wigan over at the DW, before ending second-placed Warrington's hopes of a first Championship title in 57 years at Old Trafford. Leeds winning twice against all the odds might have been tough on Warrington and Wigan, who were the most consistent sides in both years, but it was also the making of the Grand Final system.

Although they were disappointed not to go the distance and despite my being pleased that they hadn't won the title the previous year, I was pleased to see Wigan on top of the league table in 2012 because of who they decided to appoint as coach when Michael Maguire left. Rather than going for a big-name Aussie, they promoted Maguire's assistant Shaun Wane and I think that was a tremendous show of faith in a home-grown coach.

Shaun, a former prop-forward, is a massive figure and a big personality and I think he has done a tremendous job to build on the platform set down by his predecessor. As a British coach he has re-energised the traditional values of a great club and full credit to him for that.

10

*

Hell at Hull

WHEN I was sacked at Huddersfield it was the correct decision on the club's part. I was struggling, the team wasn't going anywhere and both parties needed a change, though I honestly believe nobody else could have done any better under the circumstances.

The second time I got the boot was mid-way through 2006 when Hull decided they'd had enough of me - and that time the decision was totally wrong. I felt bitter about what happened at the time and, though it didn't do me any harm in the long-run, still do.

I did a good job at Hull and anyone who says differently has got his - or her - facts wrong. In my only full season as head coach we won the club's first major trophy in 14 years, finished fifth in the league and won a play-off tie, Hull's first in the Grand Final era. In my eyes, that's an achievement I can be proud of, but I paid the price for a breakdown in my relationship with the board and especially its chairwoman, Kath Hetherington.

Coaching is Chaos

The people behind the decision to sack me would no doubt claim an early-season change worked, because after I left Hull went on to finish second in the table and reach the Grand Final. But the fact is that would have happened if I had remained in charge - and I told them so at the time. And maybe if I had still been coach we would have won that title decider.

I officially joined Hull on January 6, 2003 as first team coach, working under the director of rugby Shaun McRae. I was basically his assistant, though with a bit more responsibility than that role usually carries. Shaun left at the end of 2004 to join South Sydney, which he had hinted might happen when I joined him at Hull, and I stepped into the hot seat.

It was an exciting time to be moving to one of the sport's sleeping giants. I was on better money and in a more senior position than at Wigan and, when I arrived, the club had just left its famous old Boulevard home, so I was involved in the first game at KC (Kingston Communications) Stadium, a narrow Challenge Cup win over Halifax. We had Jason Smith and Richard Fletcher sent off that afternoon, so it was an interesting start for the new ground and my Hull career.

That probably set the pattern for the three and a quarter seasons I spent at Hull: a mixture of highs and lows, often occurring at more or less the same time. During the time I was playing for Castleford, Hull were the top side in England, boasting a star-studded side which included greats like Dave Topliss, James Leuluai, Gary Kemble, Peter Sterling, Garry Schofield and Lee Crooks. Hull KR were their only serious rivals, so the city was the centre of the British game.

When I joined the coaching staff, Hull were just starting to come out of a long period of decline, which had seen them drop into the lower divisions for a long while. The move to the KC created a lot of interest, but it was only a so-called merger with Gateshead Thunder which kept the club afloat. Gateshead were revived - sort of - in the lower divisions and the merger resulted in Shaun and some top-class players moving down the east coast. Hull had been in real strife before then, but the arrangement boosted their playing squad and gave the club a platform to build on.

I have known Shaun for a long time and he was great to work with. He has a less than flattering reputation among certain people in the game, which is completely undeserved. There's a perception that he is too laid back, he doesn't do much work on the training field and his team meetings go on too long. I would admit there's an element of truth in that final point, but the rest is a load of rubbish. When he took me to Hull he made it clear I would be doing the vast majority of the work on the training field and he would take an over-view. That was a case of playing to our strengths. I enjoy getting my hands dirty, while his analysis of the game was excellent and he was very good at getting that across to the players.

I know some of them thought he was too long-winded, but the points he made were valid and he always had a very good game plan up his sleeve to counter the opposition. I don't think Shaun has ever got a lot of credit for his rugby league nous, but he must have had it because he was very successful at St Helens, where he won the Super League and Challenge Cup, he did a good job at Gateshead and he laid some foundations at Hull. He also coached in the NRL and you don't do that without knowing what you are doing.

Working in Hull suited me in lots of ways. The city is about the same distance from my home as Wigan was, but it was much easier to get to. It could take a couple of hours going west, but it's a lot quieter east-bound once you pass the A1, so travelling time was halved.

Coaching is Chaos

I mention that because one of the first pieces of advice I was given was, 'make sure you don't move to Hull'! I know the city has got a bad reputation - I remember it featuring in a book about 'crap towns' - but that wasn't the reason. The fact is, when it comes to rugby league the city is a goldfish bowl. The interest is massive and it is the number one sport in the eyes of the population and the local media.

I'd group Wigan/St Helens, Castleford/Wakefield/ Featherstone and Hull as the three most fanatical rugby league hotbeds in this country. Cumbria should probably be included as well for the strength of its amateur game, though sadly there is no Super League club up there. But having worked in each of those three areas, I think Hull is an area apart. Shaun made sure he lived outside the city and after a few weeks I could see why. It would be impossible to go anywhere or do anything if you lived in the place; it would have driven anybody round the bend. You were constantly in the spotlight, there were always people approaching you to talk about the game and every single one of them - man, woman or child - had strong opinions on what was going right, or more often wrong.

That gives you an idea of the pressure the Hull club is under. The older generation of fans remember the glory days of the 1980s and the younger ones have been brought up on stories of the time when the Black and Whites ruled the game. Hull is a city divided - between FC and KR - but the one thing everybody is agreed on is that they want their club to get back to the top and they won't accept failure.

I am lucky to have coached some great players during my time. That word can be over-used, but I don't think too many would argue against including the likes of Kris Radlinski, Paul Sculthorpe and Andy Farrell - to name just three - in that category. But the best of them all was on the books at Hull when I joined the club in 2003, Jason Smith. He was a phenomenal rugby league player and a bit of a freak. People talk about the super-professionalism of Australian players, but Jason was in a class of his own. He had the ability to win games single-handedly, he was as tough as old boots and he had decent kicking skills, but we could never do the post-match de-brief immediately after the final hooter, because he always went missing.

It happened after every game and we all knew exactly what was going on. Someone would have to go out and find Jason and he would be skulking in a corridor somewhere having a crafty fag. That's wrong on a number of levels, not least because the KC is a non-smoking stadium and if a fan was caught doing that he or she would be booted out.

Paul King, the talented English forward who I have worked with at a couple of clubs, tended to be with him and they would both be having a light-up to get some nicotine into their lungs, so they could then come back and listen to the coaching staff's 10-minute game review before Shaun went into his press conference.

Jason liked a drink as well and there were times he turned up at early morning training and you suspected he had been on the booze the evening before, but he always arrived on time and he ripped it up. The only player I could compare him to is the ex-St Helens, Wigan and Leeds great Gary Connolly, who was also known as a bit of a drinker. Shaun McRae's attitude to Jason was that as long as he was doing his job on the training field and the playing paddock and his work didn't suffer, he would make allowances. There aren't many players you would allow to get away with that, but Jason was one, because he was so good.

He was a competitor and he had unbelievable skill. I have coached hundreds of players, but in terms of combining natural talent with in-built toughness, Jason was at the very top of the pile. When it comes to loose-forwards

Coaching is Chaos

I thought Andy Farrell was an exceptional player, but even Faz wouldn't get into my team ahead of Jason. He could also play at six (stand-off) and seven (scrum-half) and whatever game plan the coaches came up with, he would carry out to the letter - and with quality.

Jason was our best player, but Hull weren't a one-man team. Paul Cooke and Richard Horne were just establishing themselves at Super League level, Colin Best and Richie Barnett were quality imports, I am a fan of Chris Chester and we also had Tony 'Casper' Smith, until he had to pack in because of injury. We also signed the Kiwi Richard Swain, who was one of the best hookers of the modern era. He was the ultimate professional, he did everything right on and off the field and he was an 80-minute hooker, which gave us extra options off the interchange bench.

Some of the players I worked with at Hull later joined me at Wakefield, Paul Cooke among them. He was still at the rookie stage in 2003, but became a key cog in the team and he was instrumental in our Challenge Cup win in 2005. Unfortunately Paul made some wrong decisions during his career and he didn't go as far as he could have done, but at his peak he was a class act. I think I brought the best out of Paul and his finest spell was in 2005, when he wasn't far off Great Britain selection.

Our left-edge that season was a Sheffield replica; we had Paul Cooke, Chris Chester, Kirk Yeaman - who you could hit with an early ball and would use a big right-hand fend to bust through - and there was Gareth Raynor out wide, who was a good finisher. Cookie was a great reader of the game, his pass selection was first class and he was very clever. If teams were rushing up and trying to close him down, he would send a lovely kick behind them early in the tackle count and that put a bit of doubt in their mind.

Richie Barnett was also high-quality. He developed a

reputation for being a bit injury-prone, but I think that is unfair. We got some very good games out of him, but what he lacked was confidence. He'd had some of his self-belief ripped apart after a bad game playing at full-back for New Zealand against the Aussies. When he signed, Shaun promised Richie he wouldn't have to play full-back any more and we would use him in the centres.

We also had a very tough Aussie in the shape of Craig Greenhill, who was one of our enforcers. I think he typified the team we had; it wasn't a glamour side, but it was very solid and didn't take any nonsense. Gateshead, under Shaun, had the reputation of being a grinding team. That continued when they moved down to Hull, but he added some class as well in the likes of Smith and Barnett, with young talent like Horne, Cooke and Kirk Yeaman coming through.

Later, when I was head coach in 2005, Stephen Kearney spent a year with us. He has gone on to coach New Zealand and I think he may well achieve even more in a tracksuit than he did with his boots on. When he came to us he added a bit of mongrel, some physicality which we had been lacking. He had an aura about him and other players looked up to him. With him on the field we knew we would never get out-muscled; the younger forwards like Ewan Dowes and Garreth Carvell followed his lead and became much better players from having him alongside them.

Stephen did some work with our academy and I always felt he had what it takes to go on and be a great coach. He was like a wise old bird to the younger players. All the top players know how to play the game technically and tactically; what counts when it comes to coaching is whether they can communicate and get their ideas across. He could do that and he was instrumental to our 2005 Challenge Cup victory.

Coaching is Chaos

Swain was intelligent, Kearney was tough and we had Danny Brough coming through as well to give us a bit of an X-factor. Shaun Briscoe was a great returner of the ball, very brave in defence and an excellent support player, but he wasn't a good kicker. I've always liked playing with three kickers and in that team Cooke, Horne and Brough all filled the role.

Stephen Kearney's Hull career ended on a really low note at the end of 2005, when he was sent off in our elimination semi-final at Bradford Bulls. Steve Ganson is a referee who has never been afraid to make big decisions. He red-carded Stephen for a high tackle on Stuart Fielden after just seven minutes and we went on to lose the game 71-0, which is a record in the Super League play-offs.

I felt for Stephen, who deserved a better farewell. In my opinion it was a bad decision which ruined the game and cost us a chance of being competitive. We had won the Cup five weeks earlier and we were on the back of a magnificent play-offs win over Warrington, so we thought we could cause a bit of a stir on the road to Old Trafford. Warrington had beaten us at the KC in our final league game, but that was a dead rubber as far as we were concerned and we turned the tables over at their ground in the play-offs, which was a stunning result. They had Andrew Johns - one of the greatest players of all time - in their ranks, but we went over there, produced a quality performance and walloped them.

We were confident of giving Bradford a game, but looking back we would probably have lost even if we'd had 13 men on the field for the full tie, though obviously it would have been a lot closer. It was a case of a Bradford team with 13 men playing at the very top of their game against 12 men who played poorly.

Straight afterwards I held my hand up and admitted I had made a mistake with my team selection, by leaving

Danny Brough out of the side. We had a Kiwi player Sione Faumuina with us on a short-term contract and I went with him at stand-off, Richard Horne at scrum-half and Paul Cooke at loose-forward. I wanted to try and match Bradford physically and we played differently to how we had done all year. Obviously, it didn't work.

Big Lesley Vainikolo scored four tries, which was a bit of an improvement on our part. He had scored six the previous time we'd played them, a few weeks earlier! He was awesome that night and frightened the life out of our winger Nathan Blacklock in his final game for Hull.

I coached Hull for the whole of the 2005 season and eight games the following year, seven in the league and one Cup tie, before I got the push. The decision to sack me was wrong in every way. I didn't deserve the chop and even if I had, it was far too early in the season to be making a change. As far as I am concerned it was a ridiculous decision and it was a personal one, rather than being based on league matters.

Richard Agar, my assistant, took over as caretaker-coach before an Aussie, Peter Sharp, got the job. Richard was given the role on a permanent basis when Sharp left in 2007 and he led a charmed life. Though they got to the Cup final in 2009, Hull were 11th in 2008, 12th in 2009 and sixth in 2010. Richard left at the end of 2011 - ironically, to take over from me at Wakefield - after Hull had finished eighth, though by then the club had different people in charge.

I was pleased the club stuck with Richard for as long as it did. I would like to think the powers-that-be learned a lesson from my sacking and realised you have got to give a coach time. On the other hand, perhaps Richard was a little bit more popular with the board than I was. I had won three out of seven in the league when I was dismissed and the Cup game we lost was a close affair away to the Super League champions Bradford.

Coaching is Chaos

What made it all the more galling was the fact I had promised the board before the 2006 season that if we were in a play-offs position after 10 games, we would finish top. There was a directors' meeting held at the Bridge Hotel, just off the A1 in Wetherby, near Leeds. That was the venue because there were no directors from Hull; Kath lived in Pontefract and the rest were based in the north east, because they had come down from the defunct Tyneside operation.

We had a review of 2005 and looked ahead to 2006. I told the board I had no doubt we were capable of winning the league leaders' shield, if we came through the early part of the campaign in decent shape. Hull actually finished second that year, so I wasn't far off. The first 10 fixtures were really tough, but after that the road got a lot smoother. I saw any points we picked up early on as a bonus, because I could see us putting a run together over the second half of the season.

That is exactly what happened. They won three out of four when Richard was in charge and then Peter Sharp took the team on an unbelievable run of victories. Hull won 17 of their first 19 games after my exit and it is irritating when people say that run came about because of the change of coach, when I know it would have happened if I had still been in charge - and perhaps we would have done even better by finishing top and winning at Old Trafford.

The writing was on the wall for me straight after our 2005 Challenge Cup final win over Leeds. I think most people would agree a Challenge Cup final victory is special and afterwards the players - and staff - deserve to do a bit of celebrating and let their hair down. We certainly did that. Hull hadn't won the trophy for 23 years, but - despite some adversity - we pulled off a marvellous, dramatic win over the hot favourites, after beating two of the sport's other big guns en-route to the final.

As head coach I certainly wasn't going to order the

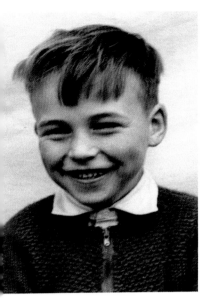

Above: Me, aged six.

Right: Me as a kid with my mate Rob Hepworth (left) and my cousin Keith Voyce. Keith went on to play professional rugby league for Dewsbury.

Above: My dad Herbert played rugby league from schoolboy through to professional level. He is pictured here (fifth from the left on the front-row) with the Wheldon Lane School team of 1933.

Above: I captained Castleford Grammar School's under-14s rugby union side (they didn't play league) in 1968. I'm at the front, with the ball.

Above: One of my first class pictures, Wheldon Lane County Infants in the 1960s. I am in the middle, back-row.

Left: My brother David was scoreboard operator at Cas' Wheldon Road ground and I used to help out, with a hot water bottle tucked under my jumper.

Above: Castleford High rugby union first XV in 1972. I am sixth from the left, front row. Gary Hetherington, now chief executive of Leeds, is second from left at the back.

Left: A shot of me kicking for Cas in a game at Wheldon Road in 1986.

Below: My dad Herbert was my inspiration. Taking the Challenge Cup home after Cas won it in 1986 was a proud moment. *Below right*: My beloved brother David congratulates me after I graduated at the end of my teaching course in Leicester.

Below: Sadly, Castleford's last Challenge Cup success was way back in 1986. Here we are, about to set off for Wembley. Jamie Sandy, who scored a wonderful try in the win over Hull KR, is to my right on the front of the picture.

Left: In action for Castleford against Hull KR in the 1984 Premiership final at Headingley.

Yorkshire Weekly Newpaper Group

Right: This is me scoring for Cas in the 1984 Premiership final against Hull KR at Headingley. I like this picture because of the reaction of the crowd.

Yorkshire Weekly Newpaper Group

Above: The proud coach of Athelstan County Primary School's rugby league team in March, 1982.

Above: My first head coaching role was at Bramley. This is a team picture from 1988 - and my hair's already beginning to disappear!

Left: The Great Britain academy squad of 1992. I am sitting between Andy Farrell and Phil Cantillon, front row.

Below: There's no place for try-scorer Paul Newlove in my Dream Team, but I was proud to be associated with Newy and England in the 1995 World Cup.

Above: My underdog Sheffield Eagles side prepares to do battle with Andy Farrell and Kris Radlinski's Wigan at Wembley in 1998. No one gave us a chance.

Above: Hull's 2005 Challenge Cup final victory over Leeds at Cardiff's Millennium Stadium was another memorable achievement.

Below: On TV duty with Brian Noble.

Above: Sadly, a fall-out with board member Kath Hetherington would eventually lead to my undeserved exit from the KC Stadium.

Left: At a press conference with Danny McGuire for England 'A' v Australia. England played brilliantly but just lost, and Danny scored a magical try with his dancing feet.

Above: Celebrating victory over my hometown club Cas in Wakefield's 'Million Pound Match' with the Wildcats' mascot Daddy Cool.

Left: Coaching Jamie Rooney at Belle Vue.

Right: Batley chairman Kevin Nicholas welcomes me to Mount Pleasant. I am enjoying my time at the club - life in the Championship offers a different set of challenges.

all rlphotos.com

Left: Dawn with me after I graduated from the University of Central Lancashire with a Postgraduate Diploma in Elite Coaching. *Below:* And on our wedding day.

Right: Rugby league is in the Kear family blood. Here my dad Herbert celebrates his 70th birthday in January 1989 with my mum Irene and an appropriately decorated cake.

Below: My proudest achievement are my twins, James and Alana.

Above right: Celebrating with my now Sky colleague Terry O'Connor at Murrayfield in 2002

rlphotos.com

players to stick to soft drinks and get an early night. I told them to enjoy the moment and they took that advice. A good time was had by all and it was a big night, which went into the wee small hours. I don't think there's anything wrong with that and I wouldn't have thought anybody could begrudge our celebration. There's a time and a place for drinking and that was it. A formal reception was held after the game and everybody had a lot to drink. Players and staff went out and about in Cardiff, where the final against Leeds was played and everyone arrived back at the hotel at different times of the morning. We were all worse for wear, me included.

I made it back in time for breakfast, but a lot of the players didn't get chance to eat before we all piled on to the bus back to Hull where a civic reception was being held later on the Sunday, the day after the game. We had to leave Wales quite early because it's a long trip. There was more drinking on the coach and, as a lot of the players hadn't eaten, I rang ahead to the Twin Oaks Motel, at junction 29 on the M1 and asked them to put some sandwiches on. I had checked with Kath if that was okay and she told me no, they shouldn't have missed their breakfast! Some people might regard that as just a tad ungrateful, considering what had happened the previous afternoon. I definitely thought it was harsh, so we went ahead and had the buffet anyway. I paid and David Plummer refunded the money on expenses, which was decent of him. After a Challenge Cup triumph, which must have brought a lot of revenue to the club and the city, I think splashing out for a few rounds of sandwiches was the least the club could do. Unfortunately, I had gone against Kath's wishes and she wasn't happy about it. I think that was the moment when our relationship began to break down. It was such a petty thing, but matters went from bad to worse and eventually she won, because I got the sack.

Coaching is Chaos

Another cause of tension between us was the signing of Sid Domic, from Wakefield, for the following season. I don't think Kath rated him as much as I did, but I pushed hard for him to be brought to the club. At the time, after the Cup success and reaching the second round of the play-offs, my stock was pretty high and I got my way. But that definitely didn't endear me to Kath. Sid played 29 games in 2006 and scored 11 tries, so he had a pretty good year. I think he was a fine signing for the club, but it was another nail in my coffin as far as being coach of Hull goes.

Towards the middle of December 2005 my wife told me I would be lucky to see the following season out at Hull. The reason was we hadn't been invited to the Hetheringtons' New Year's Eve soiree, which we had been in previous years. My wife's a smart woman, she read that very accurately as a snub and her prediction came true.

I know some people at the club were saying I had lost the dressing room or I was a victim of player power, but I believe the main reason was the lack of trust between chairwoman and coach. I was really upset about it at the time and when I think about it now it still makes me angry, because I felt Shaun and I had started to build a dynasty and all that was thrown away for no good reason. We had moulded some good young players - Shaun Briscoe, Richard Whiting, Scott Wheeldon, Kirk Yeaman, Danny Brough, Richard Horne and Paul Cooke - into a Cup-winning squad and they all had their best years in front of them.

Despite the success we enjoyed, all of a sudden I was out on my ear and when I left it was all dismantled. I couldn't believe that people like Briscoe and Cooke were allowed to leave - and not only that, they went to the nearest and fiercest rivals, Hull KR. Broughy was put on his bike as well and I think that is a decision Hull have regretted ever since. I know some of these players were regarded as my guys and after I departed things became uncomfortable for them because of that, which I regret. The players should not have been held responsible for whatever happened between me and the board.

Hull went from being a club which was very happy and had a great future, to one which - after fulfilling its potential in 2006 with a team Shaun and I had built - became one of the competition's biggest under-achievers.

FC had two great seasons in 2005 and 2006. That didn't just happen, it was the culmination of a long building process and since then it has been knocked down from the foundations, though now - years later - I believe they are back on an upward curve under new owner Adam Pearson. I found the decline after I left very sad because Hull were ready to if not dominate the competition - I think the days of one team doing that are gone - then certainly reach finals on a regular basis. They did go all the way to Wembley in the 2009 Challenge Cup, but they should have been doing that much more often.

I don't accept that the form we showed during my eight games in charge in 2006 justified sacking the coach. We defeated Castleford and Wakefield, lost to Warrington, Harlequins and Bradford, beat Wakefield, got hammered at home by St Helens and then went down away to Bradford in the Challenge Cup.

The Cup tie was shown live on the BBC and we gave a good account of ourselves against the previous year's Grand Final winners. We were beaten 23-12, but were in the contest throughout and with a bit more luck we might have won it. Kirk Dixon spilled the ball with the line at his mercy and if he had scored - which would have taken us ahead - I think we'd have gone on to win it. I am not blaming Kirk, who is a decent player, but that's just the way it was.

I was in the bar afterwards when Kath came up to me

and asked if I could meet the directors at the Cedar Court Hotel, at Junction 39 on the M1, the following day because they wanted to chat about my future. I was out of contract at the end of the season and there had been a great deal of speculation over whether I would be kept on. I wanted a renewal because I had enjoyed my time at Hull, I had brought success to the club and I felt even bigger things were just around the corner. I wasn't unduly worried when I was asked to attend that meeting as I thought the club would support me. I expected to be offered another year or two, but instead was told I wouldn't be kept on at the end of 2006.

I think they wanted to sack me there and then, but my reaction took them by surprise. It was a bit of a stormy meeting and I told them I would stay until the end of the year, finish top of the league and/or win the Grand Final and then get another job somewhere else on the back of that. The very next day I went to training as normal, at Hull Ionians Rugby Union Club and after lunch Kath and the club's chief executive David Plummer came along and swung the axe. They said they were taking away the option of me staying until the end of the season, as they felt they needed an immediate change. That was it, game over. I went back to my office, cleared my desk and drove away in a foul mood, which I think was only to be expected. Getting the sack from a job I loved at a club I loved hurt me greatly.

It was a big story in East Yorkshire and a shock not only to me, but also the vast majority of the fans. It's hard to gauge, but when I go back to the place most of the Hull supporters I meet tell me they would have liked me to stay on. In Hull, they tell you what they think and if I had lost the backing of the Faithful - as they are known - I would have heard about it. That wasn't the case and I don't believe there was any real feeling against me among the players. You can't please everyone and I am sure one or two were glad to see the back of me, but I think most of them were pretty loyal and remained on my side.

The worst result we had in 2006 was the 46-0 home defeat by St Helens in my final league game. That was a terrible evening and an unacceptable result, albeit against the team which went on to finish top of the table, win the Challenge Cup and take out the Grand Final as well.

Kath was upset that I appeared as a pundit on Sky TV the following day. The fact was I had agreed to do the TV gig well in advance and I didn't feel I could refuse to go on because we had copped a hiding. Sky drove me to the match - which was Harlequins versus Leeds at The Stoop, in London - so I did my work reviewing the Saints game on my laptop in the car en-route.

Just as a video referee can always look for ways to disallow a try, I felt Kath was searching for reasons to get shut of me. Kath, who is married to the Leeds Rhinos chief executive Gary Hetherington, remained in charge of Hull until part-way through 2011, when the new owner took over. One of the first major changes after her departure was the exit of Richard Agar, who she had backed through some very tough times.

I have no problem with Richard, who stayed on the coaching staff after I was axed. I had been Phil Larder's assistant at Sheffield and I took over following his sacking, so I have had the boot on either foot. I appointed Richard on Kath's advice and I had been aware of the fine work he did in his previous job as coach at York City Knights. It was a lesson learned though and in the future I would always make sure my staff were people I had chosen.

One person whose behaviour I really admired after my exit from Hull was the conditioner Billy Mallinson. He came out in public and said it was wrong, which was a brave thing to do. It is not easy to criticise your employer, in any walk of life. He stuck by me and it cost him his job in the end. Later, the Hull KR coach Justin Morgan rang me to ask about Billy and I could not speak highly enough of him. He got the conditioning job at Craven Park at least partly on my recommendation, because that loyalty is exactly what a head coach wants from his support staff.

I got on okay with Kath until that incident on the coach returning from Cardiff and when things were going well she was no problem to me at all. I would like to say there are no hard feelings now, but that wouldn't be completely true. I don't believe in harbouring grudges, but I have found it hard to forgive Kath for making what was a poor decision and one I still don't fully understand.

After we had lost to Bradford in the play-offs at the end of 2005, Kath had actually rung me and said: 'Don't worry about it, these things happen - we have had a great season'. I appreciated that, but two months into the following season I got my OBE: Out Before Easter. It was sad because 2005 was the best season I have ever had as a coach. What happened in 2006 was one of my lowest points.

11

*

Millennium Magic

I HAVE always enjoyed mind games. I believe if you can get one over your opponent mentally, especially before the game has even begun, you are half way towards getting a good result.

The 2005 Challenge Cup final was won by Hull's players out on the Millennium Stadium pitch, but I am convinced we gained a psychological advantage in the days leading up to the final which contributed to that. To an extent, the match was also won in the head.

The fun and games began eight days before the final in Cardiff when our opponents Leeds Rhinos played Bradford Bulls in a Super League derby at Headingley. If I could have picked Leeds' last game before the Cup decider that is the one I would have chosen. Bulls were running into a bit of form after a poor start to the season and - in their last really good campaign before they hit the skids - were still a tough, physical team, including players who were prepared to stand toe to toe with anyone. Also, in the Super League era at least, I have never seen anything less than a highly-intense clash between those two sides.

I would never wish injury on any player, friend or foe, but obviously I knew before the game if Bradford could rough Leeds up a bit that would help our cause. And so it proved as first Rhinos lost Danny McGuire to a shoulder injury after a tackle by Ben Harris and then - moments later - Bulls' big prop Joe Vagana landed heavily on top of Keith Senior, whose ankle bent nastily beneath him.

It looked serious straight away. Leeds' medical team rushed on and a stretcher was called for, though Keith sent it away. I am not a qualified lip-reader, but in my profession it pays to be half-decent at it. Watching on Sky it was clear he was telling the medical staff: 'F-off, I am not being carried off the week before a Cup final!' He hobbled off and immediately I thought that was one of their main strike men gone.

So what were my feelings when I watched Keith go off? I never like to see anybody injured in a game of rugby league and especially not a mate of mine like Keith is. On the other hand, at the time he was one of the best players in the game and we would have much more chance of beating Rhinos if he wasn't in their side. I genuinely had mixed feelings, but the injury was nothing to do with me; what I had to ensure was that we took advantage of it. Rugby league is a professional sport and a ruthless occupation and if a potential advantage falls into your lap you would be foolish not to make the most of it.

One of the first things I did when I got to work on the following Monday morning was sit down with our physio Simon Pope and watch the Senior incident again, and again, and again. We went through it frame by frame and he said to me: 'There isn't a hope in hell of Keith playing in the final, or if he does play, he'll be a passenger.'

I had already thought it was serious and from the

moment Simon said that I wanted Keith to play. Obviously I couldn't pick the Leeds team, but I did try to manipulate the opposition camp - and Keith in particular - a little bit to try and ensure he did take part. From Hull's point of view it was a win-win situation. If Keith didn't play, that was one of their better players missing. If he did, I trusted what the physio said and what my experience told me, which was that he would not be any use.

The injury was big news and when I spoke to the media early in the week I made a point of saying: 'If Keith Senior plays in the final, I'll put my boots on and play against him.' I knew I had got him when we arrived at the stadium on the Saturday lunchtime, a couple of hours before kick-off. Keith was one of the first Leeds people I saw, we shook hands and his opening comment to me was: 'Have you brought your boots?'

I told him I'd left them behind, but as soon as he said that I realised the mind games had worked and he was going to play. I walked away from the handshake with a wry smile and my confidence increased from that moment on. Keith mentions that incident in his autobiography *The Bald Truth*, which I am quite pleased about.

Keith is someone I have got a lot of time for and I also know the then-Leeds boss Tony Smith, who had taken over from me at Huddersfield, pretty well. He is a superb coach, but he is very bloody-minded. If you tell him something isn't going to happen, he will do everything he possibly can to make sure it does. That's why I made such a big issue in the pre-game build up about Keith having no chance of playing. He did play, but admits in his book that he shouldn't have done. He only lasted the first half and, as Simon had predicted, he was a passenger; he was in so much pain from the ankle he was no threat to us whatsoever.

Rhinos left Barrie McDermott out of their team that

afternoon and presumably he would have played if Keith hadn't, so they were effectively without two of their most experienced players. And losing Keith at half-time meant they only had three fit men on the bench throughout the final, sapping 40 minutes.

I also had a bit of inside information, in the form of a phone call from somebody connected with Cardiff Blues, who I knew from my time working down there in rugby union. Before the final, Leeds trained at the Arms Park, where Cardiff play. My contact had gone to watch them prepare and he rang me afterwards to say 'Keith Senior is no good, but he is going to play. He has been involved in all the team runs, but he is hobbling about.'

So that was more good news. Things went for us in the lead-up, but I still believe we would have won that final even if Keith had been fully fit and had played the full game, because we went into it as an in-form team full of confidence, we had a good game plan and the players stuck to it to perfection.

We played Super League teams all the way through our Cup run, including the top-three finishers in that year's Super League table. We started off with a win at Wakefield and then edged past Bradford by a couple of points at the KC. We beat Leigh at home in the quarter-finals and then drew St Helens in the last four.

That was probably the toughest possible tie at that stage. Saints were the holders and after we beat them in that semi-final they went on to win the Cup again for the next three seasons, so we were the only team to defeat them in five years in that competition.

The Bradford game was a cracker and when we got through that we began to think we were in with a shot of going all the way. It wasn't like Sheffield in 1998, we did not begin that year specifically targeting the Challenge Cup, but momentum and belief grew as we went along. The easiest game of the Cup run was the quarter-final. We had played Leigh at home the week before in the league and beat them 30-16 and we knew, unless something went drastically wrong, we could get through that round with something to spare.

Leigh had actually held us to a draw at their ground earlier in the season - one of the three Super League games they didn't lose that year - so we couldn't afford to be complacent, but their coach Darren Abram gave us a bit of extra motivation beforehand by saying Hull couldn't win the Cup.

There was already a bit of hype at that stage, which I get every year in the Challenge Cup. The media were referring back to Sheffield and speculating whether the 'Kear Cup magic' would work again. Darren spoke out in the build-up to the quarter-final and said he thought Hull were one of the poorer teams left. That was like manna from heaven for me and we went out there and walloped them 46-14.

The semi-final against Saints, at Huddersfield, was one of the best performances I have been involved in as a coach. I have been involved in some very good ones - like England 'A' when we nearly beat Australia and Sheffield's Cup win over Wigan - but that was the most complete display.

Everything we had practiced and all the little things we put into play came off for us and the players were sensational that afternoon. It was a surreal occasion, because we turned up at the Galpharm and we didn't have any socks: they had been left behind when the coach set off for Huddersfield. We played in our blue away kit, but the socks we wore didn't quite match. That was because they were Huddersfield Town's. We played the semi-final in Hull shirts and shorts, but Huddersfield Town socks. If you've got a copy of the DVD, have a look.

Coaching is Chaos

That caused a bit of a furore before kick-off, because obviously it was no way to prepare for such a big game. However, there was a belief among the team that we could win the tie and to the players' huge credit none of the pre-match messing about affected that.

Saints were the hot favourites because of their Cup record, but we had crushed them 44-6 at home in the league a couple of months earlier and only lost 18-10 at their place three weeks before the Cup tie, so we knew we had what it took to see them off. The players followed the game plan to the letter and the result was a sensational performance for the full 80 minutes.

Though we were leading at half-time the sense around the ground was that Saints would come back in the second half, but we scored first after the break and we went on with the job to win 34-8, which is a very comfortable scoreline, especially in a semi-final.

After seeing off Bradford and Saints nobody could claim we didn't deserve to be in the final, but in Leeds we were up against a team who were having a sensational season. They were the Super League champions and had won the World Club Challenge at the start of the campaign. Up until the week before the final, when they lost that fateful game to Bradford, they had been top of the table all year and that defeat by the Bulls was only their fourth in 30 matches.

We knew we were up against it as Hull hadn't beaten Leeds in their previous 11 meetings, dating back to 2002. There had been a draw at Headingley in 2003 in very controversial circumstances, when Steve Prescott equalised with a last-minute kick. Steve Ganson was the referee that day and he upset the Rhinos fans by penalising Leeds for offside, when they thought we had knocked on and it should have been head and feed to the home team. That was one of those occasions when the actual reason for the penalty award was wrong, but the RFL referees' department went through the incident with a fine-tooth comb and found another offence - which nobody had seen at the time - to justify the decision.

We were happy with the point, but Leeds definitely had the wood over us after beating us home and away in the league before the Cup meeting. There was a bit more refereeing controversy in the Super League game at Headingley that year, which Leeds won 34-14. In the last minute, Leeds were awarded a penalty and Kevin Sinfield told the referee, Richard Silverwood, that he was kicking for goal. Instead, he chipped the ball to the corner and Rob Burrow touched down.

Once you've said you are going for goal, you have to make an attempt to do so. Some kickers I have worked with could probably have claimed they had been aiming for the posts, but definitely not one of Kevin's ability. Richard Silverwood was completely taken by surprise and handed the decision on to the video official Robert Connolly, who fortunately knew the laws of the game and ruled 'no try'.

It didn't make any difference at that stage, but was an indication of the confidence and maybe arrogance Leeds were playing with at the time. Certainly the Rhinos were used to beating Hull and Hull were used to losing against the Rhinos. What I said to the players in the run-up to Cardiff was: 'Every time they beat us, we are one game nearer to ending that run, so why not beat them in the biggest game of the year?'

That is exactly what happened, thanks at least in part to the disrupted build-up they had due to Keith Senior's injury and the lift that gave us. That said, we had a fitness crisis of our own which began actually en-route to Cardiff two days before the game.

As first-choice full-back, Shaun Briscoe was literally the

first name on my team-sheet every week. He was a major part of our plans for the final, but unfortunately developed appendicitis on the coach down to Wales. He was feeling terrible and we grew increasingly concerned about him. Eventually he had to move forward and sit on the stairwell at the front of the bus, so if necessary we could open the door and he could leap out to be sick.

He made it down to the Welsh capital, but the club doctor took over once we arrived. He was first-class, immediately realising that Shaun was in serious trouble and we had to get him to hospital without delay. We rushed him into accident and emergency and the medics there said the appendix was about to burst. That's really serious and could have been fatal if he had not got the right treatment in time.

That happened on the Thursday and we had one training session between then and the game. At that session we ran with Motu Tony at full-back and Nathan Blacklock on the wing. That was more mind games: just as I'd had a spy to watch Rhinos prepare at the Arms Park I was pretty sure Leeds would have somebody watching us at the UWIST venue, which Cardiff Blues use for training. I was quite happy for Leeds to think that was how we would line up and I even named our team with Motu at full-back and Nathan on the flank.

In fact, once Shaun had been ruled out it was always our intention for Nathan to play as the last line of defence. He had operated at full-back on numerous occasions for his previous NRL club St George and we felt it would suit him. It worked because Motu scored a great try from the wing, when he chipped over and touched down and Nathan sent Gareth Raynor in for one on the left-hand side. That may not have happened if he hadn't been given the roving full-back role. He also missed Mark Calderwood with a one-on-one tackle so it wasn't a perfect solution, but overall I was very happy with how we coped and I certainly don't think Leeds had planned for Blacklock at full-back and Tony on the wing.

Our approach to the game was different to Leeds'. What other coaches do is up to them, but as I said with regard to Sheffield earlier, I have never believed that a final or semi-final is 'just another game', which is how Leeds treated that August afternoon. When they went for their pre-match look around the stadium they were very stern-faced, according to my spies, with no larking around and no real attempt to take in the stage they were on or the enormity of the occasion they were preparing for. I instructed my players to look around and remember everything, to take it all in and make sure they enjoyed it all, because you never know when something like this is going to happen again.

In our team meeting we emphasised the fact it is not another game. The message to the players was: 'This is one of the biggest matches any of us will ever be involved in. Get out there and give it everything you've got, so people remember your part in it for the right reasons. Use the emotion to spur you on, don't get over-awed by it or too caught up in it, but make sure it gives you an added edge.'

What you want to do in a cup final is produce the performance of your life and a lot of our players did that, particularly our scrum-half. I am a massive fan of Kevin Sinfield, who won the Lance Todd Trophy, but I have no doubt the real man of the match was Danny Brough. The problem with that award, which is one of the most prestigious individual honours in rugby league, is that the press who decide it are asked to vote with about 10 minutes of the game remaining. At the time the vote was taken Rhinos were ahead and it looked like they would win, but if the media had been asked to vote after the final hooter - which I think would be the right way of doing it - I am sure

Broughy would have got it. Kev played really well, but Broughy was the difference between the two teams. I gave him a kicking strategy and he fulfilled that to the letter, full stop and exclamation mark. He was sensational that day and, of course, his drop-goal mid-way through the second half was the one-point which ultimately got us home.

I always thought we would win the game, even when we were trailing 24-19 with a few moments left. We had been 19-12 up, but Leeds got back to within a point and then went in front. I think they took the lead just a bit too early from their point of view. There were 10 or 12 minutes left and I remember turning to my assistant Richard Agar and saying: 'We will get one more go - we'll have another chance and we've just got to take it.'

Fortunately we did and it came at exactly the right moment, because there wasn't really time left for Leeds to reply. Shayne McMenemy kicked through and if Leeds' right-winger Mark Calderwood had been able to pick the ball up, they would have completed their set, run the clock down and we'd have lost. But he didn't; he made an error almost on his own line and we got the ball back. We put into action a move we had worked on where Richard Horne switched play round the back of the ruck to Paul Cooke, who would then pick out a big, tired man to target. That happened to be Leeds prop Danny Ward, who Cookie fended off with ease. The try was a great moment and it put us a point behind with a kick to come from in front of the posts, which Broughy duly converted.

We had a scare even after that when Leeds got the ball back from Kevin Sinfield's kick-off. They set up for a drop-goal to level it, but Richard Swain raced out of the line and charged it down. That was one of the most inspirational defensive plays I have ever seen and it came from a truly top-class player. Richard had been on the field for 80 minutes, but he found the energy, desire and intelligence to read the play and deal with it. His charge-down was the real clincher, though Cookie's try will always be remembered as the match-winner.

The triumph meant just as much to me as Sheffield's Cup victory seven years earlier had done. As a one-off occasion Sheffield's win was probably the peak, but Hull's campaign was better. Nobody could claim we didn't deserve it after we had played a Super League team in every round and got shut of Bradford, St Helens and Leeds.

People felt Sheffield had snuck up and pinched the Cup, but there was no doubt Hull earned it. We were a different team to Sheffield and with respect to the Eagles, we weren't regarded as no-hopers. Leeds were favourites, but Hull were seen as having a decent outside chance, at least by people who knew what they were talking about.

At the time Hull were, rather like Huddersfield at the moment, a team on the up, who were getting closer to winning some major silverware. They were capable of winning something, but hadn't yet delivered.

We were underdogs against Bradford, Saints and Leeds and that suited us down to the ground. I always like the opposition to be the favourites because that takes the pressure off my team. If you go out and give it your best shot and just lose, everyone says 'good effort, didn't you do well'. If you go out and win it's even better. There's always the weight of expectation on the favourites and if things aren't going well, they feel that and the pressure mounts.

The 2005 Cup triumph was the club's first victory in the competition for 23 years and the reception back in Hull was unbelievable - definitely no three men and a dog scenario this time. We had a homecoming at the town hall and thousands of people turned out, so all you could see was an ocean of black and white. There wasn't a space to be had as far as the eye could see. It was phenomenal and it really drove home what we had achieved.

I am very proud of being involved in four Challenge Cup wins with different clubs, which I believe is unique, but I do get a bit annoyed when fans and the media describe me as a 'Cup king' or a coach who can get players up for one-off games. I'd like to think I can do that, but there's a lot more to me as a coach. It is nonsense to suggest I can only coach big games - you have to get teams into big games first, before you can get the players up for them.

I am not simply a motivator. I don't think I could have got as far in the game if that had been the case. As far as I am concerned, one of my greatest plus points in coaching is my man-management. Motivation might come from that because I like to think I know which particular button to press for each individual. Everybody's different, there are 17 rugby league players in a team and you always have 17 different characters. And the 14 Super League coaches will each have their own ways of doing things.

Man-management is about looking after the players in your charge and I think I have done that at every club I've been involved with and at international level as well. You have to make the players feel well-treated and respected, otherwise they won't give you their best. If you do that it tends to be reciprocated.

Some coaches choose to be disciplinarians. I do impose discipline, but I see it as agreed discipline with standards set by the group. What all team bosses need is the ability to know how to get the best out of individual players, in other words which buttons to press and when to do it. I like to think - and I believe my record bears this out - that I can draw the best out of people, but also you need to understand the game itself.

Nobody could coach at even semi-professional level

without having some technical and tactical nous, but there are as many different ways of coaching as there are coaches - and as many different ways of playing as there are players. It is a matter of highlighting the good bits and trying to negate the bad ones.

The mind games in the lead up to the 2005 Cup final helped set the platform for victory, but it was on-field tactics which won the game once the first whistle was blown. Take Danny Brough's kicking strategy as an example. We got that right and he executed it perfectly. We kicked from a specific position and aimed for a specific position in distance kicks. We had different types of kicks when we got into Leeds' 20 and Broughy had the freedom to take a one-pointer at any stage he felt fit. I was involved in the 1986 Cup final when Bob Beardmore kicked one, Tubby Aston dropped a goal in Sheffield's win over Wigan in 1998 and Adrian Lam did the same for Wigan in 2002 against Saints.

None of those were the final score of the game, but they were all crucial. We told Broughy to do it if he felt a drop-goal was an important score at the time. Ultimately that was the point which won us the game. The winning try that day came off a set play and that was satisfying as well. Those things don't just happen, they come from hours of planning and work on the training pitch. That win was down to a combination of tactics, belief, desire and determination. It was one of my proudest moments.

12

*

Wakey Wakey!

THE three months I spent out of work after I got my OBE from Hull were the lowest of my coaching career. I was totally disenchanted and for a while I really questioned whether I wanted to stay involved with rugby league.

As I have mentioned, I felt what had happened at Hull was totally unfair and unjustified and my love for the sport, which I have had more or less from birth, was on the wane. Fortunately, Sky TV rekindled my interest and then Wakefield Trinity Wildcats came along as a project I could really get my teeth into.

Time is a great healer and after a month or so to sulk, as well as recharge my batteries, read a few books and generally chill out, I began to get bored. As time goes on the phone stops ringing and you can become isolated, as I am sure too many people have found out in all walks of life recently, but I was lucky. Eddie Hemmings, the Sky rugby league commentator and his producer Neville Smith re-lit the fire when they got me back involved in rugby on the punditry side, which is something I really enjoy and I will talk about later in this book.

It was nice to have some income and to feel wanted again and also it kept me in the spotlight and ensured people knew I was still around. That's so important when you are out of work and looking for employment, because you quickly get forgotten. On top of that it made me realise how fond I am of rugby league and how much I was missing my day-to-day involvement.

Sky also played a part in me taking over from Tony 'Casper' Smith as coach at Wakefield. My path has crossed Tony's throughout our careers. He was a player at Cas when I was climbing the first rungs of the coaching ladder - it was a teenage Casper who told me he wasn't going to make his 'A' team debut on the wing, because he was a half-back - and I coached him at Wigan, Hull and in the international set-up.

He had a tough time at the Wildcats in his first senior coaching role and, in July 2006, he got the push with the team bottom of the Super League table and seemingly doomed to relegation. As it turned out, their first game after Casper left was a Sky-televised game at home to Bradford Bulls. Neil Fox, a Wakefield legend and rugby league's all-time record points scorer, saw me before the game - which I was working on for Sky - and asked me what I was doing. When I said 'nothing' he asked: 'Why don't you come here?' The answer to that was I had to be asked first!

Wildcats were thrashed 42-20 by Bradford, which was no surprise considering they didn't have a coach. Steve Ferres, the chief executive, was supposedly in charge of the team, but effectively the players were left to their own devices. Steve had been a good coach in his day, at clubs like Sheffield, Hunslet and Huddersfield, but he had moved on to the administrative side of things and didn't want to get his tracksuit back out of the wardrobe.

Coaching is Chaos

It was a shambolic performance and Neil Fox said on Sky that I should be given the job. Neil is a legend at Wakefield and people there listen to what he has to say. I had felt Steve had been avoiding my agent, David Howes, which may have been due to Steve's close connection with Gary and Kath Hetherington.

After Neil came out in support I bit the bullet, rang Steve and said I'd like to meet him and outline what I thought I could do for the team. We had a chat and I gave him my side of what had happened at Hull. I think that maybe changed some of his perceptions and cleared up a few concerns he might have had about me as a person and a coach.

We met on the Friday and two days later Dave Howes rang me, said he'd had talks with Wakefield and they had offered terms. If they were acceptable the job was mine until the end of the season, providing I was willing to take it on.

Of course I was. I was bored, looking for a challenge and it was a no-lose scenario. Absolutely nobody in the game, including Wakefield's players and management, thought they had any chance of staying up. If I took over and we were relegated it wasn't going to reflect badly on me. On the other hand, if we could pull off a miracle I would be the hero and my career would suddenly be back on the up. The players were told over the phone on Sunday evening that I had accepted the job and I met them the following day, at 8.30am. Mission impossible was in full swing.

To illustrate the size of the task at hand, the loss to Bradford was round 22, out of 28. After that defeat Wakefield were bottom of the table, two points adrift of Catalan Dragons - who were exempt from relegation - and Wigan Warriors, of all teams. Castleford Tigers were another three points ahead, along with Harlequins.

Of the 22 games so far, Wildcats had won six and lost the rest. Points for was 466, points against 626. The loss to

Bradford was their seventh in eight matches and against Huddersfield - the straw that broke Casper's back - they had been 20-0 up at half-time, only to go down 26-20. It seemed they couldn't buy a win. The situation was hopeless; they were playing poorly and not only had the wheels dropped off, the engine had blown up, the battery was dead and the oil was leaking all over the carriageway.

As Raymond Fletcher, one of the game's most respected journalists, said in his *League Express* match report after the Bradford drubbing: 'Even a miracle worker would struggle to save them from the dreaded drop now.'

I'm not a miracle worker, but what we achieved over the next couple of months was something very special. I didn't go into the job blind; I had seen Wakefield play a few times that year, both live and on Sky and I was aware of how dismal some of their performances had been. But I also looked at the personnel they had available and it was clear to me they were better players than the team's league position suggested. When I had coached against them with Hull they had always caused us problems. Any team that had David Solomona, Ben Jeffries, Semi Tadulala, Jason Demetriou, Sam Obst or Monty Betham - who later quit to become a professional boxer - in their ranks was going to be a threat, if they got their game together.

They had under-achieved all year, but there was nothing to lose and I reckoned a change could be a positive thing. I had also looked at the table with the two remaining fixtures against Castleford in my sights. I was pretty sure Wigan would pull clear of danger and my old home town club was the one I thought we had to finish above to stay up.

I went into the job full of confidence and - in an echo of the Sheffield Eagles situation eight years earlier - walked into our first team meeting and told the players: 'We will be playing Super League next year.'

Coaching is Chaos

They didn't believe me, but one of the things I had in my favour was a two-week gap until the next match, away to Castleford as I had taken over the week before the Challenge Cup semi-finals, when there were no Super League matches.

That gave me a bit of extra time to prepare, get to know the players and introduce some self-belief. I was impressed with the way they reacted. Before I took over the squad had been promised from Wednesday to Sunday of that initial week off, so they could go away for a late-season break. That wasn't ideal and I told them: 'If you've booked a holiday, I am not going to ask you to cancel it because that wouldn't be the right thing to do. But anybody who goes away won't be considered for the Castleford game.' The only person who went away was the conditioner, Anthony Hazeldine. Everybody else scrapped their plans and stayed behind to train. Straight away that gave me a good feeling. There were some proud people in that team and great competitors and they didn't want a relegation on their CV. Up to that point they thought it was inevitable, but when I came in and told them we could stay up I think they decided they might as well give it their best shot.

There was a lot of hype in the build-up to the Cas game, particularly with it being against my hometown club, but the Tigers were expecting to more or less send us down. There's a huge rivalry between the two clubs, who are only based a few miles apart and nothing would have given Cas more pleasure than being the team who condemned Wakefield to the drop.

Pride comes before a fall and ahead of kick-off someone connected with the Cas club hired a plane to fly over the ground trailing a banner which read: 'Have no fear - it's only Kear'. I have no idea what they thought that would achieve, other than good pictures on TV and in the newspapers, but I am always grateful for anything which can give me or my players a bit of added motivation - so whoever it was, thanks very much. The game went like a dream and it remains one of my favourite coaching memories. We didn't just win, we hammered them 18-0, despite playing for half of the game with only 12 men and finishing with 11.

Sky TV were there, so it sent out a message to everybody in the competition that we weren't dead and buried just yet. I think you could fairly describe it as a battling performance. Monty Betham was sent off before half-time for throwing punches at Ryan McGoldrick and Ned Catic got a red card late on, after butting Danny Sculthorpe.

The dismissals only strengthened the players' resolve and at the final hooter I could not have been more proud of them. We had put in two weeks' hard preparation for the game and that paid off immediately when Semi Tadulala scored from a planned move we had been working on in training. I could not have written a better script. When you score a try from something you've been working on just three minutes into your first game, the players immediately start thinking 'this guy must know what he's talking about'.

The first red card made it tough. We were 4-0 up at the break and I remember David Solomona asking in the changing rooms: 'What are we going to change in the second half, now we've only got 12 players?'

There was a simple answer to that: nothing. If it's not broken, you don't need to fix it. We were playing well, we were in control of the game and everything was going according to plan, so it was a case of sticking with what we were doing. It was simply a case of 12 men having to do 13 men's work. I asked them if they could do it and they all said yes. It could have been a very low half-time break, but instead it was a rousing 15 minutes and they went back out with a real belief that this could be our night.

The second-half performance was magnificent and the

nil against was a massive boost for everybody, because defence had been such an Achilles heel for them earlier in the season. We had worked on our on-line defence in the two weeks before the match and obviously it worked. The reason for that was they put their heart and soul into it. Rather than letting their heads drop when the going got tough, they responded with a never-say-die attitude which was a credit to every one of them.

After the game I could sense something in the air - and it wasn't that plane, which had scuttled off back to wherever it came from. It was a changing of attitude and the start of a belief that we really could do something special and pull off the great escape. We had good players in the team and once they started to believe in themselves they became very tough to beat.

I made it clear when I took over that we needed to win four of our six remaining games. Victory at the Jungle was just step one, but it was a double whammy because it dragged Cas back into the mire and we had them to play again in our final match. We knew now we could catch them and, just as importantly, they were aware of it too. I wasn't bothered about Wigan or Harlequins, Cas were the team I was after; not for any personal reasons, just because they were the most vulnerable of all our rivals. After that win they were just three points ahead of us with four games to play, so the pressure was back on them.

The reasoning was that if we won both Cas games, that was two games they couldn't win. I thought we could win at least one other match - home to Catalan - if we only played okay. And if we played really well we could win another, against Leeds Rhinos, St Helens or Bradford Bulls. The first Cas game, Saints and Bulls were all away and the others at home. I also looked at Cas' fixtures and couldn't see them picking up many more points.

I could not fault the players after the wonderful win at the Jungle. They trained the house down and their application was first class. That was despite the fact some of them had already signed for other clubs. Rugby league has an anti-tampering law which means clubs can't speak to players who are coming out of contract at one of their rivals until a certain date late in the season, but it is one of the most ridiculous rules in the game and nobody takes any notice. What's more, everybody in the sport is aware that it is being broken on a regular basis. Clubs won't complain about an illegal approach from somebody else, because they will be doing exactly the same thing themselves.

It is nonsense, but it meant that even though we knew certain players would be leaving at the end of the year - come what may - neither they nor the clubs they were going to could officially confirm that. I had no issues with those players; we had been in a hopeless situation and they had families to think of, mortgages to pay and food to put on the table. But with their future secure it would have been easy for them to throw in the towel; not care and let the rest of the season simply pass them by. Not one of them did that, they were just as much a part of the great escape as everybody else. They didn't want to let their mates down and full credit to them for it.

One crucial thing I did for the make-or-break final games of the season was bring David March back into the team. He was Mr Wakefield and epitomised what the team was about - he was maybe not the flashiest or the most skilful of players, but tough, hard-working and with a muck-and-nettles attitude. The same applied to the side as a whole. David was a key part in us staying up and his attitude and love for the club rubbed off on everybody else.

Jason Demetriou was the team captain and he is a player I have a huge amount of time for. I get a lot of credit for the great escape, but I don't think it would have happened without JD in the ranks. We had a lot of meetings and he gave me 100 per cent support. He was one of the best skippers I have worked with and his attitude and performances were spot on.

Someone else whose help was invaluable was another Wakefield legend, David Topliss, a former player and coach at Belle Vue who, tragically, died in 2008. David knew the game inside out and he was a regular Wildcats watcher. He had his own ideas about what had been going wrong and changes which needed to be made and I would have been stupid not to listen to his advice. He was the sort of person who commands respect. It was Toppo who suggested I brought David March back into the team and he gave me some really good advice about how to get the best from certain individual players.

Next up after Cas were Catalan, good opponents for us because they were exempt from relegation and effectively had nothing to play for. We were without Monty Betham and Ned Catic, who were both suspended. I had expected them to get bans, but I thought two and three games respectively was very harsh. All that did was add to our siege mentality and we produced another good performance to beat Catalan 34-14, again in front of the Sky cameras. Jamie Rooney scored three tries and seven goals, which equalled his own club record of 26 points in a Super League match. Afterwards, the Catalan coach Mick Potter said he thought we could stay up. Meanwhile, Cas lost 72-4 at home to St Helens so now we were only a point behind.

After Catalan we took on Leeds Rhinos at home and we lost that one 14-12, but Cas were beaten 48-10 at Bradford and there was no real harm done. Obviously I wanted us to beat Leeds, but I didn't see that as a make-or-break game. I thought we could afford to lose that one and possibly one more and still stay up, if other results went our way. Leeds had lost their previous five matches and we almost made it six. It was 12-12 about 10 minutes into the second half when Kevin Sinfield kicked a penalty goal and that completed the scoring. I was happy with the performance, though we lost another player through suspension after Darrell Griffin was placed on report for a supposed spear tackle and banned for one match.

We had another week off before our trip to Knowsley Road to play St Helens, because of the Challenge Cup final. Saints were in that, against Huddersfield Giants, so I was hoping they would win and spend the entire week on the beer. They did win the final and they might have had a long celebration, but they still defeated us, though only just. It was 34-12 to Saints, but we might have come away with something if Michael Korkidas hadn't been sent-off after 63 minutes, for nutting Jamie Lyon. That was our third red card in three matches, plus Darrell's one game ban, though Korky got a sending-off sufficient verdict when he appeared before the disciplinary committee and therefore wasn't suspended for the next match.

I will admit it, we were sailing a bit too close to the wind with some of our aggressive tactics. But we were fighting for our rugby lives and I think that's understandable. We were up the creek, or - to use another metaphor - our balls were on the line. When you are desperate you do desperate things and on occasions we stepped over the edge. It's not ideal, but I have absolutely no regrets and I'd much rather we stayed up through scrapping, fighting and battling for everything, than go down meekly or playing a pretty, but ineffective, style.

We had started off at a high level against Cas and the performances got better and better every week, despite the back-to-back losses to Leeds and Saints. Unfortunately we played Saints on a Friday night and Cas were at home to Harlequins the following day. When they won that one it lifted them three points clear of us with only two games left to play.

After round 26 we were 1/8 to finish in the relegation position which, because of Catalan's situation, was either bottom or second-bottom. We now had to win both our remaining games, away to Bradford and home against Cas - and we needed them not to pick up another point. Because we played Cas in the final round, effectively if meant if we won at Odsal and they lost away to Salford City Reds everything would go down to a one-match, winner-takes-all shoot-out. But if we lost to Bradford and Cas beat Salford, we were down.

I watched Cas' game against Harlequins on Sky and they definitely counted their chickens before they had hatched. Their players and staff all claimed afterwards that they didn't think the job was done, but the evidence said otherwise. It looked to me like they had put their cue on the rack and I thought that might prove to be a fatal error.

I remember one of their players, Danny Sculthorpe, bringing his dog - a bulldog - on to the field at the end and they all did a lap of honour. They would claim it was the usual thanks to the fans following the last home game of the year, but as far as I was concerned they were celebrating staying up.

Our game at Bradford and theirs against Salford were both staged on the same night, a Friday, kicking off at 8pm. For us it was a cup final, it was win or bust and - until we'd got two points in the bag - it didn't matter one jot what Tigers did. We produced another great performance and there were three plays in that game at Odsal which I think kept us up.

David Solomona had a magnificent match and scored a

wonderful try, a little short-side move, dummying, going down the blindside and shoving a couple of their fellas off on the way to the line. Then there was Jason Demetriou running the ball out of his own in-goal area. They kicked over the line, JD - who was playing on the wing because of injuries - picked the ball up, beat four players and just got his head into the field of play. That allowed us to start a set on our own line rather than having to drop the ball out to Bradford, which would have meant another six tackles to make in our own danger zone. And thirdly, David March played on after getting knocked out. I have never seen anything like it, he was out cold; the physio went on, stood him up and pointed him in the right direction and he made the next tackle under our posts to prevent a try.

We won 20-12, in yet another televised match. We knew Sky were there for the last rites and we were happy to disappoint them - though I know nobody at the broadcaster actually wanted to see us go down, they just felt they had to be at the game which saw relegation confirmed.

There were no celebrations when the hooter sounded. The players all walked over towards the Wakefield fans, who were standing on the open terrace at one end of the ground, with the Sky big screen behind them. We all stood and waited for the Cas score to appear and when it came up that they had lost 26-16 everybody erupted.

Almost everybody. Monty Betham brought a quick halt to the celebrations, telling us all: 'We're not there yet, we've still got one game to play - it's a grand final and we've got to win that, then we can let our hair down.' After that speech we took the plaudits from the fans, walked into the changing rooms and immediately began to focus on the following week. We had worked hard and given ourselves a chance of escaping relegation, but that's all it was - a chance.

We were still a point behind Cas, but believe it or not, we

actually went into the last game as favourites to stay up. They were 2/5 for relegation and we were 7/4, according to the bookies. That is quite a turnaround from the previous week, but we were on a roll and had home advantage, while Tigers were on the back of a defeat.

I don't think there has ever been another Super League game like that Saturday evening sudden-death shoot-out at Belle Vue. A full house of 11,000 turned up, Wakefield's biggest crowd for more than 30 years, and you could cut the atmosphere with a knife.

As it turned out it wasn't as tense as I might have expected. We were nine points behind early on, but the belief in the team never wavered. Despite us having a perfectly good try disallowed, the players dug in and we ran out comfortable 29-17 winners. That was it, the great escape completed and my fortunes restored. The transformation in emotions over 13 months was incredible. I had been on top of the world in August 2005 following the Challenge Cup win at Cardiff, at rock-bottom the following April when I got sacked by Hull, then up in the clouds again in September. It was absolutely incredible. We had achieved something nobody in the sport thought we were capable of and that will live with me forever as my proudest achievement. It's why I am involved in sport; nothing else can give you such lows, followed by amazing highs - or vice versa.

Before I took over there had been nothing in Wildcats' performances to suggest they could turn it around. I sorted some things out structurally in the way they were playing, but more than anything else I gave the players some self-belief and managed to convince them they were good enough to pick up the four wins needed to survive. The win at Cas in my first game was a major step, Bradford was do or die and then for them to keep their composure the way they did in the final match was credit to every one of them.

In the process, we sent Cas down. If I'd had a choice I would have picked any team other than my home town club to be relegated. You don't operate the scoreboard at five years old, support them throughout your childhood and then play and coach there for a number of years without developing a real affection for the club and the people there. But it is a dog-eat-dog business and I didn't shed any tears. I had an opportunity to resurrect my career and in those circumstances you put self before emotion. I was ready to battle with anyone; if I'd thought it would have helped the cause I'd have nutted, gouged, kicked or punched anybody who stood in our way. I would have done anything it took and I think that attitude filtered through to the players, which is probably why we picked up so many red cards. We were desperate people in a desperate situation and we applied desperate measures.

We stayed up on merit and the fact is Castleford weren't quite good enough in the end. They thought the job was done after the Harlequins game and they hadn't really played well since beating Leeds at home in July, so they could have no complaints.

Unless something changes, we won't have an end to the season like that again. In 2009 the RFL introduced a licensing process which meant places in Super League were allocated on factors like fan base, financial stability and ground facilities, rather than how teams did on the field.

There's no doubt in my mind rugby league is poorer for the decision to scrap automatic relegation. I understand the argument that relegation is destructive and that it means clubs can't plan ahead, but I think the benefits far outweigh the advantages. Cas went down in 2006, came back the following year and have been in a better state because of that experience. I can only admire people like their Aussie player Ryan McGoldrick and coach Terry Matterson, who struck with the club and got to enjoy better times when they returned to the top-flight.

There is a big Australian influence in our game and relegation is not part of their psyche, but it is integral to British sport. Fans love the excitement and drama that promotion and relegation produces. Without it you don't get a situation like the million pound match in 2006 and lower division clubs are denied a chance to live their dream. Hunslet won the old Northern Ford Premiership in 1999, but then weren't allowed a place in Super League because their ground wasn't up to scratch. They have never really recovered from that. In my eyes that's not what sport is about; it is all about fairytales and emotion, not reports and written applications. I have never been to a rugby league game and sat and admired that stadium and I would never support a team because they have nice toilet facilities. I go to watch two teams battling it out head to head and that's all that interests me. I believe the fate of a club should be decided on the pitch, not in an office somewhere.

If there had been no relegation I doubt I would ever have worked at Wakefield. They would have been quite happy to meander on and allow that season to drift away from them; there would have been none of the drama that surrounded the great escape and one of the best stories of the Super League era wouldn't have been written.

St Helens won the title in 2006, beating Hull at Old Trafford. The season wasn't about that, it was all about who stayed up. More people remember the million pound match than can recall the Grand Final. Perhaps we should focus more on success than failure, but in sporting terms life or death struggles are what capture the public's attention. We have lost that now and there are far too many meaningless matches as a result.

13

*

Highs and Lows

THOUGH my five and a bit seasons at Wakefield started and finished with a battle to stay in Super League, it wasn't all a struggle against adversity. Well actually it was, but we did achieve a measure of success, by Wildcats' standards.

After the great escape in 2006 we finished eighth, an improvement of two places, in each of the next two years and we were fifth in 2009, which is Wakefield's best Super League finish. It was an expanded, 14-team competition for the first time that year and we qualified for a home play-off, which I think is a measure of success for an under-resourced club like Wildcats, though that turned out to be a damp squib as we fell at the first hurdle to Catalan Dragons.

In the two seasons before that, when the top-six teams qualified for the semi-finals, we were right in the play-offs mix. In 2008 we also reached the semi-finals of the Challenge Cup, the first time Wakefield had got that far in 29 years.

For a club spending as little of the salary cap as we were, I think that is a decent record. We also brought some young kids through, we reduced Wakefield's reliance on overseas players and revived the career of one or two who had been thrown on the scrapheap. From easybeats, Wakefield became a team the opposition knew they would have to play well against if they were to get the two points. Obviously 2009 is the complete season I remember most fondly; we came home with a wet sail, winning our last five league matches and everything seemed to be coming together.

Danny Brough was developing as an accomplished Super League half-back and I think he was a much better player then than when he won the Challenge Cup with Hull four years earlier. He ran the team and he had great support from players around him, like Jason Demetriou, Brad Drew and Scott Grix. There was also plenty of strike-power, Ryan Atkins especially, and some hard-working forwards. We were more than a competent team and finished where we deserved to. Over the season you can't achieve a home play-off without a level of consistency in your performance, which is what I was always after at Wakefield. They were the most consistent they had been since getting into Super League in 1999. I know Shane McNally took them to the play-offs in 2004, but they sneaked through in sixth spot that year.

What Shane achieved and I didn't was a play-offs win. That's something I think every team should aim for; if you win a play-off you have had a decent year, in my opinion. In 2004 Wakefield came to Hull, where I was coach and beat us in an elimination game. Five years later we should have been too strong for Catalan, but the occasion got to us and we were turned over quite convincingly, which is something that still disappoints me when I think about it now.

We were over-confident and a little bit complacent in our approach and, fatally, we were looking further down the line, at what the following week could offer. Catalan were no mugs and with Greg Bird featuring prominently they taught us a very painful lesson. I am sure we'd have been better for that experience if we had managed to get that far again, but things began to unravel after that season.

The Cup semi-final the previous year, against Hull at Doncaster, was a highlight of my stint at Wakefield, though it was another result which still smarts. I thought we were going all the way that year, which would have made me the first head coach to take three different teams to the final.

You need a bit of luck in the Cup and we had it in the shape of a very favourable draw. We played Salford, then a Championship club, away in our first tie - the fourth round - and then visited Barrow, before a home quarter-final against Oldham. So when we took on Hull in the last four that was the first time we had come up against Super League opposition.

The BBC chose our game at Salford for live coverage, so they obviously thought there was a chance of an upset. The Willows was never an easy place for opposition teams to go and play well, because its facilities made even Belle Vue seem palatial. The changing area was the size of an average front room and it was always a case of going there, doing as professional a job as you could and then getting the hell out of Dodge.

That's just what we did: we beat Salford 38-8, won 58-6 at Barrow and crushed Oldham - coached by Steve Deakin - 46-4. Hull were obviously going to be tough semi-final opponents, but as the alternatives were Leeds Rhinos and St Helens, I was happy with the draw. Unfortunately, I don't think the players really believed they could get to Wembley. They realised we'd had the luck of the draw and knew we had a great opportunity to create a bit of club history, but deep down - it seemed to me - they felt they had over-achieved by getting that far. When it came to the big day, they were like rabbits caught in the headlights. It was a bizarre start and we found ourselves 18 points down after just 10 minutes. That cost us in the end and I still think if the players had really believed in themselves and been at the races from the start, we would have won. We made a game of it and we got the final scoreline back to 32-24 so you could argue we were the better team for the majority of the game, but that terrible start cost us. Damien Blanch had a try ruled out by the video referee, Ashley Klein, in the second half and that was probably the most crucial moment of the game.

That was my first semi-final defeat as a coach, though I played in two semi-finals - both against Hull, ironically - when I was at Castleford and we lost both of these. I would have played in a third, but for injury. We drew that one and lost the replay. It is not a nice time to lose because you are so close to something every player and coach dreams of being part of, which is a big day out in the final.

It didn't sink in how much it upset me until I got home after the game. It was a bit like an out of body experience; I was absolutely distraught for about 36 hours and I think that defeat had a serious effect on our season. There were five league games after the semi-final and we lost four of them, which cost us any chance of making the play-offs.

I copped some criticism for the performance at Doncaster. The players lacked belief and I have to accept some blame for that, but I was also accused of getting my team selection wrong. I left Jamie Rooney and Matty Blaymire out of the team and played Paul Reilly at full-back, with Brad Drew and Danny Brough as the halves. I think the Drew-Brough thing worked, but Reilly didn't. Whether playing Matty would have made any difference to the result I don't know, but decisions like that are a big part of being a head coach. I like to think I get seven or eight out of 10 right, but it tends to be the two or three you get wrong that you're remembered for. Anybody can be a good Monday morning coach, but there aren't many good Sunday morning ones.

Even after our poor start we matched Hull try for try - it was five each - but goalkicks cost us. Ultra-reliable Danny Brough missed four shots which he would have back-heeled over on another day. I would never blame a kicker for a defeat though; they can win matches, but don't lose them.

Danny is a player I have got a lot of time for and I am proud of the part I played in his development from a promising lower division half-back, with Dewsbury and York, to one of the best in Super League. When he was sold to Huddersfield in 2010 that was the first time I realised Wakefield were in a dire situation financially. You don't get rid of a player as influential as Danny without a good reason. We did have our differences at times though. The main one was in May, 2009, when I suspended him for a breach of internal discipline, along with the prop-forward Danny Sculthorpe.

We had a club policy that all official team camps were dry and so were all coaches on the way back from matches. By dry I mean there was to be no alcohol drunk, under any circumstances. The players agreed to that, but both Dannys stepped out of line on the way home from a game against Harlequins in London. I was totally unaware they'd had a drink, but Scully gave himself away by giving the driver £20 to pay for the booze. It was a commercial bus and drinks were kept in fridges for use on long foreign trips. It wasn't a hanging offence, but they had broken the rules. It might seem a bit harsh, but in the modern era players have to look after themselves in terms of recovery for the next match. They needed to get some energy drinks down them and make sure any bumps and bruises were iced. Alcohol just inflames sore bruises, so they weren't being professional.

All the players had signed a code of conduct, which they

agreed to adhere to, so there was no excuse. I called the two miscreants in, drew their attention to the rules they had broken and told them they wouldn't be considered for selection for the following game. To his credit Danny Brough accepted he was wrong, paid his fine and was welcomed back into the fold after his enforced week off. Unfortunately Scully took a different approach, he became confrontational and that resulted in him leaving the club and joining Huddersfield on loan. It was an untenable situation, so he had to leave.

That sort of thing happens from time to time. I think any coach - or manager in whatever business - will have bust-ups with his players or staff at some stage. I always make sure I am covered by drawing up a code of conduct and ensuring all the players are aware of what they can and can't do. As employees of the club they have legal rights, just like everyone else, so it's important you make it clear to players what is and is not acceptable. It's equally important, from the club's point of view, that the players sign the code, so you have the evidence there.

It was accepted that our buses on the way back from matches - even ones in the south of England or France - were dry. After a victory in Catalan if the players approached me and asked for permission to have a drink, I would almost certainly say yes. There are times when that is acceptable, particularly in the euphoria of victory which is, after all, what you play sport for.

But that time against London we hadn't played well, we'd lost the game and there was nothing to celebrate. It was a sombre bus on the way back and by breaking the rules I felt the players involved had flicked two fingers at the coaching staff and the management, plus their team-mates who did obey the rules. We had to take action and I don't regret that for a moment, even though it cost us a good player in Danny Sculthorpe. I wonder if he regrets it too, as his career hasn't really taken off since he left Wakefield.

I was pretty sad about the situation because I always had a good relationship with Danny, his dad and his older brother Paul, who was one of the great players of the Super League era. The fall-out over the drinking on the coach incident soured that to some extent.

Things like that do happen. Another infamous occasion was a Mad Monday which got totally out of hand. That's an Australian tradition which has begun to take off over here since the top division went full-time and it means players go out and get blathered on the Monday after their final game of the season. On that occasion the players went out in Wakefield and made an exhibition of themselves, caused uproar in various pubs and managed to shock even some hardened landlords, who are quite used to dealing with boozed-up groups of lads on a weekend night out.

This got reported in the local paper and as a result we had to write a new clause into the code of conduct stating that no Mad Mondays would be allowed in or around the Wakefield area. The players should have had more sense than to go out in their home patch. That was just asking for trouble and they got it. If they had gone to Newcastle, Manchester or even Leeds nobody would have cared much, but the Westgate Run - which is a notorious pub crawl in Wakefield - was a poor choice of venue. By the time they had got to the far end of Westgate they were in a pretty sorry state and their behaviour was unacceptable.

The club had to take firm action; severe fines were handed out, the players were told not to go out socially in the Wakefield area, some of them had to visit the landlords concerned and apologise face-to-face and we also imposed some extra community work and fund-raising, for charities of the aggrieved publicans' choice. So you can see we took it seriously. That list of punishments was accepted by the players, the slate was wiped clean and the code of conduct was re-drawn, which happens time, after time, after time.

My entire time at Wakefield was eventful both on and off the field. Right at the start of this book I wrote about the tragedies which struck the club in 2009 and 2010, but there was another fatality which also greatly affected me, the Wakefield club and many people in rugby league.

At the end of the 2009 season Wakefield signed the former Great Britain hooker Terry Newton from Bradford Bulls. Terry was a top-class player; tough, uncompromising and skilful and a great competitor. He was going to be one of my leaders for the next couple of years and I felt he was one of the best recruits we had brought in during my time at the club.

Sadly, Terry only made two substitute appearances for Wildcats before his career ended in disgrace, something which led to an even greater tragedy a few months later. I don't know if we were targeted because we were seen to have over-achieved the previous two or three years, but we were frequently visited by the drugs testers both in-season and during the pre-season and they were targeting members of the squad as well as ones chosen at random.

They came to see us at a gym in Castleford, during a pre-season wrestling session. There were 28 players there and the drugs people wanted to test a dozen of them. That was pretty severe and it was also the first time I had known them carry out blood tests, rather than taking the urine, which is what normally happens. That was a concern, because one of the players chosen at random was Cain Southernwood, who was only 17 and therefore not an adult. I pointed this out to the drug testers, who included the former player Shaun Irwin, an old team-mate of mine at Castleford. I insisted on being there when they tested Cain, as his responsible adult.

I saw that test being done and I assume it was the same for everyone else.

That sort of thing is an inconvenience, but it's part of modern sport and you accept it. I wasn't worried in the slightest, because afterwards there was nobody acting strangely, looking concerned or skulking about; everyone - Terry included - carried on as normal. When the drugs testers turn up you do tend to watch out to see if anyone breaks into a cold sweat, but that definitely wasn't the case. There was plenty of banter and everyone was in good humour afterwards.

The storm broke a little while later, a few games into the season when we found out Terry had tested positive for human growth hormone. That's why they had done blood tests, which can detect that particular substance whereas urine can't. It's the sort of news every coach dreads. I found out from a solicitor called Andy Bailey, who had played at Hull and Featherstone and was then acting as Terry's advisor. He had helped negotiate his contract and he rang me up, said Terry had told him what happened and had asked him to pass the message on, because he couldn't cope with the idea of telling me himself.

I said I wanted Terry to ring me, because I was keen to speak to him. I wanted to hear his version of events, from the horse's mouth. To his credit Terry did phone me and he was then called in to a hastily-arranged board meeting. Club officials Diane Maskill, Eric Timmins and Ted Richardson were all there and they acted very professionally. There wasn't any option other than to ban Terry from the club until the issue had been fully investigated and the end result was his contract was torn-up and he was sacked; inevitable with a two-year ban from the sport just around the corner.

Sadly, that led to a decline which resulted in Terry's suicide just six months or so later. That sent shockwaves through rugby league and deeply upset everyone who knew Terry, including me. He had made a mistake, but I always rated him as a player and liked him as a person and while I felt let down by the fact he had been taking an illegal substance - which effectively is cheating - that opinion didn't change.

I was shocked to the core when I heard news of Terry's death. He was running a pub near his home in Wigan, had just had his autobiography published and was beginning to give interviews and talk about what had happened. I wasn't in close contact with him, but it seemed to me he was beginning to get things back together. We will never know for sure what caused Terry to take his own life, but it definitely caused a lot of soul-searching in the sport. There was a feeling that Terry had been abandoned and if more care had been shown to him then perhaps things would have turned out differently.

It's easy to be wise after the event, but the RFL have taken more interest in player welfare since Terry's death, though in my opinion that's nothing more than window dressing. The RFL have state of mind presentations to players, about mental health, but a presentation to a full group is a waste of time.

When we took part at Wakefield, a couple of nurses came to give a talk to the whole group. They asked a number of questions and if you answered 'yes' to so many, that was an indication you might have a problem. I am sure we could all have answered in the affirmative to several of them. It was very thought-provoking, but there was no follow-up, which is where the system falls down. The game needs regional welfare officers who are tasked with making contact with every player at least twice a year, to see if there's any issues or problems. It shouldn't just be about state of mind - or depression - it also needs to concern finance, investments, mortgages, pensions, advice for players who are going through a break-up or divorce and bereavement counselling as well.

This obviously isn't just a rugby issue, but if you have got troubles one of the best solutions is to have someone to talk to. I would like to see one welfare officer appointed by the governing body to look after every three or four clubs. I know some clubs have now put their own person in place, but the RFL needs to get involved in this as well.

Super League now devotes a whole round of matches, the State of Mind weekend, to mental health issues, which I think is a good idea, but we need to go further. Obviously if people are going well in their lives it would just be a matter of meeting for a coffee and having a chat, ticking a few boxes. But if a player did require help, the duty of the RFL welfare officer would be to bring in outside assistance to deal with the problem, whether that's depression, financial worries, drug abuse, gambling addiction of whatever.

There is alcohol and social drug abuse in rugby league and gambling is a major issue. I imagine every coach could name players he at least suspects of having those problems. The RFL needs to address it, which they aren't doing at the moment. They are raising the issue, but not dealing with it. There has to be an avenue for players to go down; if all you are doing is organising presentations that's nothing more than political correctness. Raising awareness without providing a follow-up is what my dad would have called 'fur coat and no knickers', all show and no substance. We need to raise awareness and then take action. Everybody should have access to people they can talk to, who in turn should have access to specialist agencies to provide whatever assistance is necessary.

Rugby league is a very macho environment and players often don't want to admit when they've got an issue, certainly not in a group situation. I am pleased that depression is becoming less of a secret topic in sporting circles and some top athletes are now coming out and admitting they've got - or had - a problem. I don't think depression is anything to be ashamed of, it's an illness, but there is a stigma to mental health issues.

I am sure everyone is under pressure in his or her own job, but with sports people success and failure is very public. Everyone has an opinion and with the advent of social media and internet message boards it is very easy to express that view. You'd have to be very thick-skinned indeed not to be affected by some of the comments made on message boards, for example, even if you know they are completely wrong and are based on nothing more than spite and ignorance. It certainly depresses me, some of the things I read.

Obviously I regret what happened with Terry, the entire situation, but I don't feel any guilt. I think Wakefield handled it the only way the club could. The reason I feel so passionately about player welfare is what happened to Adam Watene and Leon Walker. The Rugby League Benevolent Fund provided great help to both families, but that was reactive. I feel as a sport we need to be more proactive and if we had been, perhaps Terry Newton would still be with us today.

I would say that Wigan were very supportive of their player Gareth Hock, when he tested positive for a so-called recreational drug in 2009 and was banned for two years. They didn't wash their hands of him, they attempted to support him through the period when he was banned from the sport. The signs are now that he is a reformed character, he is toeing the line and he is going to be a big part of their team for years to come. His career is back on line.

I hope lessons have been learned since Terry's death. In

2012 a very high profile player, Martin Gleeson, was also banned after failing a drugs test. He did bring shame on the game, but he is obviously a troubled individual and in my opinion we need to support him and people like him.

The Terry Newton situation raised concerns over the use of performance-enhancing substances in rugby league. There are failed tests every year, so obviously players are taking things they shouldn't. That has to be stamped out. I am as anti-drugs as anyone in the game, but I believe we also need to provide help to the individuals involved so they can get themselves back on track, rather than just casting them out and forgetting about them.

14

*

Make Do and Mend

WHEN someone is flogging off the family silver, you begin to suspect that they may have financial problems. In 2009-2010 Wakefield players Ryan Atkins, Jay Pitts and Danny Brough were all sold to rival Super League clubs. I may not be Sherlock Holmes, but even I could tell there was trouble brewing.

Jay was a young, talented forward who I believed had a big future as a Super League regular. If he had maintained the progress he was making, he would have been a big part of our team in 2010 and 2011, but he was sold to Leeds for something like £25,000. That was a steal, an absolutely ridiculous deal. Obviously Leeds had a stronger squad than we did and it was going to take him time to get established in their senior team, so I could not see why we had let him go. It was a backwards step and a clear sign the club was in bother. That was before Ryan and Danny left. They were both much higher-profile players who were a big loss, but they would have been able to move for nothing when they came out of contract and I could understand, to an extent, why the club cashed in.

Ryan had joined us from Bradford, who didn't seem to think he had a Super League future. I am sure that is a decision they have regretted ever since. He wanted to play Test rugby and to win trophies and it was obvious he would not sign a new deal, so when Warrington Wolves offered big money it made sense to take it. He has gone on to play for England, as I knew he would.

It was a similar scenario with Broughy, who went to Huddersfield Giants, though he was the heart of the team and we couldn't really afford to lose a player of his ability. We hoped another of my old Hull lads, Paul Cooke, would fill his boots. Paul had been paid off by Hull KR and he was a cheaper option, but he was a different type of player to Danny and it didn't work out.

Danny's departure was a big factor in our poor finish to the 2010 season, but even so I felt worse about losing Jay. He was a young lad we had developed and brought through to a stage where he was just beginning to dip his toe in the Super League waters. For me, the decision to sell him was the most worrying of all the departures, but it was only one of a number of indicators of stormy times ahead.

Early in my tenure at Wakefield we went to Brown's, in Portugal, on pre-season camps. I felt they were very successful, the players did as well and they allowed us to get a lot of work done, which we wouldn't have been able to achieve in the damp, cold and dark of an English winter. Eventually though we were told there would be no more overseas camps.

Wakefield was never, at least in my time there, a club dripping with money. One of the problems we had from a rugby point of view was the lack of our own training venue. We used a community facility at Crofton, just down the road from Belle Vue, but I lost count of the number of times we were told we couldn't go there because the bill hadn't been paid. When you aren't allowed to go on pre-season camps and you can't train at your usual venue because nobody has settled the bill you do tend to think 'we aren't in great shape financially'.

Our groundsman Steve Dutton was one of the best in the business. The pitch at Belle Vue was always first class, whatever the weather conditions or however much it was used, but Steve didn't have thousands of pounds to spend on it. He was lucky if his budget got into three figures. He used to beg and borrow equipment from wherever he could: Barnsley FC, Crofton, the local Queen Elizabeth Grammar School (QEGS), anyone who could lend a hand. In the circumstances he did a marvellous job and there were plenty of people like that at Wakefield, really keen, enthusiastic individuals who had a passion for the club and who were doing their very best on limited resources.

All that was very much in my mind when - in 2010 - an opportunity came up to join Catalan Dragons for the start of the following season. It was an attractive proposition; it was pretty obvious that one club, Catalan, were on the up while the other, Wakefield, were teetering at the top of a slippery slope. The French outfit were spending the full salary cap, attracting big crowds and in vibrant health. They were an ambitious club with bags of potential and no worries about a Super League licence in 2011. Everything, in other words, that Wakefield were not. We had problems with the stadium, no money and little chance of a new licence, so I don't think I could be blamed for fancying the move.

A lot of Wakefield people view the former management, led by Ted Richardson, in a bad light. I think that's unfair; without Ted and his fellow directors there wouldn't have been a club, though obviously not everything he did worked out for the best. Ted put a lot of time and money in and I can understand his reluctance to hand over control for next to nothing. I got on really well with Ted, Diane Maskill - his daughter who was also on the board - and Eric Timmins, but I certainly won't ever forgive them for preventing my move to France.

Catalan did everything by the book. They asked if I was interested and I said I would be, but pointed out I was under contract until the end of 2011. I then spoke to the Wakefield board and they gave me permission to speak to Catalan. We held talks and agreed a deal, but the fly in the ointment was that Wakefield wanted to finish paying me the Monday after the end of the season. I was contracted for several weeks after that, so they would be saving a considerable amount of money - a five-figure sum. I was prepared to accept that, but then they asked Catalan for £20,000 compensation as well.

If I hadn't done a good job they would have been pushing me out of the door. Before I joined, Wildcats had six coaches in as many years and they weren't exactly averse to a change of team boss when it suited them. As I had done a good job they felt they could ask for an unrealistic fee.

That deeply upset me because I was all set to go. My wife had even arranged a three-year secondment from her job so we could move to France. I had agreed a two-year contract, with an option for a third season at the end of that. I knew the house I would have been staying in and even the car Catalan were going to provide. It had got that far, but it all broke down because Wakefield weren't prepared simply to release me. I felt I deserved better. Catalan had approached me in the first place and everything was done properly.

When the two clubs failed to agree terms Catalan instead appointed an Australian, Trent Robinson. He was a former assistant-coach at NRL side Sydney City Roosters who had moved to the French Elite competition and who had a

Coaching is Chaos

French lady as his partner. He did a marvellous job in Perpignan before returning to the Roosters as coach at the end of 2012 and he was a good appointment by Catalan. He speaks French, knows and understands the culture and has proved to be a very good coach, but I can't help thinking it could have been me. I would have taken a similar approach to the one he put in place, developing the French culture at the club. I speak a bit of French, I would have been confident of picking up some more pretty quickly and I would have implemented a policy of 'If you play for Catalan, you speak French'. Trent did that and it worked really well.

What Wildcats should have done is let me go, then use the money they had saved on my contract to put a less experienced coach in place. It would have been easy to promote my assistant Paul Broadbent, give him an extra - say - £10,000 and appoint a recent ex-player as his number two. To rub salt into the wound, within a few months of effectively blocking my move Wakefield were struggling to pay the rugby staff's wages and then the financial situation really took a turn for the worse.

As time went on money became even tighter. Though I was director of rugby and attended board meetings, I wasn't kept in the loop and, despite all the little signs, when the financial storm finally broke I was shocked how bad it was. In September, 2010, HM Revenue and Customs - in other words, the tax man - served a winding-up order. That was shortly after the chairman, Ted Richardson, had offered to hand over control of the club to new investors. The following month Sir Rodney Walker donated £164,000 to clear the tax bill, but that was just a temporary reprieve.

It was a tough time and not exactly an ideal situation for a coach looking to build a team for a new season. The main focus of every month in the 2010-2011 off-season wasn't what plans we had for the following year or who we were going to recruit, it was how many season tickets have been sold ... is there any money coming in ... can the club meet the wage bill?

As a coach, when you start preparing for the following season you always draw up a wish list of who you'd like to sign. At the top you have the stars of the game, people like Leon Pryce. Then it goes down in quality and in the autumn of 2010 we were signing people at the bottom of the list. We weren't looking at ability or if a target would fit in with the Wakefield culture or the way we wanted to play. The only criteria was, is he cheap?

It was a sorry situation and people on the outside didn't understand the circumstances. I lost count of the number of times I was asked 'why have you signed so and so?' The reason inevitably was he was all we could afford. Not that I could say any of that in public. I had to be smart enough to come up with a positive way of justifying the signings I was making, to sell my recruitment to the fans and the game in general. Much though I would have liked to, I couldn't say: 'We've got this much in the piggy bank and we can't afford anyone better'.

First of all, we had the 'young and British' scenario. Official explanation: We want to sign home-grown kids, who have the potential to develop into Super League regulars. Real reason: They are all we can afford. Then there was the 'players with a point to prove'. Official explanation: We're looking at people who have been finished at other clubs or who've dropped out of Super League, because they are hungry to get back to the top. Real reason: We can afford them too.

All that said, I don't think we did too badly at all in terms of recruitment and I wouldn't want anyone to think the players we brought in for the 2011 campaign were any old rubbish. As an experienced shopper will tell you, bargains can always be had if you know where to look. Jimmy Elston - the chief executive, who had returned to the club after a spell at Hull KR - was very good. Together we went to watch all the lower grade play-offs in 2010 and that is how we picked up Chris Dean, Paul Johnson, Stuart Howarth and Josh Veivers, all players who did a good job for us the following year.

We put a fair few miles on the clock in order to get players we could afford. They were all kids who wanted a chance at Super League level. Veivers and Howarth weren't regarded as being good enough for Wigan, there were other props ahead of Johnson in the queue at St Helens and it was a similar story for Dean. I won't hear a word said against them, because they did a very good job indeed for themselves, me, the team and the club. Paul was the only one who survived the clear-out at Wakefield at the end of 2011, but I think he would have been a key man in Wildcats' pack for a number of years if Hull had not signed him at the end of 2012. Chris Dean got an opportunity at Widnes and Josh Veivers and Stuart Howarth both went to Salford, so all of them have proved they are genuine Super League players. I doubt any of them will gain international caps, they are not going to be superstars of the sport, but they are good, solid professionals.

At the start of 2011 the club held a meeting with shareholders to appeal for funds, but the response wasn't enough to keep them afloat and, on February 1, Wildcats entered administration. That was exactly two weeks before our first Super League game, against Castleford at the Magic Weekend in Cardiff. There were people interested in taking over, but they were smart businessmen and obviously they were waiting to see what would happen. The favourite was Steve Parkin, one of the owners of Guiseley Football Club. He has a very successful logistics business and I was excited at the possibility of him coming in as our new owner.

Guiseley's manager Steve Kittrick is a Wildcats fan and he painted a bright picture of what Mr Parkin could bring. For a start, there was talk of money being injected so I could bring players in. I am not sure how far negotiations went, but in the end nothing came of it, though Steve Kittrick later did join the board as a director. Instead Andrew Glover, of West Yorkshire Windows, became Wakefield's new owner. I think that was as much a shock to him as everybody else. Jimmy Elston had brought him in as a sponsor the previous autumn and he ended up in charge of the whole thing.

Peter O'Hara is an insolvency expert who has done a lot of work with struggling rugby league clubs and he was appointed as the administrator. He called everyone to a meeting and basically those who weren't involved on the rugby side of things were sacked. A lot of them then got their jobs back, but the people who had been most closely associated with the previous regime - including the general manager Francis Stephenson - found themselves out of the door. It was a really difficult time for everybody concerned, especially the office staff. I think as a coach or a player you are always aware that you could end up out on your ear at the whim of a chairman, an injury or a few bad results. If you work behind a desk you tend to think you have a bit more stability, but that was taken away.

The meeting with O'Hara and Co was horrific. There were women in tears and a lot of harsh words were said. Blame was thrown around, accusations were made and some harsh truths were spoken. To put it bluntly, it was a shit fight. I was in the thick of it when I should have been getting my team ready for the start of the season. Things were so bad for a while I genuinely thought there was a chance we would not fulfil the opening fixture. I was telling the players everything was hunky dory when I knew full well it wasn't. I kept my fears to myself and as far as the players were concerned it was business as normal, but in reality it was anything but.

As it turned out, we did go to Cardiff. By that stage Andrew Glover was being strongly linked with the club and there was a glimmer of light at the end of the tunnel. We played Cas in our opening game and were well beaten, 40-20. Fans weren't happy with the performance, but all I could think was 'if only they knew'. From my point of view it was an achievement just to get a team out on the pitch.

Two days after the opener in Cardiff the administrator sold Sam Obst to Hull. The following day, Dale Ferguson went to Huddersfield Giants and the day after that Catalan signed Darryl Millard - and then, 24 hours later, Andrew Glover completed his take-over. And after all that, we went to France for our second league fixture and beat Catalan 38-14. It was, to put it mildy, quite a week.

We had a small enough squad as it was, in fact we'd had to draft a player - Russ Spiers - in from outside the full-time set-up for the Castleford game, so to lose three key men was a huge blow. I think maybe things could have been handled a bit better, but I had no quibble with the departed players themselves. I couldn't have had, as I would have gone to Catalan less than a year earlier if the club hadn't blocked the deal.

Sam had himself and his future to think of and he did what he thought was best for him at the time, though it didn't work out as well as he would have hoped and he was released by Hull at the end of the year. It proved to be a tremendous move for Darryl and the same for Dale. My admiration for the Catalan club only grew over the way they handled the Millard transfer. They paid the club up front, did everything by the book and behaved like a professional sports club should.

Dale is a very exciting prospect and a player I have a lot

of time for. He is two days away from being exactly the same age as my twins and I felt I had played a fairly big part in his development. I know he thought highly of me and we got on very well. I was in the bath at home when I heard he was leaving, on the Monday night. My wife answered the phone and took a message, asking me to call Dale as soon as I could. When I rang back he told me: 'I am terribly sorry, but I have gone to Huddersfield.' He also tipped me off that Aaron Murphy might be going as well. I called Aaron straight away and persuaded him to stay put.

Because of that Aaron will always be near the top of my list of favourite players I have worked with. He could have gone and nobody would have blamed him for it. Collectively we were at the end of our tether, but he decided to show loyalty to me, the club and his team-mates and I will always be grateful to him for that. And I'd have fancied my chances of talking Dale round too if I had got to him first. As it was, Aaron joined Huddersfield at the end of the season so he got to help his team-mates through a difficult year and still moved to what is probably perceived as a bigger club. That season I wished we had five Aaron Murphys, because he was our best full-back, winger and centre.

It was a good job Aaron stayed, because we only had 18 players to take to France. That win in Perpignan was phenomenal. I honestly thought we would go there and get our backsides spanked, but it was Roy of the Rovers, Dunkirk and Rorke's Drift all rolled into one. With everything that had happened we had no right to be competing with Catalan, but the whole team pulled together and they produced a performance full of grit and character. We got off to a great start and the self-belief grew. I would rate it as one of the best victories of my coaching career, but I'm not going to take credit for it. It was down to the players and I was proud to be associated with them.

Coaching is Chaos

When the club went into administration we were docked four competition points. After that I sat down with my assistants Paul Broadbent and Colin Sanctuary and I told them my motivation for the season was to make sure I didn't become the first coach to go through a whole Super League campaign without winning a game. I really thought there was a chance that might happen.

After we won in France I said I don't want to be the first Super League coach to finish on minus points and then when we'd got into the black we wanted to overtake Crusaders - who had also been docked four points - and Harlequins. We set small targets so we had things to play for. We needed something to keep us as staff going and the players as well.

In the end we won seven games that year. It was more victories than Harlequins managed, but the points deduction meant we finished below them in the table. But we didn't come last; Crusaders were two points adrift after round 27. That may not be something to highlight in red ink on my CV, but it's still an achievement I am proud of and all the players should be as well.

The big achievement in 2011 was staying in business and remaining in Super League, which came as a massive surprise to everybody concerned. When Andrew Glover took over I am pretty sure he was expecting Wakefield to be a Co-operative Championship club for the next three years; that's what everyone in the game thought, including me.

We were down near the bottom of the table, we'd had continual financial problems, been in administration and made no progress on improving the ground or moving to a new one. You could argue that Wildcats, at the start of 2011 at least, were in a far worse state than when we'd been awarded a licence three years earlier.

The season started in February and the new licences, for

2012-14, were announced in July. The RFL had already said one Super League club would be relegated to make way for Widnes coming up. You would get very short odds indeed on which Super League club was in the firing line.

I had no hope of us keeping our Super League place, even though - because of our playing record - I thought we deserved to. The club had been in a mess financially and the ground wasn't up to scratch, but as I mentioned earlier, in my opinion it is what happens on the field that matters the most. To be eligible to apply for a Super League licence Championship clubs have to either win the Northern Rail Cup or reach a Grand Final. Once they have done that they can submit a bid and things like the ground, fan base, financial record and so on will be considered before a final decision is made.

For clubs already in the top-flight, the playing record wasn't considered. I said publically before July 26 that I thought only clubs who finished bottom of the table during a three-year licence period should be eligible for relegation. Of course I would say that, but it happens to be something I strongly believe. For all the club's other problems, Wildcats have never finished at the foot of the table since entering Super League in 1999. I think that is a record to be proud of and the club should be given some credit for it.

That is a flaw in the licensing system, which I don't agree with anyway. Supposedly it gives clubs stability and allows them time to bring on young, British players who would not get a chance during a relegation dogfight. The number of overseas players is on the decline, but that is largely due to economic conditions, rather than chief executives' decisions not to recruit them. Rather than putting long-term plans into place the majority of clubs have still gone for the here and now, which involves bringing in foreign journeymen rather than giving home-grown players a chance.

Coaching is Chaos

The licence system breeds complacency; none of the clubs who were warned in 2008 that they needed to upgrade their facilities were in a new stadium at the start of 2011. St Helens and Salford were well down that route, but neither Castleford nor Wakefield had so much as chopped a tree down or laid a brick.

Anyway, our relatively good playing record - one fifth-place finish and a Challenge Cup semi-final appearance during the licence period - wasn't going to save us. The only hope we had was that one of our rivals' applications might have been lost in the post. The licence announcement attracted a lot of media attention; it was broadcast live on Sky Sports News - from Old Trafford, in Manchester - and we had press men and broadcasters camped outside the gates at Belle Vue.

The drawbridge was pulled up. Over at Castleford they invited fans and the media into the restaurant to listen to the announcement. We decided to keep everybody, other than staff, outside. Livelihoods were at stake and we wanted people whose jobs were under threat to have time for it all to sink in before the media came asking questions. The plan was to hold a press conference about an hour after the announcement to give the club's reaction to it - in other words, to talk about how we were going to cope with three years, at least, in the Championship.

I had given it some thought and I was coming around to the idea of coaching Wildcats in the lower division. I had decided I would rather coach them in the Championship, when we might have a chance of winning it, than continue on with my back to the wall, constantly putting out fires and wondering 'how am I going to survive this'?

I'll never forget the day of the announcement. The admin employees watched it on a television in the second floor learning zone in one of the stands at Belle Vue and the rugby staff were gathered around a set downstairs. We had begun training, but broke off to watch the announcement. The Grade A and B licences were announced, then it came to Grade C. Richard Lewis, then the sport's executive chairman, read the successful clubs out in alphabetical order: Castleford Tigers, Harlequins......

Having been a bit of a swot at school I had learned my alphabet and I knew Crusaders should have come after Castleford. Something was obviously up. When Richard Lewis read out 'Wakefield Trinity Wildcats' there was a moment of stunned silence and then the place erupted.

I've read that we were told in advance, but in fact we genuinely didn't know until that moment. It turned out that Crusaders had withdrawn their bid at the 11th hour, meaning we were reprieved. I have no doubt that had Crusaders not done that they would have been in and we'd have been out, but that doesn't matter now. The few hours after the announcement were surreal; the doors were thrown open and the media invited in and the press conference was held an hour earlier than planned. There was even some champagne, though I am not sure where that came from.

I was shocked, but pleased because I had invested half a decade of my life into Wakefield Trinity Wildcats. I will freely admit the club were very, very lucky to get away with it, but it was the right verdict in the end. It is a big club, potentially at least, with a rich rugby league heritage and a decent playing record over the summer era. There are some very good people at Wakefield and I was delighted for them, though I did realise it probably meant I would be out of work at the end of the year. I was out of contract at the end of the season and I had made it known that I fancied taking over from Terry Matterson, who was returning to Australia, at Castleford. That is my hometown club, a club I still support and it would be my dream job. I didn't get it, they opted for Ian Millward instead, but I think the new Wildcats board were less than impressed by the fact I had been so keen to move to their nearest and fiercest rivals.

Soon after the licence announcement I had a meeting with Jimmy Elston and Andrew Glover and they told me they felt it was time for a change. I agreed with them, it was. I did not want another season struggling along trying to put out a competitive team on limited resources. If they had told me they were going to spend the full salary cap I might have felt differently and I'd have scrapped a bit harder to stay there, but that wasn't the right approach. My advice to the club was to make sure they didn't splash out on the team all in one go. We spent £850,000 on the team in 2011 and I suggested they went to £1.1m in 2012, £1.4m the next year and then the full cap in the final year of the licence. That way they wouldn't have to pay people off to get rid of them and they could add quality, but also keep the younger lads coming through. Towards the end of my time at Wakefield we did have some very promising kids, like Matty Wildie and James Davey. They needed nurturing, alongside some quality signings.

When the board told me I was on my bike at the end of the year there were no hard feelings at all. I thought Jimmy and Andrew handled it very well, they were honest with me and I felt it was the right decision for all concerned. Unlike what happened at Hull, I did not feel I had been unfairly treated. When I took over in 2006 I was enthused and excited by it; had I stayed on beyond 2011 I would have been doing so because it was a job and better than being on the dole. I was as ready for a new challenge as everyone else at the club was.

After the licence announcement our season went off the rails. Lack of numbers, plus the quality of players we had recruited, began to take its toll. I'll be honest and admit that some of our recruitment before and during 2011 had been based on playing in the Championship the following year. The lads we brought in were willing and keen, but they lacked experience and in some cases just weren't up to the job of week-in, week-out Super League football. The plan had been to stay full-time in level two and we were building a Championship team, anticipating the fact we wouldn't get a licence. The players were as shocked as anyone when we did. I know some of them had already agreed deals with other clubs, expecting us to go down, so the announcement left them in a sticky situation.

We got hammered 40-6 at home by Crusaders, of all clubs, the weekend after the licence announcement and didn't win again until the final game of the campaign, against Bradford. That was my final fixture in charge and the victory ensured we didn't finish bottom, which I thought was an appropriate way to bow out. Above all else, I was chuffed to bits to be handing over a Super League team.

Wakefield was good for me and I think I was good for the club. We never finished bottom and we twice survived, in 2006 and 2011, when everybody had written us off. We came fifth one year, which is the highest they have ever finished in Super League and reached a Challenge Cup semi-final. The academy teams improved and began to reach finals and the number of British players increased. I am proud of how we coped with sub-standard training facilities and the fact we managed to put a team out when we were down to the bare bones. We may not have won a trophy, but I enjoyed every moment. I would have swapped some of the experiences I had; I would much rather have been able to sign better quality players and to have spent up to the full salary cap, but Wakefield will always hold a special place in my heart. It is a good club, with some good people and I hope and believe they can have a long-term Super League future.

15

*

Little Drummer Boy

THE best thing about rugby is getting paid to play. Second best is being paid to coach and the third best? Being paid to talk about it, which is what happens in my role as a media pundit.

That first came about through Sky and my involvement with the academy. I was working at the RFL as head of the youth structure when Neville Smith, Sky's rugby league producer, came up with the idea of covering under-18s matches. At that point the war between BARLA (the amateur game's governing body) and the RFL was raging over youth players and putting lower grade matches on TV was seen as another way of attracting teenage talent to professional clubs. It was decided to stage academy games as curtain-raisers to first team fixtures and to film some of them for broadcast later in the week.

Neville spoke about it to Maurice Lindsay and me and the fact was I knew more about the top academy kids who were coming through at the time than anybody else did. Sky needed a summariser to help their commentator Bill Arthur and I was the obvious choice. This was in the early 1990s before Super League and I used to sit alongside Bill and give my views. It was a really far-sighted thing for Sky to do and it underlined their commitment to rugby league.

Academy matches were shown on Sky during the early years of Super League as well, before - sadly in my opinion - the concept was scrapped. Unfortunately we used to find that a lot of the curtain-raisers were called off, to protect the pitch for the main game, and I think that's one of the reasons Sky lost patience with it. In my opinion it's a real shame the clubs didn't buy into it more.

Before Sky got involved nobody had broadcast youth matches on TV since the 1960s, when Roger Millward was coming through as a hot prospect at Castleford, so it was the first opportunity many fans got to see future big name stars, kids like Iestyn Harris, Paul Sculthorpe and Kevin Sinfield, in action. It was great for me because it provided an opportunity to raise my profile and gain some broadcasting experience. It definitely gave me an appetite for co-commentary, which is something I have done for various TV and radio companies ever since.

My involvement in radio also began during my time at the RFL. I was invited by a local station, BBC Radio Leeds, to do some co-commentary for them. Following on from that, I started working for 5 Live, with their commentator Dave Woods and producer Alastair Yeomans.

Peter Fox, the legendary old school coach, tended to be their summariser and I was groomed as his successor. I used to make some observations from the touchline while Peter was the main summariser up in the stand. We were the commentary team for Super League's first game, Paris versus Sheffield in 1996. Peter and Dave were in the commentary box, with Alastair and me on the sideline.

Coaching is Chaos

Working for BBC 5 Live gave me an in at BBC TV and as I became more well known as a Super League coach I began to get involved more and more as a pundit for Sky. It is something I really enjoy for a number of reasons: I like talking, I like watching rugby league and I like passing opinions. Being a summariser/pundit allows me to get paid for doing all three. I feel like I am pretty good at it and I like to think my passion for the game comes across on the air.

As a Super League coach it was handy being paid by Sky to go and watch other teams in action, but there were also drawbacks. To be honest, I think it would be better if all their pundits were neutral, rather than them using people attached to top-flight clubs. When I was coaching in Super League I did find it difficult to give a totally honest opinion; you are always a little guarded, especially if you are commentating on a match involving a future opponent. I was always anxious to avoid giving any opposition added motivation. I also tended to be careful with what I said about individual players. You never know who you are going to be coaching - or trying to sign - in the future.

Using neutrals, people from outside the competition, or not directly involved as a head coach, is the way to go in my opinion. It is tough for head coaches to go on Sky or the BBC and pass comment, though I think the ones who do, do a pretty good job.

I have never had any real media training, though I've been given plenty of good advice. Again, my teaching background has helped because education is also about communication. If you can't communicate, you can't get your message across and that applies to broadcasting and teaching. When I went to college in Leicester I did have elocution lessons, because of my broad Castleford accent. It was called English Speech and Reading. There was me, a Cockney lad and one or two others, all with heavy local accents. The idea was to make us understood by one and all. The course worked and I thoroughly enjoyed it, not just because of what it did for my speech. The main reason was the lecturer, a woman who had the most enormous breasts I have ever seen. That made the breathing exercises very interesting; we were a lot more captivated by the rhythm of her chest than what she was saying about controlling our breathing.

Both the BBC and Sky get criticised for their coverage of the game, but I will defend each of them for the good job they do. When I left Wakefield to join Batley I also stood down from the BBC, because Sky were offering me work on a more regular basis. That was a tough decision to make and I do miss working with people like Sally Richardson, Dave Woods, Ray French and Clare Balding.

In my opinion, Clare's involvement is one of the best things to happen to rugby league for years. She is a lovely person and a magnificent broadcaster and journalist and she absolutely loves the game. Since the 2012 Olympics she has become a national treasure and she is never afraid to tell anyone of her love for our sport. I was watching her present the TV comedy quiz *Have I Got News For You* around the time I was finishing this book and she even managed to give rugby league a mention then. That's unusual because rugby league doesn't have enough high-profile friends in the media, but Clare's involvement has made the sport respectable in a lot of broadcast people's eyes.

She is not a typical rugby league fan; as she will tell you she is a posh southern bird, but I think she was genuinely overwhelmed by the welcome she received when she first started covering the sport for BBC *Grandstand*. When she had a cancer scare a few years ago a lot of rugby league people made the effort to send their best wishes and I know she was touched by that.

Coaching is Chaos

We get on very well and I learned a lot working with her. I know in the past - and this is changing now as she gets more into the game - some fans complained that she didn't know enough about rugby league, but they were missing the point. As presenter Clare's job was to make coverage accessible to non-fans, to ask the sorts of questions people who haven't been brought up in the game would want to put. It's the presenter's job to draw the knowledge from the experts, people like me.

Working in live TV can be hair-raising at times and I remember one of the first occasions I worked with Clare, on the BBC's Challenge Cup team. It wasn't just a rugby league broadcast, we were supposed to be sharing air time with some swimming, but that finished early, leaving us with about 20-25 minutes to fill. Clare was very new to it at the time, but we blagged our way through it and the feedback we got from the director and producer was that we had done it pretty well.

Clare is very knowledgeable and enthusiastic about sport in general and she loves horse racing, which I also enjoy. I always think if you take any sports fan to a live rugby league game, he or she will be hooked. That was the case with Clare. She likes the action, the skill level, the combat - between ball carrier and defence - and the bravery players show, when they are diving at an opponent's feet or taking a high ball under pressure. I think the 2012 Grand Final made a particular impression on her, when first Kevin Sinfield, of Leeds, got up after being knocked out to win the man of the match honour, then it was revealed Warrington's Paul Wood had played the entire second half with a ruptured testicle, which later had to be removed.

I think in the past some of the BBC's presenters were just going through the motions when it came to live rugby league, but that has not been the case with Clare. She pushes the game a great deal and we need people like her on board to spread the word. It's not just the fact she is well-known, she is also well-liked and respected. When she says rugby league is a sport worth watching, people pay attention. And I wouldn't want to be on the wrong end of some of Clare's questions. She can be very Jeremy Paxman-like when she's interviewing someone in authority.

I would struggle to name more than a handful of high-profile rugby league fans, but I think it's important we attract celebrities to the game. When big names are talking about our sport, it gives it an air of respectability. I know Joey Barton, the footballer, regularly tweets about rugby league and is a big Saints fan. Before the 2011 Super League Grand Final Wayne Rooney tweeted to say he was at the game and he was a keen Rhinos supporter. The following year he met the team in their Manchester hotel and he tweeted congratulations to them all individually after they had won the trophy. Roy Keane spoke to Warrington before that year's play-offs and I know Sir Alex Ferguson has passed on words of wisdom to various rugby league teams in the past.

Bradley Wiggins, who won the 2012 Tour de France and an Olympic gold medal, is a Wigan season ticket holder and his son's big hero is Sam Tomkins. When he returned from France, after winning the tour, one of the first things Wiggins did was take his lad to a Wigan summer rugby camp. I thought it was a nice touch by the RFL getting Wiggins to present the award when Tomkins was named Man of Steel later that year.

Ryan Giggs' dad was a rugby league player, for Swinton. I know he still has a lot of time for the game and Rio Ferdinand is another Wigan supporter. Rio has been to games and visited the changing rooms to chat to the players afterwards, as he did when they won at Leeds in 2012.

Coaching is Chaos

Backing like that is priceless and I think we should make more of it. It is a sure-fire way to increase our audience: if football fans see their idols admiring and enjoying our game they might decide to have a look for themselves. I'm sure that would pay off in terms of viewing figures on the TV and paying customers through the gates.

The BBC is heavily criticised by some rugby league people for the way it covers the game, but that's totally unfair. The BBC has a very tough job on a relatively limited budget and the people directly involved in its rugby league coverage, the likes of Carl Hicks, Sally Richardson and Jill Crabtee, love the game just as much as Clare Balding and the commentators Ray French and Dave Woods do.

Unfortunately, higher up in the BBC rugby league isn't as well thought of and I think there are senior managers who still regard it as a minority sport, played and watched by northern oiks. That's illustrated by the fact coverage of the opening few rounds of the Challenge Cup was halved from two matches per weekend to one in 2012. That said, the decision was partly the game's fault. The BBC were fed up of broadcasting ties played out in front of crowds of a few thousand, which is what happens in the early rounds and doesn't make for good TV.

That upsets me, because it is depriving people who don't have Sky of the opportunity to watch the game live on TV. The BBC was behind moving the Challenge Cup from a pre- and early season competition, with the final in April or May, to its current slot with rounds spread throughout the spring and summer and a final on the August bank holiday weekend. That hasn't worked and I'd like to see it shifted back to a May final. Crowds have been dwindling and the competition doesn't have the aura it once did, which to me - as one of its biggest fans - is a crying shame. At the moment all the big games, other than the World Club Challenge, are staged at the end of the year and I think that's tough on players, coaches and fans alike.

There's the Challenge Cup final at the end of August, then the play-offs start a couple of weeks later followed by the Grand Final in early October. And once the domestic season is out of the way the autumn internationals begin. It seems to me we are putting all our eggs in one basket. If I was in charge I would bring the Cup forward - maybe even with a June final - and keep the title decider where it is, then fans aren't being expected to splash out for two big games in the space of a few weeks.

At the moment the Challenge Cup is on the BBC's golden list, which means it has to be shown by the national broadcaster. I'd have no problems with it being taken off and allowing Sky, or whoever else is interested, to bid for it. The people who fill Wembley are the ones who go to games every week and treat the Cup final as a party weekend. It's difficult to do that at the end of August and then fund all the Super League play-offs - which don't count on season tickets - and the Grand Final as well, plus maybe four international matches. I think packing all the big games together at the end of the season has an adverse effect on attendances and it's something that needs addressing.

The BBC wanted the Cup final moving so it didn't clash with events like the Grand National, Boat Race and the end of the football season. But, so what if it does? If we can't go up against the Boat Race - a bunch of posh southerners splashing around on the river and about as interesting as watching paint dry - then we've got a real problem.

I actually think the BBC's rugby league coverage is very good, though I would like to see more of it. Dave Woods is an excellent commentator and the production values have definitely improved over the years. I get the impression though, that at times the BBC is almost embarrassed to be broadcasting our game, which is why it doesn't get promoted the way their Six Nations rugby union coverage, for example, does.

You certainly couldn't accuse Sky of lacking enthusiasm. When Sky began covering the Challenge Cup in 2012 that was a positive step for the sport, because that particular broadcaster's influence is growing and there's one thing you can guarantee about Sky, if they have the rights to cover an event they will pull out all the stops to ensure they do it right. The satellite broadcaster has revolutionised how the game is covered, with innovations like 3D, multiple camera angles and the video referee, which was Neville Smith's brainchild. That's yet another example - like blood-bins, sin-bins and play-offs - of a rugby league innovation which rugby union has copied; it makes me laugh that they call it the TV Match Official, to avoid using the term video referee.

Rugby league fans like to moan about Sky as much as they do about the BBC, though usually for exactly the opposite reason. I remember someone describing their commentary duo of Eddie Hemmings and Mike 'Stevo' Stephenson as Hype and Tripe, which made me laugh, even if it is very unfair. The BBC gets criticised for not being enthusiastic about rugby league, the complaint about Sky is that they are too enthusiastic. You can't win.

As the lead commentator Eddie has a very tough job and I think he does it really well. He is not appreciated for the amount of research he carries out, with the help of stats guru Ian Proctor who knows everything about anything. Stevo's job is to analyse and cause a bit of controversy and he does that very well. I think people misunderstand what Stevo is all about; he is definitely not a buffoon, but he is being paid to play the clown a bit. That's his role, not to please everybody but to have a black or white opinion, which viewers will either love or hate him for.

The younger generation of fans won't realise how good a player Stevo was at his peak; he was - without a shadow of a doubt - one of the best hookers of his era. He is a few years older than me and I watched him a lot when he was playing at Dewsbury in the early 1970s, because my cousin Keith Voyce was his understudy. He was a hell of a player and years ahead of his time; as a hooker he was playing a modern 21st century-style of dummy-half game and he was very quick. He didn't just lumber from scrum to scrum, he also contributed a lot in open play. That's why the Australian side Penrith signed him and anybody who plays in their top competition has to be an outstanding player. Not many Englishmen get to do that and even fewer make a success of it. I think Stevo should get more respect, both for what he achieved as a player and for his knowledge of the game.

Sky pour money into their coverage and that's why it is so good. I know a lot of people think they have too much influence and maybe they have a point when it comes to kick-off times etc, but their money allowed all the clubs to go full-time in the mid-1990s and without it I think some clubs would probably have gone bust by now.

One thing I feel could be emphasised less in Sky's coverage is their obsession with coaches. During matches, every few minutes they cut to a shot of one of the team bosses in the stand and I think that's an unnecessary distraction for viewers and it's also very annoying when you are on the end of it. I have no problem with the media focusing on coaches before and after games, because it's natural for people to want to know your opinion. The coach knows the ins and outs of his own team and what they are trying to achieve and he will attempt to have similar knowledge of the opposition. But I can't see what it adds to the coverage during a match, especially as all coaches are aware they are being watched and they alter their behaviour accordingly.

Coaching is Chaos

As soon as something controversial happens, the cameras are on the coach. At Wakefield if I was unhappy with something one of my players, the opposition or the referee had done I would always turn my back and walk into the box behind my viewing position, to have a rant and rave in there, in private. The added advantage of that was we had a TV and video recorder in there, so I could have a look at a replay and confirm my view, then compose myself and get on with things. A lot of coaches talk to their staff with a hand in front of their mouth, so nobody can lip-read what is being said. That's something else to think about during a game, when you've got enough on your mind as it is.

You do try to be detached and unemotional, but some coaches are better at that than others. It is an emotional game. Everybody who saw it will remember Matthew Elliott, the Bradford Bulls coach, falling out of his seat when St Helens scored a try after the hooter to beat his team in a play-offs tie in September 2000. I remember Neil Kelly, then in charge of Widnes, kicking a drinks container - on camera - during the interval of a televised Challenge Cup tie at Wakefield. And I am sure Leeds will have been lifted by the sight of St Helens coach Daniel Anderson laying into his players at half-time during a Grand Final. Leeds won't have been watching, but you can be sure they would have heard about it pretty quickly.

One thing the TV cameras have picked up on is the habit I have of drumming my fingers at times of great stress. It has become a bit of a trademark and it is simply a nervous reaction, I am not really conscious I am doing it. But I am sure if my heart was wired up to a monitor during a match the machine would blow a fuse. There are occasions when you feel totally calm and in control, but they are few and far between. I wouldn't have it any other way; rugby league is a huge part of my life, it is how I make my living and I have to feel emotionally involved. If I start turning up at games and I'm not feeling nervous it will be time to pack it in.

Unfortunately, I think the focus on coaches is going to get more intense, rather than less. Sky have had remote control cameras in the changing rooms for years now and they usually want a word with one of the coaching staff early in the second 40 to get an insight into what was said at half-time. Sky's changing room cameras have no sound, so they aren't much of an intrusion. Most modern Super League dressing rooms now have little areas out of sight of the cameras, so you can always take players in there if you want a chat totally in private.

I do understand why Sky do it, because it makes good television and it gives viewers a glimpse into a world they would otherwise have no access to, such as Daniel Anderson's now infamous rant. That made fascinating viewing, but I am not sure it did Daniel or Saints - who went on to lose the game - any good. I felt for him and to me it seemed a bit like his privacy had been invaded.

During my Super League coaching days when Sky wanted to know what had been said in the changing room at half-time I would designate someone else to speak to them on my behalf. And generally what I'd instruct my staff was 'tell them any old rubbish, but don't tell them what's been said'. So all they'd get was 'we need to complete a bit better and not miss as many tackles' - the sort of mundane stuff anybody could have picked up on.

That goes back to the Challenge Cup campaign in 1998. Steve Deakin used to talk to the BBC during games and he was really good at it; he would manage to come up with something that sounded like it made sense, but bore absolutely no relation to what was really going on. The BBC were happy because they got a nice quote or two and I was delighted, because nothing was being given away.

Coaching is Chaos

I think Sky realised that they were being fed a lot of bull, so they don't bother so much now. You couldn't tell them the truth: that we are going to change our attacking structure because it isn't working, or that we are doing a good job on so and so and he can't handle us so keep going at him. I can just about put up with a camera in the changing room and someone speaking to one of my staff at half-time because I recognise the game needs television coverage, but what I don't want to do is speak to a reporter during a game or have a camera crew in the changing room at any time, other than maybe half an hour after the match has finished.

That was tried a few years ago in a BBC show called *Rugby League Raw*, which was a fly on the wall-type series about the lower division play-offs. The language was pretty fruity and I thought it took things too far, it didn't show rugby league in a good light and, when things are being edited, often you don't get the true picture. They say the camera never lies, but it can certainly distort things.

Rugby league prides itself on being a family game and a large percentage of crowds are made up of women and children. That's obviously a good thing, but - and maybe I am being a bit old-fashioned - I don't like to see women and kids exposed to the sort of language that gets used in the heat of battle, on a male-to-male basis. Some home truths are spoken in private, behind closed changing room doors and you certainly don't want a TV camera poking its nose in. You have to be honest with your players, but you can't do that in front of thousands of television viewers.

I can't imagine Premiership football managers giving television the sort of access it gets in our sport, but the media is a big issue for rugby league. Ask any fan for a list of pet hates and lack of coverage on TV, radio or in the national newspapers will be near the top.

That's not a problem in Yorkshire, Lancashire or

Cumbria, where the regional papers and local radio do a fantastic job. I am a huge fan of BBC Radio Leeds' rugby league output and it will be a massive shame if local radio coverage falls victim to BBC cuts. Radio Leeds covers all parts of the game, from amateur to the elite level. They send reporters or commentators to all matches in their areas and they really take the sport seriously and give it the respect it deserves. Local newspapers, like the *Yorkshire Post, Yorkshire Evening Post, Hull Daily Mail, Wakefield Express* and *Castleford and Pontefract Express* are the same, though it is getting harder for them as staffs and budgets get cut, but when it comes to the national press they just don't seem to be interested.

I suppose that's partly because they are all based in London and rugby league-land is a long way away, but that's no excuse. Most of them manage to cover northern rugby union - or what's left of it - pretty well, so it's probably more a case of them simply not being interested. It is a shame, because rugby league people are very open and accessible and I think they speak a lot of sense. The national media would do very well out of rugby league if the powers that be could be bothered to take an interest. The BBC moving its sport operation to Salford may help, but I am not confident of that. It's not geography that's the issue in the BBC's case; it is the attitude of the people at the top.

It is very sad that virtually all the national newspapers' rugby league writers have lost their jobs over recent years. Rugby league journalists are good people; over all my time in the sport there's only one I have ever had an issue with and that's the writer who tried to make a mountain out of a molehill about my expenses when I was assistant-coach at Wigan. I felt like I had been stitched up on that occasion, but the rest of the time I have been reported fairly and accurately and I count a lot of the writers as friends. Most of them are fans as well as journalists and they want to see the game thrive and prosper. I enjoy their company, I will take the mickey out of them and if they've written something I don't like I will have a bit of a dig back, but it's done in good spirit and that's how it should be.

During the 2000 World Cup Andy Wilson, of *The Guardian*, wrote an article which upset me, but I could see where he was coming from and I didn't fall out with him about it, because he was doing his job. If you are a public person you have to accept that people are going to have an opinion about you. Most of the time that is positive and it gives you a warm glow inside, but you also have to cop it on the chin when it's not.

Dealing with the media is part of the job in modern sport, for players and coaches. It's not the same in the lower divisions, where there's not as much interest, but at Super League level you are expected to cooperate with the Press and broadcasters, especially Sky who have privileged access.

You are selling your product and you have to respect that. Post-match press conferences are a bit of a necessary evil, you have to do them and they can be great when you've had a good win, but after a defeat it's not a nice place to be. Fortunately, most of the time the winning team is the story, so if you've lost you don't get much of a grilling, though the questions can be tough when you're in a bad form slump or pressure is supposedly mounting on the coach's job.

The RFL tell coaches to cooperate with the media and to attend post-game briefings, but they want you to do it with one arm tied behind your back. There is a coaches' code of conduct which severely restricts what you are allowed to say; in other words, you are not allowed to criticise match referees or other match officials.

Personally, I think that's out of order. If I am asked a question by a press man or a radio interviewer - for example, 'what did you think of the referee's performance today'? - I should be allowed to give an honest answer. Press men - and there are a few women as well - aren't stupid and if they see a referee make a poor decision they are going to ask about it. They wouldn't be doing their job if they didn't. I don't believe in blaming referees for a team's poor performance, but sometimes things out of your control have a major bearing on the result and it's not easy dealing with the media when that happens.

In 2011, Wakefield lost a Challenge Cup tie against Castleford in sudden-death extra-time, when Kirk Dixon landed the winning points for Cas with a penalty goal. I was dying to say something about that in the press conference afterwards, but I kept my thoughts to myself because I didn't want to get in bother with the RFL.

I think if you could come out and give the referee, or an opposition player or coach, a serve - like they do in football - it would create more interest and talking points. Unfortunately, the RFL wants coaches to be politically correct and not to say what they think. You have to be diplomatic; if there has been a controversial decision - which there is in most games - you will get asked about it and you'll probably have a strong opinion, but it can be costly if you voice it. You have to bite your tongue, because if you don't you will cop a fine. That happened to me once, when I was at Hull and I have been very careful ever since. I passed an opinion about a decision - and that opinion was right - but the RFL didn't like it, so I was £300 out of pocket. I was told it was public criticism of a match official and that wasn't allowed. If I'm asked 'what about that no try decision John'? I would love to give an honest answer; I will have had a look on my monitor or the Sky big screen and I'll know full well it should have been a try, but I am not allowed to say so.

I also think it would be a good idea if the match

commissioner or referee had to face the media after games. Match commissioners attend press conferences, but only to listen to what the coaches are saying and make sure they don't speak out of turn, not to answer questions themselves. I would love to see them put on the spot after controversial incidents. Coaches and players are accountable, so why not the referees' department?

When coaches get together we tend to have a good moan and groan about referees, the RFL and the state of the game, because that's the only time we can get away with it. The RFL is concerned about lack of media coverage, but it is determined to stamp out what would be a rich source of stories.

Obviously anything that's controversial will capture the press's attention. For example, what was the most famous match staged at a Magic Weekend? It was Bradford Bulls versus Leeds Rhinos in 2007 - everybody remembers that because of an error the referee made. Leeds were losing by two points with a few seconds to go when they were awarded a penalty just inside Bradford's half. That was a poor decision, made on the video referee's say-so. Then Kevin Sinfield kicked for goal, the ball bounced off the cross bar and Jordan Tansey followed up to touch down. He came from an offside position, but the referee - Steve Ganson - awarded the try without asking for the video official's help. That created a huge storm and got masses of column inches. I'm sure the RFL would like everything to be rosy and all the headlines to be positive, but that can't always happen. Tanseygate got people talking about the game and that can only be a good thing.

16

*

Family Guy

THE years 1998 and 2005 were significant ones for me and not just because of the Challenge Cup victories. I met Dawn the year Sheffield Eagles won at Wembley and we married seven years later, the same year as Hull's Cup triumph in Cardiff.

I was married before to Karen, the mother of my now grown-up twins, Alana - who is a teacher in Leeds - and James. He has recently been travelling, but has just returned to manage a Power League soccer centre. They have both done pretty well for themselves and I am massively proud of both of them.

Dawn also has three adult kids from a previous relationship: Kane Chambers, the youngest, works in the midlands as a community rugby league officer for the RFL; Jamie is the eldest and has his own business as an Independent Training Consultant and the middle one is Cara, who is the football secretary at Wakefield Trinity Wildcats.

Coaching is Chaos

She worked closely with me and my football department and now does the same for Richard Agar. The job was advertised when Sam Teagle moved from Wakefield to the governing body, the RFL. Cara saw it and applied. Three people were interviewed and I sat in when the other two came in, but withdrew for Cara's because of a conflict of interest. She was appointed by Diane Maskill and Francis Stephenson, got the job on merit and has done really well.

I am a family man, but I will freely admit my job can put personal relationships under strain at times. Anybody who works in sport has to have a very understanding spouse or partner and kids as well, because your whole life tends to revolve around work. All our kids go to the games and that's one way you can have regular contact with them. Being a coach, especially in Super League, is a 24/7 occupation. It's not just training and matches, there are media demands and public appearances, you are dealing with players out of office hours and your phone rings constantly. It's almost impossible to have any time to devote solely to your partner or family and obviously that can make things difficult. You never really switch off and your mood is often very much influenced by how things are going at work.

It is hard for Dawn, in particular, because as a Personal Adviser with Barnsley Council she has a very demanding job herself. It is a job she loves, but there are pressures which come with that. I know people in the game say rugby league coaching is a tough job, but it all gets put into perspective when Dawn comes home and has a moan about what has happened at work. There's always a bit of one-upmanship between the two of us and sometimes we compare how rotten our days have been, but being honest, Dawn has to cope with far tougher situations than I do. She is dealing with often quite troubled and vulnerable people and some of the problems they have make what happens on a rugby league field seem quite insignificant. At the end of the day, sport is part of the entertainment business. We all care deeply about it, but it's not a matter of life and death.

My wife knows that at times she has to take a back seat to rugby commitments, which can't be easy for her. As a Super League coach I tended to get more evenings at home, but now much of my time off is during the day, when Dawn is at work and I am working more on an evening. Plus, I have greater media commitments now.

Take the week I am writing this - early in the 2012 season - for example. From Sunday to Sunday: We played London Skolars at home, which occupied my morning and afternoon. After that I drove straight down to London to appear on Sky Sports' *Super League Full Time* show, which is filmed on a Sunday evening. When that was finished I jumped in the car and drove immediately back up the M1 to my home in South Yorkshire, arriving at about 3am. So in terms of my relationship, Sunday was written-off.

Monday was a day when I could work from home and get various things done, though I was pretty tired after the previous day and I had a bit of a lie-in. Tuesday was training day, so that was busy with preparation and then the session itself in the evening. On Wednesday I had a meeting with Peter Smith, who is helping me write this book, in Leeds at lunchtime and then I was due to go to the RFL's referees' department to collect a DVD of our next opponents Toulouse in action. There was a mix-up over that, which took some sorting out; then when that was done I took Alana out for a meal in Leeds. That's something I aim to do once a week. I got home 7.30-8pm, but Dawn was over in Hull on a case and she didn't get back until after 9pm.

Thursday was training, so I had to finalise what I planned to do in the team meeting and preparation for training and then take the session itself, so that occupied the afternoon and evening. On Friday I worked for BBC 5 Live on their coverage of St Helens versus Catalan, which was an 8pm kick-off. I had to be there a couple of hours early and on a Friday afternoon it is at least a two and a half hour drive from my home, so that didn't leave me with much spare time beforehand and I got back at just after midnight. Saturday was matchday, with a 2pm kick-off and on Sunday I was back down in London at the Sky studios for the *Full Time* show.

When I left Wakefield and went into part-time coaching people said to me 'aren't you going to get bored - how are you going to fill your spare time?'. I really wish I had some, but that is the nature of the beast. It's not a job it is a vocation and, to tell the truth, I am aware that working in sport is a privileged occupation, for all the stresses and strains it puts on you. In the Championship it is less pressure, but the time commitments for me are equally as great because of the media work I am doing.

I had been thinking of doing a Masters degree this year, but there's no way I could fit that in at the moment, so it's something I will have to put on hold for further down the line. The week I've outlined above is not uncommon; it was a pretty standard seven days and so you can see why I need a supportive wife and family. They are very understanding and they realise how much rugby league means to me and they also accept that sport is not a Monday to Friday, 9am-5pm occupation. Games have to be played when 'normal' people aren't at work, otherwise nobody would ever draw a crowd. That is the way of the world and I would not want to change that, but it is very demanding.

It is hard to switch off, because there is so much to do. I am constantly thinking about either the last performance or the next one. I try not to let what's happening rugby-wise affect my mood, but it's difficult to be detached. I am not very good on the morning of a game; I like to be left alone. I need to make sure I've got my last minute team talk sorted out, that I have got my little key words - that I am going to speak to the pivotal players about - in my mind and that all my equipment, my computer and so on, is prepared. I don't like noise, so on the morning of the game I'll read a paper or do some ironing, which is my favourite way to relax. Honestly, there's nothing better - put a shirt on the ironing board, iron it and hang it up, it's the perfect way to chill out.

After a game a lot depends on how it has gone; if the team has played particularly well you can feel a glow of satisfaction and a zest and enthusiasm for looking at the match again and reviewing it. If it hasn't turned out so well the first thing you question is yourself, could I have done anything differently? Did I get my team selection right, were the interchanges handled properly; was there something wrong with the game plan? I enjoy reviewing the game when we've won, but I have an even greater desire to re-watch matches we've lost, because I want to know where we messed up. That is usually where you can get some solace, by working out where you - as a team - have gone wrong and knowing you can put it right. It's when it has gone wrong and you can't put your finger on why that a sense of frustration creeps in.

I think about rugby league most of the time, but that's no great hardship because I love the game. I read all the trade papers, I listen to the radio when there's rugby league on and I watch it on television whenever I get chance.

I think that goes back to my dear old dad. Being from Castleford, which was a mining area in those days, he had one ambition for me: 'You're not going down that black 'ole.' If ever I was straying in my studies, at junior or grammar school, he made sure I kept my focus on what was really important, which was getting a good education and

successful exam results, so I wouldn't have to go down the
pit. My mum and dad's families had been down the pit and
it had affected their health. It was also a very dangerous job
for that generation. It is much safer now, with the modern
machinery, but most pits had suffered at least one big fatal
accident at some point in their history. My dad worked in
pretty grim conditions when he was a collier, he had got out
of it and he was going to make damned sure I never had to
go down a mine. It was the same with my brother; he was a
pretty hard task master when it came to education and
academic achievement, because he saw it as a way out of
Castleford's traditional industry.

So, despite all the pressure and the hassle any coach gets,
I will always know it beats having a real job. It is a pleasure
and a privilege to work in any sport, especially rugby
league, which I believe is the greatest game. Even when the
team's not playing well, you've got a major injury crisis and
you've just been thrashed 52-0 at home by Huddersfield
Giants, I would sooner be in the thick of that than working
down t'black ole.

Every team boss gets criticised and we all know the old
saying 'the only certainty about coaching is you're going to
get sacked at some point'. I can handle that, because it comes
with the territory. What upsets me is when it becomes
personal and it begins to affect my family. When I am getting
a hard time, I try to take a leaf out of Gary Hetherington's
book. The Leeds Rhinos chief executive is probably the most
thick-skinned person I have ever come across. He has done
a fantastic job at the Rhinos and is a die-hard rugby league
man - even considering his involvement with Leeds
Carnegie rugby union. He cops plenty of stick at times, but
he doesn't let it bother him. He sticks to his guns and more
often than not he comes out on top.

Gary's a Cas man, as is the Rhinos' owner Paul Caddick.

The club has been transformed since they took over and six Super League titles from 2004-2012 tells its own story. If he listened to what people were saying about him, he would have packed it in years ago - and if he'd taken any notice of the critics in 2011, Brian McDermott would have been out of a job mid-way through the campaign. Fortunately for Brian, Gary was always confident he had got the right man to replace Brian McClennan, who had taken Rhinos to two Grand Final wins in three years as coach. Leeds were in danger of missing out on the play-offs with two thirds of the season gone, but they circled the wagons, stuck to their guns and it all came good in the end as Leeds won their last six matches and took out the title from fifth spot on the league table. I think that's a lesson for every club.

Of course fans have a right to their opinion, but that doesn't always make them right. The ones who were calling for Brian McDermott to be sacked in August 2011 were left with egg on their faces when he was showing off the Super League trophy at Old Trafford two months later. If Brian hadn't been strong enough to put that to one side and carry on and if Gary had listened to what just about everyone was telling him, that title win would probably not have happened. Brian got more stick in 2012 when Leeds had a bad run during the regular season, but he proved his critics wrong again when Rhinos went on to retain their title.

It's tough at the top, when the expectations are on you. It's also hard when you're at the other end of the table. I have been in both situations and I have copped my fair share of criticism and abuse from the terraces. I like to think I am pretty laid back about it: I have got great self-confidence, in that I know I am good at what I am doing and I have got a great knowledge of the game, which you're bound to have after being involved for so long.

I am self-assured and I can ride the criticism, though

there are odd comments that do hurt. At times like that, you want to have a pop back and that's the frustrating thing. The keyboard warriors are the ones who really annoy me, the anonymous critics who sit at their computer all day spouting bile on internet message boards. I don't think they are real fans; they are playground bullies who just like to have a go at targets who can't hit back.

I remember Peter Fox, who was one of the great coaches of the 1980s. He showed me his little black book, which listed every player in the Stones Bitter First Division - including me - and outlined their strengths and weaknesses. He had his own fact-file, years before we all started doing something similar on computer. Peter did summarising on BBC 5 Live before me and told me about a fella at Bradford who continually slagged him off, saying his team weren't worth the admission money. Peter said: 'One day he was having a go at me, so I got a fiver out of my wallet and told him to f-off.' I love that story, but you can't do that nowadays because most of the critics are keyboard warriors who wouldn't say boo to you face-to-face and if you do react to someone in the crowd you are accused of inciting trouble.

I am all right with the pressures of the job, but it hits home when the abuse becomes personal and, even worse, if it gets aimed at your wife or family. I had an issue with Radio Leeds once when their breakfast show ran a so-called news story claiming I had resigned as Wildcats coach. My son heard it and rang me up, very upset, asking why I had done it and why I hadn't spoken to the family first.

There was absolutely no truth in it whatsoever. It was all speculation and rumour, which the presenter had delivered as fact. I rang him up, gave him an ear-bashing and fair dos, he apologised. But the damage had been done and my son and daughter had been deeply upset, because they thought their dad had walked out of his job.

I can think of a few coaches in the past who have called it a day because they've got fed up with the abuse their family has been getting from so-called fans. I don't understand that on a number of levels. One, why make it personal when things are going wrong? You might not agree with what a coach is doing and you might not believe he is the right man for the job, but he will certainly be trying his hardest to get things right. I have never met a coach who didn't care about how his team are performing. Secondly, why would anyone take their anger out on someone who has absolutely nothing to do with the situation at all, such as the coach's wife or kids?

I wouldn't stop Dawn going to a game, because she's quite feisty and can give as good as she gets. She works in a tough environment and if anyone turned on her at a match, they'd end up regretting it. But I wouldn't expect her boss at Barnsley Council to get stuck into me because she hadn't done well on a case. It would be nothing to do with me, just like my selection decisions or game plan are nothing to do with her. My family are supportive and understanding, but they don't take part in any decision-making, which is why they should be free of criticism or potential abuse.

Criticism is all right and I am prepared to take that on board, but abuse is unacceptable. I often find that when I speak to people face to face, they will go away with a different opinion. I'll talk rugby with anyone and if someone has got a point to make about the team - and they are prepared to voice it in a reasonable manner - I'm happy to hear it. But they have also got to accept that I will give them something back; as long as they are prepared for that I will talk to anyone. Sometimes decisions are made and the reasons aren't obvious to the general public. You might have an injury or a disciplinary issue which you want to keep behind closed doors. If someone has got a rib injury, you may want to rest him for a week, but not say that's what you are doing because you don't want him targeted the following game. Coaches always make what they believe to be the right decision, for the right reasons. If you can explain that to people, nine times out of 10 they will understand, even if they don't agree. And the one in 10 who doesn't, I can always give him a serve back, which I quite enjoy.

One of the best things about rugby league is the contact between fans and players and coaches. At Super League games quite often the coach - especially of the visiting team - will sit in a seat in the stand, next to paying spectators. Players and fans mingle after matches, in the bars or wherever and that keeps everybody grounded. It's another reason why the keyboard warriors upset me. My successor at Hull, Richard Agar, suffered so much at the hands of the internet message boards and that was sad. Often it's a snowball effect, someone voices an opinion and everyone else joins in, because they want to feel part of the pack. It's uncalled for in my opinion and it's cowardly, but you have to have a thick skin. If you are going to have a public profile, you've got to be able to take that sort of thing on the chin.

What I can't understand in the modern era is players going on Twitter and sharing their thoughts with the world at large. Sadly, some of them aren't smart enough to handle social networking. I know of a case at a Super League club - not one I have coached - where a player had posed for a gay lifestyle magazine. Another player tweeted him calling him a 'puff' and one of the gay rights organisations was straight on the phone - quite rightly - to the club concerned, demanding an apology. The player wasn't being homophobic; it was a bit of ill-judged banter - but if he wanted to make a comment like that, why didn't he send a text message? Once something is on Twitter, it is in the public domain forever.

My mate Keith Senior is as bad as anybody. He caused a storm when he went on Twitter swearing and carrying on after Crusaders withdrew their Super League licence application in 2011. He had every right to be upset, because he had signed a two-year contract a few weeks earlier, but I'm not sure why he would want everyone to know what he was thinking. Richie Mathers is another one who uses it a lot. When Wakefield played the first game on Widnes' artificial 4G pitch in 2012 he went on Twitter complaining about grazes to his knees and elbows. The Vikings coach, Denis Betts, had a pop back, telling him to 'man up'. It's fair enough having an opinion like that, but I reckon you should go through the proper channels. When Luke Burgess, the Leeds prop, got a broken jaw in a game at Castleford in 2010 he tweeted a picture of the wound from the ambulance on the way to hospital. Maybe I am an old fogey, but I don't understand that at all.

Most of the time, the chat on Twitter is just gossip: 'Just finished training - am off to Nando's now' - that sort of thing. I can't imagine why that's of any interest to anybody. I prefer to actually talk to my mates, who include some fellow coaches. As a group we generally get on pretty well together. We aren't the best of friends and there's probably one or two coaches who can't stand the sight of each other, but it's a small community and it makes life easier if we all at least cooperate. There are some coaches I like more than others, but that is human nature and it would be the same for any group of 14 people, in whatever walk of life. There is an unwritten respect because we all know it's a pretty tough place to be and we will all have bad times and some good times.

It very much keeps you grounded because you know full well that if you are experiencing a high, everyone else in the same line of work has been through the same thing - and the same in reverse. It's good, if you're in a bit of a slump, to look around at a coaches' meeting - or at the league table -

and think 'he was at rock bottom a few weeks/months ago and now he is absolutely flying', so you can draw a bit of comfort and inspiration from that.

I have always really liked Ian Millward, who has probably been one of the more controversial coaches of the modern era. An Aussie, he came to England in the late 1990s to coach Leigh and then took over from Ellery Hanley at St Helens. He had great success there, but was eventually sacked after falling out with the people who ran the club. He got the job at Saints' nearest and fiercest rivals Wigan and struggled there, then went back to Australia for a spell, before returning for a second stint with Leigh. After that he got the Castleford job when Terry Matterson left at the end of 2011. That's a role I had been hoping for, but I certainly wouldn't hold it against him. Just like me, he needs a job to make a living so there were no hard feelings.

The media like Ian, or Basil as he's known, because he gives them good copy. He comes up with interesting quotes and is not afraid to speak his mind. That hasn't always made him popular with the game's authorities or fans of rival clubs and a lot of people thought, when he was in charge of Saints, that he was arrogant. When he was struggling with Wigan some of his critics enjoyed that, but I felt it was unfair. I have always enjoyed his company and valued his opinion and I'd like to think he feels the same about me. In my opinion, he is a genuinely good guy.

Ian was involved in a tragedy in 2012 when his son Robbie, who was only 19, died suddenly of a massive heart attack. I don't think you can fully appreciate how terrible that must be unless it happens to a member of your family, but as a father myself I really felt for Ian. Once again, as they did when we had our tragedies at Wakefield, the whole of rugby league rallied around to support Ian and I was proud of the way the game looked out for one of its own.

Another one I have got a lot of time for is Nathan Brown, who came over here to coach Huddersfield Giants and joined St Helens ahead of the 2013 season. He has done a good job at Huddersfield, has a bit of character about him and is another one who is not scared to say what he thinks. On a couple of occasions he has spoken out in public about an opposition player or a referee's performance and while that's not always the wisest thing to do, it does sometimes liven up media coverage of our sport.

I thought it was very unfair when he was fined by the RFL for some remarks he made following a game at Leeds in 2011. Huddersfield had a player sent-off, along with Rhinos' Ryan Bailey. Nathan accused Bailey of targeting his small men, the half-backs and said he'd encourage his forwards to 'knock him out' if it happened again. That got massive coverage and Bailey got a ban, whereas the Huddersfield player didn't, so it probably had the desired effect as far as Nathan was concerned.

Mind you, when Tommy Lee nearly decapitated one of Warrington's little fellas, Lee Briers, in a game the following season, Browny said he didn't think there was much in it! Fortunately there is no law against hypocrisy or every coach would get locked up. We all do it. You are always out to try and get the best possible outcome for your own player or team.

Brian Noble has been probably the most successful British coach of recent times and I think it's a shame he has been out of work since things went wrong at Crusaders. He did a great job at Bradford, stabilised things at Wigan and managed to get the Welsh outfit into the top-eight in their first season, which was remarkable. He also did well at international level and he is a good bloke as well, who really cares about the game.

I think the best coach in the Super League era has been

Coaching is Chaos

Tony Smith, the man who succeeded me at Huddersfield. Another Aussie, he backed himself and paid his own way over to England to get the job at the Giants. They were relegated that year, but bounced back the following season and he turned them from easybeats into a solid mid-table team. Then he took over at Leeds and won the title in his debut season, 2004. That was their first Championship for 32 years. He won it again three years later, in his final game before taking over as Great Britain coach. He didn't have the best of times in charge of the national team, but returned to Super League with Warrington Wolves and won the Challenge Cup the first two years he was there and finished top of the table at the end of the third.

He is, in my opinion, the best modern day coach and I would rate him above Brian Noble, who has also been a great team boss. Wherever he has been Tony has improved the club, the squad and the team and that's what it is all about. Not everybody can win trophies, but I reckon if you can say when you leave that the team's in a better state than when you took over, you have done a good job.

There aren't any coaches I have really disliked. If there's anyone I am not particularly keen on I will be polite, but keep my distance. It is a small world and it pays to be nice to each other. You have to be guarded to some extent, but if a rival coach calls me up for advice, I'll give it. We don't talk tactics very often and you wouldn't call someone else to discuss a game plan, because it's your job to devise things like that. But you might ask for an opinion on a playing surface for example or possibly the best way of handling a trip to France to play Catalan, what the training facilities are like over there, is it best to travel a day or two days before the game and that sort of thing.

When I was at Wakefield we used to fly late on a Thursday to Perpignan, where games are usually staged on a Saturday evening. Following a chat with a coach at another club I altered that to going during the day on Friday, because the way they did it was working better and it would be foolish not to.

I am also quite happy to share videos. If we have just played Keighley Cougars, for example and the coach of their next opponent asks me for a DVD of the game, so he can do his preparation, I will happily provide one. Most coaches are the same. You try to be cooperative, open and honest and you expect the others to be the same with you. The Keighley coach will be passing on a tape to whoever we play next, so there's no problem. It's the old saying 'treat others like you'd want to be treated'.

We have coaches' meetings and the RFL say they listen to the feedback from those, but I don't know if that's really the case. Coaches probably should have more input, because we are at the sharp end and we probably watch more rugby than anyone else, both live and when reviewing our own team's performance and looking at future opponents.

Take an example: I think the law regarding shoulder charges should be changed, so they are made illegal. In 2012, Hull's Sam Moa was sent off for a shoulder charge against London Broncos. That sparked a lot of controversy, with some in the game saying it was a fair hit. In my opinion, and Moa pleaded guilty and got a ban so this must be right, it was the correct decision to dismiss him.

You can shoulder charge, but you can't tackle above the shoulder. Sam hit the London hooker Julien Rinaldi around the head and he was knocked spark out. If he had made contact with an arm, nobody would have questioned the decision. Because the contact had been by the shoulder, he had people defending him, but the simple fact was, it was a high shot, that's foul play and he deserved to go off.

I would not encourage my players to shoulder charge,

because I want them to hit and stick and I think the majority of coaches are the same. In rugby union shoulder charges are illegal and I think there's a case that our sport should follow suit. There's no doubt that sort of tackle does lift the crowd, but I don't think it's good technique and it's not ideal for the image of the game. If you had an 11-year-old kid and your wife saw the sort of tackle Moa committed on Rinaldi, she wouldn't be rushing him down to the local rugby league club the following evening. She'd probably buy him a cricket bat.

The spear tackle - picking a ball carrier up and dumping him - has been outlawed because it is dangerous, and rightly so. I feel the same way about the shoulder charge. If the governing body asked for my opinion I would be happy to tell them that, but so far they haven't asked and - to be honest - I don't expect them to. The RFL has its rule-makers and fair play to them, but I do think it would be a step forward if they canvassed more opinions from the people who are actually at the sharp end.

17

*

Dream Teams

I MENTIONED earlier that I would not have picked myself as a player in any of the teams I've been in charge of. That set me to wondering about who I would select if I had a choice of everybody I've played with or against, or have coached - the John Kear Dream Teams.

I'm going to select two; one from my playing days and the other made up of players I have worked with since I hung up my boots.

I played in the 1980s, at a time when the British game was awash with talent. We had homegrown players like John Joyner, Ellery Hanley, Andy Gregory, Garry Schofield, Joe Lydon and Andy Platt ruling the roost, to name just a few - and on top of that the cream of the Australian competition came over, at their peak, for short stints in our game.

At that time both competitions were played in the winter so the Aussies had their off-season when our campaign was in full swing - and the other way around. That allowed a host of top British players to go over there and do well in the

Coaching is Chaos

Sydney competition and we got the benefit of seeing the world's best individuals over here, even if only fleetingly.

The difference between then and now, in terms of imports, was that in the 1980s the Aussies and Kiwis who came over were doing so in their pomp. It was a privilege to share a field with some of them. Sadly now, in most cases, we get players who are a little past their best and who can no longer hold down a regular place in an NRL team.

I think the 1980s was a golden period in terms of the quality of players on show, even if the game had some serious problems off the field. Picking 15 players - there were only two subs in those days - from that pool was an almost impossible task, but I think I've come up with a side that would be a match for any that has ever played the game. It's a shame it is only a fantasy team because I would have paid good money to watch it in action.

For full-back I did consider Geoff Wraith, who I played with at Cas. He also spent a bit of time in the Brisbane competition and at Wakefield. He was a great leader, really good under the high ball and a fine attacking full-back. He played more than 200 times for Cas and also had a spell as Malcolm Reilly's assistant-coach. Putting head before heart though, Geoff would just miss out. As would Gary Kemble, a Kiwi, who played at Hull and was absolutely sensational. He would have to be considered, but Joe Lydon would be my pick. I have always felt he would be one of the true greats of the modern era, because he was superb at receiving kicks, was a deceptive runner, could link in the line and had a good pair of hands. He was also a classy finisher.

One of my wingers would be Des Drummond, who pound for pound was the toughest player I ever went up against. He launched into you when he made a tackle, he was fast and brave in any attacking situation and he could finish. He would have been a really good winger in the modern game, where they have to get to dummy-half, scoot out and finish well. He could be a bit shaky under the high ball, but I am sure he would have mastered that with full-time training. He was a high-quality player and someone I have a lot of time for. And like I say, hard as nails.

The other winger in my team was a shoo-in. He only played 16 matches over here and one of them was against Castleford, though he was in the centre that day. I tackled him once and I am still feeling it, nearly three decades later. I'm talking about the great Aussie, Rolling Thunder Eric Grothe. He was big, fast and strong with a very awkward running style. It was like tackling a heavy sack of elbows and knees. He really did cause problems for any team. Eric scored 14 tries in his stint with Leeds, including a hat-trick on his debut, against Leigh on New Year's Day, 1985. Stuart Duffy, who was a Leeds fan and later became football manager at Bradford Bulls, once told me that his daughter Louise was born that morning, but he left his wife and baby at the hospital to dash to Headingley to watch Grothe play. He claims he told his family: 'I can see you any day, but Eric Grothe's only going to make one debut for Leeds.'

I would have Eric on the left wing with Des occupying the other flank. Between them they would score plenty of tries and there'd be no prisoners taken.

In the centres I'd have John Joyner and Mal Meninga. John was one of the best players I have ever seen. If he played now he would be commanding £165,000-plus per season and worth every penny. John was an absolutely exceptional player, the only one I have ever seen who could beat an opponent just by raising his eyebrows. He had so much deception about him; he was big, strong and fast. On top of that he was a very, very good centre. He also played at stand-off and loose forward, but coming through in his early 20s he was a centre and he was one of the best around.

Coaching is Chaos

Mal is an Australian Test legend and current Queensland coach. He had one season at St Helens and fans over there still talk about it now. I was fortunate - or unfortunate, depending on which way you look at it - to play against him just the once and looking back I can honestly say it was an honour. Size-wise it was a mis-match and to be honest, he had the sort of ability I could only dream about.

He was part of the great Aussie sides who went through Great Britain unbeaten on tours in 1982 and 1986 and didn't lose a Test to us between 1978 and 1988. Mal was one of the reasons for that and I remember him breaking my heart in 1990 when he scored the winning try for the Kangaroos in the second Test at Old Trafford. Great Britain had won the opener at Wembley and the scores in game two were level with a few seconds to go when Mal struck. If he hadn't scored, Great Britain would have at least shared the series - and we haven't got anywhere near that close ever since. Mal shoved Carl Gibson out of the way in the back-play and with a video referee I think the try might have been disallowed, but it was still a sensational touchdown and proved what a ruthless player he was.

Another of the reasons for the Aussies' dominance in the 1980s was their half-back combination of Wally Lewis and Peter Sterling, who would take that role in my Dream Team. Wally came over for a short stint with Wakefield in the 1980s on £1,000 a game. He only played a dozen or so matches, but we saw at first-hand how good he was when we faced them on Boxing Day. Cas had a better team than Wakefield and we won quite convincingly, but he kept them in the game. He was an astonishing player; I remember one particular tackle when he nearly knocked Steve Fenton into the middle of the next week. He fired out a couple of 30-yard passes for their tries and they were right on the button. I thought then that he was years ahead of his time - he was playing a future style of rugby and the rest of us were years behind. I was in awe of him and I think just about everybody else on both teams was as well.

Peter Sterling spent a number of years at Hull in a couple of spells, so I played against him several times. He was instrumental in knocking us out of the Challenge Cup on a regular basis. We tried to spot him up and intimidate him, because Malcolm Reilly - being an aggressive sort of player and coach - felt that was the best way to keep him in check. It is one thing saying it and quite another doing it, Peter stood up to whatever we threw at him and more often than not, he came out on top. He was a great organiser and a world class ball-player and also a really tough defender.

I'd have to pick both Lewis and Sterling, which means no place for Shaun Edwards or Garry Schofield in my starting line-up. That was a tough call, because they were both great players, but I think it would be hard to beat any team whose backline included Meninga, Grothe, Lewis and Sterling, as various opponents found out for a decade or more.

Big Kevin Ward would be one of my props. He won all the top honours playing for Cas and then St Helens and was one of the few British players truly feared and respected by the Aussies. You don't achieve that without being great and Kevin was. I liked the fact other teams knew he was a handful. When you ran out alongside Kevin, you knew the opposition were looking at him and thinking 'we're in for a tough afternoon - I wish he was on our team and not theirs'.

He was the type of player every successful team needs. He was tough and fast for such a big man. He had an offload, but what appealed to me was the fact he was a leader without really knowing it. He led by deed.

Kev Beardmore would be my No 9. At Cas we called him Gripper. One of the top kids' television programmes in those days was *Grange Hill*, set in a comprehensive school. There was a character called Gripper, who was a bully and used to pinch all the other kids' dinner money. Kev used to do that to everybody at Airedale High School!

He played a bit in Canberra and also for Great Britain and I'd identify him as one of the first modern-style hookers. The way Kevin played wasn't about being the best cheat in the scrum - which was how old-style rakes did it. Instead Kev played more like a modern-day dummy-half, he was a big fella who could defend. He also had a great engine and would have had no trouble doing 80 minutes every week in Super League.

I lost a bit of sleep mulling over my other prop, so I am going to cheat a bit and push Mal Reilly up there. I have to have Mal in my team, because he is one of the all-time greats and also I wouldn't dare not to. He did finish his career in the front row and he was pretty good there, if not at his absolute best. Everybody knows how tough Malcolm was, but he was also skilful. He had a kicking game, a pre-line passing game and an offload. And crucially, he could defend. He was an all-rounder and if he was playing now he would be worth a fortune.

That allows me to have Bob Lindner, an Australian international who played 19 games for Cas in 1986, as one of my second rowers and Steve 'Knocker' Norton in the other slot. Bob made a big impression with his barn-storming runs and he was an absolute pleasure to play with, while Knocker was a Cas lad who - unfortunately - played probably his best rugby for Hull. He was a one-off, a remarkable player who could basically do whatever he wanted to with the ball.

Sadly that means no place for Keith 'Beefy' England. Leaving Beefy out was a tough call, because he was as tough as teak and played more than 300 games for Cas, which is a notable achievement. He was a top-quality rugby league player as well as a good team man.

I had to do some shuffling around to accommodate Ellery Hanley at loose forward. Ellery was the best British player of his generation and one of the greatest of all time. He could do things nobody else could and was a very complex individual on and off the field. Putting it simply, he was a genius - the sort of player who was top class at every asset. He was a playmaker, he could score tries, he was a tough defender and also a decent goal-kicker if he ever needed to be. He could play three, four, six, seven or 13 and even had a spell on the wing, though why any coach would want to play Ellery Hanley on the wing is beyond me.

Garry Schofield would come into contention for a place on the subs' bench, but again he just misses out and I am going to opt instead for the late Wakefield and Hull great David Topliss. Schoey was still emerging when I played against him, but I came up against a peak Toppo and there weren't many better. My forward sub is Beefy, because I could play him anywhere in the pack and he could do whatever job I asked him to.

I think all the 15 players I've selected in my Dream Team would be successful in the modern, full-time era, but the one who would blow everyone away would be John Joyner. The modern player I would liken him to, at least during his time as a centre, is Leeds' Kallum Watkins. He is a kid I think will go all the way in the game and he is very Joyner-like. John never got tackled first up, he always made a half-break, or got the ball away to his winger or split the line, or got a quick play-the-ball to keep an attack moving.

Malcolm Reilly would be my captain, mainly because if he wanted the role, who would stop him? If I was unavailable as coach for any reason Malcolm would get that job too. He was the only coach I ever had; assisted by wise old sage John Sheridan, he was head man throughout my 12 years at Cas and was as good a coach as he was as a player.

Coaching is Chaos

I haven't bothered selecting an out-and-out specialist goal-kicker, because I don't think we'd need one. But Mal Meninga could do the job and there's a few in there who could back him up.

Now, moving on to players I have coached was even tougher, because I am looking at a longer period. I've considered everyone I have worked with through my club and international career and have come up with another side that would be capable of winning Super League!

Full-back was again a difficult one. I coached Joe Lydon so I considered backing him up, but I also thought about Graham Steadman, Kris Radlinski and Paul Wellens. I thought Graham was superb as a full-back for Cas and Paul Wellens has been one of the most consistent players of the summer era. I also like Rads, who was so instrumental in Wigan's 2002 Cup final win. He was a great professional, a threat in attack through his support play and defensively he was brave and solid. He knew when to close space down and when to back off, a first-class full-back. However, in the end I plumped for Jonathan Davies, who made such a big impact in league after moving over from Welsh rugby union. I was involved with him in the Great Britain set-up and he was a class act. He will forever be remembered in rugby league for his try in the 1994 first Test win over Australia at Wembley, after Shaun Edwards had been sent-off.

The wingers are easy: Jason Robinson on the right and Martin Offiah down the left. Two Wigan and Great Britain greats; one who came from rugby union and the other who went there. Only great players score as many tries as they did. They were different sorts of players and complemented each other because of that.

Martin was the fastest player in the game; impossible to stop when he got into a bit of space and he popped up and scored tries anywhere. His strike rate was phenomenal and

I know people might point to one or two defensive deficiencies, but if he let one in he would score three to make up for it, so it wasn't really a problem.

Jason manufactured tries out of the blue. When you thought there was nothing on, he would stand somebody up, beat them and score, as he did to Leeds in the first-ever Super League Grand Final. I coached him in the Great Britain academy when he was a scrum-half, but he would be a winger every day of the week for me. He did start off as a stand-off in junior football, but that was because he was the best player around. It was a case of giving him the ball and he'd score. I remember watching him at the Buslingthorpe Vale ground in Leeds and he was absolutely amazing with his balance, footwork and evasive skills. I know various people claim to have 'spotted' Jason playing as a youngster in Leeds, but you didn't need to know much about the game to do that; he was so far above everyone he was playing with and against. Wigan picked him up and he developed into a world-class wing three-quarter in both codes.

There's lots of choice in the centres, but three stand out above the rest: Keith Senior, Gary Connolly and Paul Newlove. I will always have a soft spot for Keith from our time together at Sheffield. I think there's a special bond between everyone involved in the 1998 Cup win, which will last forever. I also coached him for England in the 2000 World Cup and he never let me down. He is a natural rugby player, had speed and strength, an eye for the line and was a winger's centre. Given a choice between scoring himself or putting his winger in, Keith would take the unselfish course. He was incredibly durable as well. Though a knee problem ended his Leeds career in 2011, he rarely had a serious injury in 19 seasons at the top level, which is phenomenal.

So Keith's in there, which leaves a choice between Gary Connolly and Paul Newlove. If Paul had Keith's attitude he would be remembered as one of the all-time greats, but sadly he was so laid-back it was unbelievable. We'd get him into a Test camp and he seemed more bothered about his pigeons. Even when half-asleep he could do things you wouldn't have thought possible and his record with Featherstone Rovers, Bradford Bulls, St Helens and Great Britain speaks for itself.

If he had really applied himself, he would have been unstoppable. I think that's one difference between us and the Aussies; we have players with as much talent and ability, but - certainly in the past - I don't think we've been as professional or applied ourselves as well as they did. Maybe part of the problem was that Paul was an automatic choice for Great Britain, whereas in Australia, no matter how good you are, there's always a few players snapping at your heels. You have to turn up and give everything - not only in every game, but every training session as well.

Gary Connolly was a freak. Defensively, as a centre he was awesome. He played against some great Australians, Gene Miles and company, and kept them quiet. He was a good footballer as well and was creative, despite not having - shall we say - the ideal lifestyle for a rugby player. He liked more than the occasional beer (he used to be known as Gary Lager), but that didn't seem to affect him once he got over the whitewash. He gets the nod, just ahead of Paul. He was also a very good full-back.

In the halves, I would have Garry Schofield as my stand-off. He has been a bit of a controversial figure since he hung up his boots, but there's no doubt he was a great player. I remember the second Test in Melbourne, 1992, when Great Britain took Australia to the cleaners: he was phenomenal that night. I was fortunate enough to join the coaching staff for part of that tour, when Phil Larder came back, and Garry was superb throughout. You have to acknowledge greatness when it's there and you don't get more than 40 Test caps without being one of the very best. He is known as a poacher, but he was a lot more than that. He could play, he had the ability to create tries for his team and he could defend if he put his mind to it as well. I would pick Garry ahead of Shaun Edwards because I think he had more to his all-round game, though I have a lot of time for Shaun as well.

My No 7 is Jason Smith, who I coached at Hull. As I have mentioned, he is one of my favourites out of all the players I have worked with. His creative ability and his toughness was second to none. He had a kicking game, he could put people through a gap and he could go through a gap himself if necessary - though he preferred not to do that, because he didn't much like running. Like most of the players I have selected, he was also a strong defender. I think Schoey and Jason would complement each other pretty well. Jason could play a structure as well as deviate from one and Garry would be there as the maverick, drifting in and out of the game and doing more or less whatever he wanted to.

I am selecting two modern day greats at prop, Adrian Morley and Jamie Peacock. That means leaving out people like Paul Broadbent, Kelvin Skerrett and Andy Platt, who were all among the best of their generation, but Moz and JP are two players who have done it all in the game, have been at the top level throughout their career and earned the respect of Aussie opponents. Moz was fantastic for Leeds a decade ago and then went off and proved himself in the toughest competition in the world, Australia's NRL. He came back and has been sensational for both his country and Warrington Wolves. A good bloke as well.

JP is one of the fiercest competitors I have ever come across. Like Moz, he is a converted second-rower and never knows when to quit. He has won more Super League Grand Finals than anyone else and I think his move from Bradford

Coaching is Chaos

Bulls was the key piece in the jigsaw for Leeds as they won five titles in six years from 2007-2012.

The role of prop has changed over the years, but I think Moz and JP would have been great in any era. They are both big, tough men, they each have a good engine, they can defend and aren't just battering rams, they can also play. You could argue that Moz was at his peak as a second rower; he actually converted to prop during his spell at Sydney Roosters. JP was a fine back-rower, but I'd play him at prop and I think that's where he has produced his best form.

I never coached Kieron Cunningham, because he played his international rugby for Wales and wasn't involved when I linked up with Great Britain. If I had taken the St Helens job back in the late 1990s, working with Kieron would have been one of the attractions, because he is someone I very much admire. That rules him out, so my hooker will be Richard Swain, who did such a good job for me at Hull and who I think is very under-rated in terms of Super League No 9s. He was the model professional. Jason Smith played like Tarzan, but was a bit strange off the field, whereas Richard did everything right - watched what he ate and drank and prepared for every game in the same, efficient way. That's why he was so consistent. He was a great attacking hooker, who also had a good kicking game out of dummy-half and he was a quality leader.

The second-rowers are Stephen Kearney and David Solomona, which means no place for Paul Sculthorpe, unfortunately. Stephen would play on the right, as a tight second-rower, in a prop-type role. Sol - the only player I've selected from my Wakefield days - would be on the opposite side, giving us a nice combination. Sol would give us toughness, flair and creativity, while Kearney provides go-forward, aggression and some creativity with his offload. I think they would bring the best out of Schoey. I think Sol was at his athletic best during his Wakefield days, when he had explosive power as well as the ability to offload the ball out of impossible situations.

Locking the scrum is Andy Farrell, at loose-forward. I relished working with him during the 2000 World Cup and he is one of the modern day players I admire the most. He has got the Richard Swain attitude and is highly skilled; you could use him as a ball-playing loose-forward, but he would be equally happy to tuck the ball under his arm, rip in and provide some go-forward as an auxillary prop.

On the bench I am going to go for Paul Sculthorpe, Andy Platt, Gareth Ellis and Rob Burrow. Scully could come in and cover six, 11, 12 and 13 and he was a great player. Andy Platt was a really good, tidy player; he wasn't the biggest, but he oozed quality. He gets the nod just ahead of Craig Smith, who was on Wigan's books when I was assistant coach there. He was a mean machine, but with Morley, Peacock and Platt you'd be able to rotate your props without losing any effect. I would have liked James Graham and/or Sam Burgess, but unfortunately I never coached either of those.

I did coach Gareth Ellis when he was with England 'A', though he left Wakefield the year before I took over. He could play at centre, second-row or loose-forward. He was a fantastic player for Leeds, improved during his stint at Wests Tigers and is a magnificent signing for Hull.

Rob Burrow is a player I like a lot and always have done, since we worked together for Emerging England. He can play in the halves or at hooker and is a fabulous impact player. At only 5ft 4in he doesn't look like a rugby league player, but that's what makes him special. He has got plenty of pace and is unique in the modern game in the way he plays, with his dodging, weaving, ducking and diving. He is also tough and brave and a good character to have around.

He edges out his Leeds club captain Kevin Sinfield, who

is the best goal kicker in the game at the moment and has been so instrumental for Leeds during their glory years over the last decade or so.

I am going to coach the team, obviously and will have the late Mike Gregory as my assistant, alongside Paul Cullen. As players, they epitomised what I value greatly, hard work, ability, durability and toughness. Andy Farrell is captain and goalkicker.

You will have your own ideas, but I think this team has got every eventuality covered; there's big men, fast men, creative players and tough guys. Perhaps we wouldn't go through a whole season undefeated, but it would definitely take a special side to beat us.

Dream Team of players I played with or against:

1. Joe Lydon
2. Des Drummond
3. John Joyner
4. Mal Meninga
5. Eric Grothe
6. Wally Lewis
7. Peter Sterling
8. Kevin Ward
9. Kev Beardmore
10. Malcolm Reilly (*captain*)
11. Bob Lindner
12. Steve 'Knocker' Norton
13. Ellery Hanley.
Subs
14. Dave Topliss
15. Beefy England

Dream Team of players I have coached:

1. Jonathan Davies
2. Jason Robinson
3. Gary Connolly
4. Keith Senior
5. Martin Offiah
6. Garry Schofield
7. Jason Smith
8. Adrian Morley
9. Richard Swain
10. Jamie Peacock
11. Stephen Kearney
12. David Solomona
13. Andy Farrell (*captain*)
Subs
14. Paul Sculthorpe
15. Andy Platt
16. Gareth Ellis
17. Rob Burrow

18

*

The Future

AS I wrote earlier, in 100 years' time there will certainly be rugby league played in the heartlands at both amateur and semi-professional level. Whether we also have a hybrid code or the top level of the game has been swallowed up by rugby union, I'm not sure.

I know rugby union's powers-that-be admire our game, secretly in some cases and openly in others. They realise we have a sport that's very entertaining, highly skilled and fan-friendly. It is an easy code to watch and understand and it doesn't allow spectators to take their eye off the ball for even a second. In union, the action isn't quite as free-flowing; in fact you could go for a pint, come back and not have missed anything.

I have already made it clear I am not anti-union and I can see the merits in that particular form of the game, but I do find it hard to come to terms with a sport in which a try can be scored without anyone being able to see the ball. That hasn't stopped it becoming increasingly popular over the last couple of decades. Obviously we have to respect what rugby union is doing and recognise that it is growing at a phenomenal rate, thanks largely to regular money-spinning World Cups and the Heineken Cup. What union has done very successfully is grow their club game on the back of the international one. We have tried to do things the other way around and it hasn't worked.

Recent financial problems at Crusaders, Bradford Bulls and Wakefield - among others - have highlighted issues in Super League. Crusaders would have been given a licence for 2012-14 if the club hadn't withdrawn from the process at the last minute, recognising that they couldn't sustain a top-flight, full-time operation. That saved Wakefield and that particular club now looks to be reasonably healthy, but only after going into administration and being taken over by a new owner. In March 2012, I - along with most others in the sport - was stunned to hear of Bradford Bulls' financial crisis. Club officials announced they needed to raise £1m - half of it by early April - to stay afloat. This, remember, was a club that led the way on and off the field in the late 1990s and early 2000s, won the Challenge Cup twice, Super League four times and the World Club Challenge on three occasions.

In the early years of Super League Bulls boasted some of the best players in the game - the likes of Robbie and Henry Paul, Lesley Vainikolo, Jamie Peacock and Stuart Fielden - and regularly played in front of high five figure crowds. I'm not going to go into where they went wrong, as I am not party to inside information, but I do know they were granted a B licence in 2011 after a supposedly thorough investigation into every aspect of the club's operation, including the financial side.

If a club as big as Bradford can get into such desperate trouble, it is a worrying sign for everyone else and is another indication that a 14-team Super League competition isn't working. Fortunately, Bradford seem to have come through their crisis and the club does now have a future. After going into administration, the Bulls were eventually bought by a consortium led by local businessman Omar Khan and I wish him all the best for the future because the sport needs a strong club in Bradford, attracting five-figure gates.

Bulls managed to finish ninth in the 2012 Super League season, despite having six points deducted as a penalty for entering administration. That was two points more than we suffered at Wakefield, but on the other hand the administrator didn't sell any of their first-team players, which allowed them to remain competitive on the field.

The coaching staff spent the last couple of months of the season working for nothing, which was a huge credit to them. Mick Potter did a tremendous job under very difficult circumstances and was rewarded for it by being named coach of the year. I was delighted the new owners promoted his assistant Francis Cummins after Potter decided to go back to Australia at the end of the year. Franny has a tough job ahead of him, but another British head coach in Super League can only be a good thing.

The potential demise of a successful club like Bradford highlighted the problems we have got and I think it is clear changes need to be made to the sport at the top level. I have thought for a long time that what we need is a two-division Super League, of 10 clubs each. I honestly believe the game should be able to generate enough television, sponsorship and corporate income to sustain 20 full-time teams.

That would obviously be a gamble at first, because it would mean an increase in the number of full-time clubs and some of those are struggling as it is. But in my opinion, two divisions in Super League would raise standards and make the competition more attractive to fans and sponsors and would thus generate more income.

Coaching is Chaos

Under my plan the top division (maybe the Super League Premiership) would have a higher salary cap than the second tier (the Super League Championship, perhaps) and that would create a more intense competition. The only way we'll get that is by reducing the number of teams.

At the minute, Super League is effectively a two-tier competition anyway, with a huge and growing gap between the top six or so and the rest. There are surprise results every now and then, but far too many blow-out scores. For every time a Widnes beat Wigan, Salford defeat Warrington or Leeds slip up against London, there will be half a dozen occasions when one side loses by 30, 40 or more points and that's not healthy for the competition as a whole.

If we had a two division Super League, that would pave the way for the return of promotion and relegation, which is something I think has been badly missed. It is part of our sporting culture and fans demand it. It creates huge interest in sports like football and rugby union, but we lost that when we went over to the licence system. Having been in the thick of it on a couple of occasions, especially 2006, I know how exciting a relegation dogfight can be. I accept that it does cost people's jobs, but that wouldn't be the case if we had two full-time divisions of 10.

Of all the games I have been involved in throughout my career, the one league fixture that has created the most interest was the winner-takes-all relegation battle between Wakefield and Castleford in 2006.

Critics of relegation claim we should all focus on the top of the table rather than the bottom, but realistically you look at what's most interesting and if the battle against the drop is more exciting than the title race, so be it. Ultimately, when the Grand Final comes along everyone will be focusing on that, so there'll be positive interest as well.

We have to face the fact that, at the moment, clubs like

Wakefield, Castleford, Salford, Widnes and London can't compete with Leeds, Wigan, St Helens, Huddersfield or Warrington on a consistent basis. Salford against Wigan is likely to be a mis-match and that's of no interest to anybody. But Salford versus Featherstone, Leigh, Sheffield or Halifax would be competitive, if the latter four clubs were full-time.

At the moment it is very tough for teams who are promoted into Super League to compete, as the likes of Crusaders, Castleford, Salford and Widnes have found out. Playing in a lower division, with a reduced salary cap, would allow them to develop their team and grow the business, so they are ready to step up if and when they get promoted.

The difficulty at the moment is making the transition from part-time to full-time. A lot of players are happy doing a proper job, training in the evenings and playing at weekends and good luck to them. There's a hooker up at Workington, Graeme Mattinson, for example. When we played them in the Challenge Cup in 2012, I did some preparation work on Workington and he stood out like a sore thumb. He was exceptional and he reminded me a lot of St Helens' outstanding No 9 James Roby.

I spoke to some of the Workington people about him after the game, but they said he had a good, well-paid job up there in Cumbria. He wouldn't give that up to take a chance on making it as a full-time player in Super League, on £25,000 a year. There is talent out there in the lower divisions, but the way to build a successful Super League club is by either developing your own juniors or signing lads who have come from a full-time environment.

I am sure two full-time divisions of 10 could be sustained. Taking the 14 clubs who were granted licences in 2011, you'd probably add Featherstone Rovers, Leigh Centurions, Halifax and then see which others felt they could handle a move up. It would be a great way to develop clubs like Oxford, Hemel Hempstead and Gloucester, who were all ear-marked for the semi-professional game in 2013.

London Broncos haven't been a success. They have reached a Wembley final and finished second in Super League, but it's about more than that. On Easter Thursday in 2012 they played Catalan Dragons at Twickenham Stoop and 1,829 people turned up to watch. As a rugby league fan, I am embarrassed by that. There were more people at Featherstone, Halifax and Leigh in the Championship that weekend and almost as many at Barrow and Whitehaven in Championship One.

Without their owner David Hughes, I doubt London would have survived this long. In 2011 - when they were called Harlequins RL - they won only six matches and they'd recorded only two victories by Easter of the following year. Fans want to watch a winning team and in London they haven't got one. If they dropped down into a second full-time division they would be competing on more of a level playing field, would get more victories and their support would increase. That would also prepare them better for advancement into the top flight, when the time was right and their squad was good enough to win promotion.

Rugby league in London is a controversial subject and a complicated one. A lot of good things are being done in the capital, but the area that is weak is the elite club. Rugby league is played in most London boroughs now, at school and amateur level and some good players are beginning to emerge. The sport will only benefit if we have got more players to choose from and obviously there are a lot of athletic kids in London who might make good rugby league players, if we can get hold of them. A Surrey side, Howard of Effingham, won the 2012 Champion Schools tournament, beating Cas High in the final at Wembley. That shows there is the talent out there.

I would hate to see all the development work that has gone on down in the capital go to waste, but I am not sure how having a struggling Super League team, playing in front of a few men and a dog, benefits anyone down there. Maybe the Super League club should move. They have tried grounds all over London, but the current Twickenham base hasn't worked. Maybe a more working class area would be better. There was talk of the Broncos moving to Gillingham, in Kent, but they have now decided to remain at the Stoop, which is not a venue where rugby league can take off.

It is no good having a team which isn't competitive. I do feel for the small hard-core of Broncos fans, who turn up every week and have had absolutely nothing to cheer about for several seasons. That would test anybody's resolve.

It's often said that the national media won't take rugby league seriously without a team in London. The problem with that is, we do have a club down there and they still don't take us seriously. I am supportive of a side in the capital, but we can't stick with a failing operation forever.

The other Holy Grail for rugby league development is south Wales. Ever since the game was founded we have been trying to get a foothold in what is a very strong rugby area, without much success. Crusaders didn't work, unfortunately, but I am confident that rugby league will take off in south Wales eventually. The original Crusaders club played out of Bridgend and did pretty well down there, despite the wrong location. The stadium there was the worst in the competition and I think the club should have been based somewhere with Super League-standard facilities. Cardiff would have been a better option, in my view.

I also think Crusaders were given a Super League licence too early. In my opinion it would have been better if they'd had another three years to grow in the Championship, but the RFL were worried that their backer would pull out if they didn't get the nod. As it was, they did get a licence and he still withdrew. Moving to Wrexham was another mistake. North Wales isn't really a rugby area, though it's only half an hour's drive or so from Warrington and Widnes.

Though it meant a reprieve for Wakefield, I was sorry to see Crusaders' demise and just as pleased that a new club was formed in Wrexham to play in Championship One, alongside South Wales Scorpions, who were established when the Super League club moved north.

Wales has the raw material; a steady supply of talented, young rugby players. Some of them who don't have the physical attributes to play union could be a big success in league. Barriers between the two codes are being broken down and I know a lot of people in Wales admire our sport, so there's the potential to grow a support base. They are the two raw ingredients for a successful club: local players and potential fans.

The midlands is another area which could fit the bill and I also feel we should be looking towards the student game as a way of growing rugby league. If you have a strong student team in the midlands, Loughborough for example, you immediately have another resource to draw from.

Cumbria is one of this country's best breeding grounds for rugby league players and a successful team up there would attract massive support. It is a real shame we haven't had a Cumbrian Super League team since Workington, in the inaugural 1996 campaign. The problem there is geography: where would you put a team? Cumbria has three pro clubs, Barrow, Whitehaven and Workington. The latter two are on each other's doorstep and a merger would seem an obvious solution, but there is a fierce rivalry and the current fans up there wouldn't go for it.

There's some great players up there. I have already mentioned the Workington hooker Graeme Mattinson, but I also have a lot of time for players like Ade Gardner, Rob Purdham and Kyle Amor, who all made it at Super League level. Kyle was signed by Leeds from Whitehaven and then joined me on loan at Wakefield. He was raw, but with bags of potential and I am sure he will go on to have a long and successful career. It is just a shame he had to give up his job and uproot himself and his family. There are plenty more where Kyle came from, but they need a pathway.

When I set out I knew where I wanted to go; I wanted to play for Cas and there was a ladder there for me: schoolboys, to Cas juniors, to the intermediates and so on. If there was a Super League club in Cumbria there would be a route for talented local kids to follow, either being identified and going through the academy system, being picked up from an open-age amateur club or playing for Barrow, Whitehaven or Workington, getting spotted and being offered the chance to step up.

With the local talent available, plus shrewd recruiting and the overseas quota as well, I think a competitive team could be built in Cumbria, especially if they were to first of all play in the Super League Championship.

The south of France is another hotbed and that is a rare development success story. Catalan Dragons have definitely added to Super League since they entered the competition in 2006. They haven't always been successful on the field, but they did reach the 2007 Challenge Cup final. They play to decent-sized crowds in a fine stadium with a fantastic atmosphere and they have a pool of local players to choose from, so they tick all the boxes. If you haven't been to a game in Perpignan, I would recommend you give it a go.

This discussion of where we should be headed and what we should be doing is typical of rugby league, but I think if you stop evolving you begin to stagnate. Rugby league has always been innovative and that's one of its strengths:

Coaching is Chaos

almost 20 years after we introduced video technology, football is still arguing about it. Our history is built on bold decisions, right back to the first meeting at the George Hotel in Huddersfield in 1895, when Yorkshire and Lancashire clubs voted to split from the Rugby Football Union.

Within a few years, northern union - league's original name - was almost unrecognisable from its parent code, due to a reduction in the number of players, the abolition of line-outs and the play-the-ball. They are three initiatives which instantly made league more attractive to watch, something which was needed as league clubs were professional and had to raise money through the gate to pay players' wages.

We are open to fresh ideas and I applaud that. Unfortunately, other sports are more than willing to pinch our ideas. Rugby union, for example, has introduced video referees and adopted a Super League style play-off system to decide the Premiership champions.

It is not all one-way. In the lower divisions we have introduced a bonus point system, which was something union did first. I believe sport is about winning and I don't like the idea of being rewarded for failure. I think if you win you should get the spoils, if you draw you share them and when you lose, you get nothing.

The thing I can't understand about the bonus point is the fact it is uneven: there are four points available in some games and only three in others. If you win by 12 points or fewer, you get three points for the victory and the other side gets a defensive bonus, but if you win by more than a dozen you still receive three points and the opposition gets nothing. Surely if you're going to award a bonus for losing by 12 or less, there should be an extra point on offer for victories by more than that.

In my view there should be four points available in every game. The argument in favour of a losing bonus is that if a team is losing by - say - 18 points, they will try a bit harder to close the gap. That is utter rubbish and whoever thought of that has obviously never played the game. Anyone who has ever set foot on a rugby field knows you try, from minute one to minute 80. Even sides who are getting their backsides kicked are trying. It might not be working for them, for whatever reason, but they will be putting the effort in. You don't make people try because there's a bonus point on offer; they do that anyway.

In Australia's NRL they have golden point extra-time in matches that are all-square after 80 minutes. That's a terrible concept. At Wakefield we went to golden point in a Challenge Cup tie against Castleford in 2011 and it was one of the worst periods of rugby I've ever seen. All structures, systems and good sense went out of the window and players were trying ridiculous attempted drop-goals from every part of the field. It was a farce. We lost to a penalty goal and afterwards I was angry with myself for not preparing the players for the possibility of sudden death. We spoke about it as a group and decided if we ever got in that situation again we'd just play normal rugby league and try and score on the back of that.

Other than Cup ties, if you're not going to have replays, I think a draw is a legitimate result. In football, which is pretty well supported, draws are commonplace and that doesn't seem to deter anyone from wanting to go and watch.

Because the Australian game is a few years ahead of ours, we try to copy from them a bit too much. Maybe copy is not the right word, but we certainly try to follow. There are cycles in their game which inevitably happen in ours a couple of years later. That doesn't bring us level with them though, because they are moving ahead all the time.

When he was Wigan coach, the Aussie Michael Maguire brought over those wrestling tactics and techniques we have already discussed, which proved to be hugely successful for his side. Those techniques had been tried a few years earlier in Australia, mainly by the all-conquering Melbourne Storm, where Maguire was an assistant-coach. In the NRL, it was decided that way of playing didn't appeal to fans, so they brought in two referees to stamp it out. That made the game more skill and attack-based, and more entertaining.

I would be in favour of two referees at every game, but we simply don't have enough match officials to make that possible. It is a similar situation to the one we have with players; the Aussies have a far deeper pool. When I was over in Australia with the Great Britain academy I was deeply impressed by the fact the Parramatta catchment area had as many young players as we did in the whole of England.

That's why the standard of players is better over there and it is the same with referees. So I can't see the dual-ref system being introduced over here, but I do think we have to find some way of eliminating wrestling tactics. They are designed to slow the opposition down, but it's not good to watch. If we can't legislate against it, through having two referees, a change of philosophy has to be the answer.

I think there is now more of a risk-taking approach being developed, as played by teams like Leeds, Warrington and Catalan. Wigan were very clinical and professional under Maguire, but they weren't as much fun to watch as Leeds or Warrington. Credit to Shaun Wane, he has kept them very structured, but I think there's more passing involved in their game now.

A few years ago the NRL went to unlimited interchanges, so players could be rolled on and off the field at any time. Over here we decided against that, it didn't work and the Aussies went back to a limited number of changes. We recently dropped from 12 changes to 10 and I think it will probably be reduced further to eight. That's something I am in favour of but, like all law changes, it is how you handle it that counts. The reduction in interchanges has benefited Leeds, who are now using converted scrum-half Rob Burrow to great effect at hooker. You can't keep resting your big fellas and Burrow, with his pace off the mark, has exploited that.

When I played there were only two substitutes and before that it was one, and changes could only be made up to half-time. Substitutes do introduce a tactical element to the game and I think eight changes from four players on the bench is probably the ideal we should be striving towards.

Assuming we are not going to merge with union or introduce a hybrid game, reducing the number of teams and creating more intense matches has to be the number one priority for league going forward. Eventually that would make the English team stronger and more able to compete with Australia and New Zealand, which is the key to gaining credibility among the wider sporting public.

If we can raise our level and start beating the Aussies and Kiwis on a regular basis - something we are some way off doing at the moment - that would create a fantastic triangular series, which would pack out stadiums in both hemispheres.

So rather than changing the rules, it's the structure of the sport we need to deal with as we move forward. Of course there are rules that need tinkering with. I don't think 50 or 60-point blow-outs are good for anyone, so I would swap things around so the scoring team restarts play. That was tried for a while and I would go back to it.

I would also make the 30-metre line the restart mark. If you have to restart after a try there, you aren't going to opt for a short kick-off to regain possession. You're more likely to kick long and that is going to hand possession back to the opposition.

Coaching is Chaos

One tactic coaches use on a regular basis, me included, is kicking the ball dead, so the opposition restart on the 20 metre line. That was the law which was changed half a century or so ago, after Cas' Dougie Walton kicked Leigh to death in the game which sparked my interest in coaching. Now things have moved on and coaches encourage their teams to boot the ball out of play so they get chance to reset their defence and also take the opposition's back three out of the equation. I'd like to see a change to a situation where if you kick the ball dead from outside the 30-metre area, the tap restart would be on the 30-metre line.

These and a few other alterations would make our great game more even and challenging and would force coaches to innovate, altering tactics and making the sport more interesting and better to watch.

19

*

Bulldog Spirit

I HAVE worked at some of the biggest clubs in the game, and Batley Bulldogs. It's actually hard to think of a less glamorous side than the outfit I joined after leaving Wakefield, though you would struggle to come across more dedicated rugby league people.

In July 2011, the Wakefield board, Jimmy Elston and Andrew Glover, told me my contract there wasn't going to be renewed at the end of the season. As I've mentioned, I felt - deep down - that was the right decision. I needed refreshing and it was going to take a change of scenery to do that.

I genuinely left by mutual agreement, though that is normally a euphemism for 'sacked'. There was no acrimony or ill-feeling and I still speak to Jimmy on a regular basis. I have a good relationship with everyone at Wakefield, as far as I know, and we continue to help each other. I've signed a couple of players - either permanently or on loan/dual registration from there - and I'm quite prepared to help them out if there's anything they need from me. I still have a lot of affection for the club, but I really do believe a parting of the ways was right for both parties. I was probably there a bit too long, I required a new challenge and they needed some fresh ideas.

I would have loved to have stayed in Super League, but English coaches were going out of fashion at the time. There were jobs available, but Hull and Hull KR both appointed from Australia's NRL. Castleford, which is the job I would really have liked, took on Ian Millward, who is an English-based Aussie and Salford did the same with Phil Veivers. Only Wigan, who replaced Michael Maguire with his assistant Shaun Wane, put their faith in an Englishman.

I applied for the Cas job, spoke to their then-chief executive Richard Wright and was very disappointed when I didn't land the role, having hankered after it all my career. I built my hopes up and I took it hard when they offered my dream job to someone else, especially as it was fairly well known that several other applicants turned it down before Ian got the post. It did make me question why they didn't think I was the right man for the job and I was quite upset at the time, but Ian is a personal mate of mine, he is a good fella and when he was eventually appointed I wished him all the best. I would like to think I showed some dignity and respect and handled the whole business in the right manner.

This is nothing against Ian, but I would have liked to see an Englishman get it, because I think it's important for the future of the game over here that we develop our own coaching talent. I was equally disappointed when Hull KR and Hull both also took the overseas options and one of those appointments cost me a very long-standing friendship.

I didn't apply for the Hull job and I don't suppose, even under a change of ownership, it would have been a realistic option. I am not sure it's ever a good idea to go back, but obviously I would have spoken to them if they had come knocking.

I did, though, throw my hat into the ring to succeed Justin Morgan at their rivals on the other side of the city. My agent, David Howes, led me to believe I had a good chance, but then I read that Hull KR's chairman Neil Hudgell had flown down under looking for an Australian coach and later on they announced that Craig Sandercock, from Newcastle Knights, had got the gig. That was disappointing, because I felt I could have done a good job there. My specialism has been making silk purses out of sows' ears and I think I would have fitted the bill at Craven Park. It was well documented that they were cutting down their expenditure on players and it could have been a hand in glove fit.

Dave was heavily involved in getting another Aussie, Peter Gentle, the job at Hull and I felt there was a conflict of interest. He was representing me and supposedly peddling my wares, but was also pushing the case for an overseas coach to be brought into the British game. It was my view that he should be doing everything possible to get me a job and, in my opinion, he wasn't doing that. Dave disagreed with that view and he likened himself to an estate agent, saying he had so many houses on his books and if someone wanted to buy one, he'd sell them it.

But you only pay an estate agent if your house is purchased. I wasn't happy with the job he was doing for me and we fell out over it. It was a shame because I have known Dave a long, long time and we had always got on well. He was team manager when I was England coach for the 2000 World Cup for example. But maybe you shouldn't mix business with pleasure and perhaps I made a mistake by being on his books and he erred by having me as a client. I am sorry things turned out as they did, but you live and learn.

Coaching is Chaos

Phil Veivers being appointed as Salford coach was a different matter. I was linked with the club while I was still at Wakefield, but my preference at the time was to stay where I was. Phil is an Aussie by birth, but he has been over here for a long time and I view him as a Brit. He has gone through the ranks here, he's a good bloke and I was delighted for him when they gave him the job. He was definitely the right man for it.

Anyway, there wasn't an opening for me in Super League and it appeared I would have to spend quite a bit of time out of the game and then see what came up. I was quite at ease with that because I had been speaking to Sky TV about an extended role there and there were plenty of other avenues to go down.

I was actually interviewed by Derbyshire County Council for a post as consultant with their elite sport department, which would have meant me working there eight days per month. There was no rugby league involvement - sports like basketball and badminton were part of it - but it was an interesting concept. They have a Team Derby brand, linked up with the local university, and I think if I had been offered it, I'd probably have taken the job.

That didn't come about, but I was looking at options outside the game. That changed when the Batley chairman Kevin Nicholas rang me in August 2011, just as I was preparing to go down to Wembley to be part of the BBC's Challenge Cup final coverage.

As a club Batley weren't on my radar. I think a lot of people in the game have a soft spot for one of the perennial underdogs who have somehow managed to keep their head above water in the face of all manner of adversity and indifference from the local population, but I'd not had any inkling they were thinking of me as their new coach.

Batley were founder members of the Northern Union in 1895 and won the first two Challenge Cup titles in 1897 and 1898, plus again in 1901, but it has been more or less downhill ever since. They have, however, been in the second tier - the top division outside Super League - ever since the leagues were restructured and under the previous three coaches, Paul Storey, Gary Thornton and Karl Harrison, had become something of a force in what is now the Co-operative Championship.

Under Karl they won the Northern Rail Cup in 2010, which was an amazing achievement and - even more impressively - finished third in the table in 2011. They have a reputation as being a well-run club, with a good chairman, who live within their means and are happy to be a growing fish in a fairly small pond.

I had only ever heard good things about Kevin, but I was taken totally by surprise when he called me out of the blue and offered me the head coach's job there and then. He didn't even ask me if I was interested, just said he wanted me and the job was mine if I was willing to take it. I told him I wasn't going to accept a job over the phone, without having spoken to my wife or done any research, but we were heading for a weekend away so that was an ideal opportunity to give it some thought. My wife and I spoke extensively about it and when we got back we went to a game at Mount Pleasant, Batley's ground, to watch them play Toulouse. Kevin and the whole club made a big fuss of me and Dawn and they were very welcoming and friendly. It seemed like a good place to work, with plenty of potential, so I found myself saying yes, I'd take the job.

There was no contract, we sealed the deal with a handshake and the agreement was if I wanted to leave they'd let me go and equally if they wanted shut of me, that would also be all right. It is an informal arrangement, but it's a good one. Kevin read my character correctly, that I am very competitive and even if I was doing things on a part-time basis I would still give it 100 per cent.

There is no doubt coaching a club like Batley is a challenge, and a different one to those I had faced in the past. The amount of time you get to work with players is the big difference between Super League and the Championship from a coaching point of view. Every Super League player and club is full-time, so you have a lot more opportunity to cross the t's and dot the i's. Being full-time allows players an opportunity to recover after matches and rehabilitate injuries and it gives coaches chance to prepare and plan and work on the tactical elements of the game.

In the Championship, the vast majority of players are part-time and a coach probably gets three two-hour sessions with his troops every week. The key then is to ensure that within that time every minute is used properly. People talk about players having a professional attitude, but it's actually the ones who are part-time who have to show the most dedication. The only way they will progress is by putting in little extras, away from training and when they are not getting paid. That might mean extra time in the weights room or arriving early at sessions to practice kicking, for example.

Though I am not full-time I probably do almost as many hours as when I was at Wakefield. I put the hours in because of personal pride and the fact I want to do a good job and make a success of it, but Batley are relaxed about me also doing media work and other commitments.

The job at Batley means just as much to me as any of the others I've had in the game, though the profile is much lower. At Wakefield I was used to working with limited - at best - resources, but the situation at the Bulldogs is even more make do and mend. I think Batley should be a model for many other clubs, because of the way they have managed to be relatively successful while still living within their means.

Batley don't spent what they haven't got. Before the 2012 season we splashed out all of £90,000 on guaranteed contracts and for 2013 the plan was £92,500. That's what the board know they can generate and spend without sending the club into the red. It's a similar way of doing things to how Leeds Rhinos operate in Super League. My old school mate Gary Hetherington doesn't break the bank, but Rhinos have still managed to be successful on the field at the same time as improving their facilities off it.

The highest-paid player at Batley is on £8,000 per year, plus match fees and incentives. A lot of Super League stars wouldn't get out of bed for that amount of money, per month. I'll let people guess who our top earner is, but it's one of the more well-known members of the squad. For that he is expected to train a minimum of three times every week and play once per week, plus do a full pre-season. These people play the game because they want to and that's one of the things that appeals to me and that I like about working with players at this level.

It is also one of the frustrations; you can't spend as much time working with players as you can at a full-time club and they aren't looked after as well. That's no criticism of Batley, who are a fantastic club and do everything they can, but there simply aren't the resources at Championship or Championship One (division three) level to make player welfare a priority. Players aren't even covered by private insurance; if they get injured they have to go and join a queue and wait for treatment, just like everybody else.

There's cover which allows them to be diagnosed and scanned, but if an operation is required that either has to be done by the club's own insurance - some have it and some don't - or on the NHS, which obviously takes a long time. That is why injuries which are resolved in four to six weeks at Super League level take up to four months in the lower divisions.

As an example, in my first season at Batley we had a player - Chris Buttery, who has since moved on to Hunslet Hawks - who had a knee injury which, if it had been covered by private medical insurance, would have kept him out of action for about 10 to 12 weeks. He wasn't insured so he had to get his treatment on the NHS, which meant waiting in line. As a consequence of that he missed the entire season.

The RFL push - and rightly so - things like the State of Mind campaign, which is aimed at protecting players' mental wellbeing, but the sport does not look after them well enough physically and I think that's a scandal. My players at Batley put their bodies on the line every game, just as much as Super League stars do. I think they deserve the same protection.

The fact most players in the lower divisions have full-time jobs alongside their rugby commitments makes things even tougher. Ash Lindsay, one of my mainstays at Batley, broke a hand during the 2012 season, but continued to work, which meant it took longer for the injury to heal and for him to get back on to the field and up to his best level of performance. He wasn't being particularly brave or foolish, but it's simple economics. As Bruce Springsteen says in one of his songs, he don't work and he don't get paid. In Super League, he would have gone for a scan and an X-ray, seen a specialist, had it operated on, potted up or pinned and got plenty of rest until he was able to get back to training. Ash just had to tough it out and let the bone heal naturally.

I have always admired rugby players, at any level, but the dedication and attitude of the part-time lads in the Championship and Championship One staggers me. Take another of the Batley players, Danny Maun, as an example. He's a dustman, he gets up early to start at 6am and does a full, fairly demanding shift, gets a kip for an hour or two after work and then goes training in the evening.

Danny lives in the real world and that's something a lot of Super League players have never experienced. My mate Keith Senior was one of the last of the generation of players who crossed over from the part-time days pre-1996 into the modern, full-time era. Lads like Keith knew what it was like having to earn a living and they were better for it.

Most Super League players now have never experienced that, because they've been full-time since they left school. In fact, we are now starting to get lads coming through who were born after the competition kicked off.

I think it would do a lot of Super League players some good to taste a dose of reality and to find out what it's like out in the real working world. For one thing, it would help prepare them for the day - which comes to us all - when their body can't do it anymore and they have to hang up their boots for good. Rugby league players don't earn enough to set themselves up for life, so they have to find another way of making a living.

Also, it would teach them just how lucky they are to be a full-time professional player. In Super League, every day you hear players moaning about the training surface being poor or their hamstrings are sore, but they'd be even sorer if they had to get up and empty dustbins for eight hours and then turn up for training after that.

All that said, going full-time was a huge step forward for our sport and I really wish I'd had the opportunity in my playing days. The competition has advanced rapidly, it is making strides forward all the time, but I do believe there should be some way of keeping players grounded, so they realise how lucky they are.

Coaching is Chaos

I enjoyed my first season at Batley and I think we had a good year. We finished fifth in the Championship and went out to Sheffield Eagles in the opening round of the play-offs, but we beat all the other teams at our level - other than my old club - at some stage or another, we were competitive every week and I think the players improved individually and as a team.

The playing standard in the Championship impressed me greatly. It is less skilful than Super League, but that is because they are part-time athletes and they don't have as much time to work on things as the top flight players do. But I am pretty certain if you took the top six teams from the Championship, made them full-time and put them in a division with the bottom four teams from Super League, you would have a pretty competitive and entertaining second-tier competition.

There are some good players operating at Championship level, either those who have dropped down from Super League, young kids released from the top division's academy or ones who have come through from the amateur game.

For me, one of the most pleasing things about the 2012 season was the fact two of our players left the club at the end of it to move into Super League. No coach likes losing his best talent, but that's something you've got to accept as a fact of life; players are always ambitious and they want to better themselves and move on to a higher level. It gives me a sense of pride and satisfaction if I can help them do that. It's also a feather in the cap of the club and it proves we are doing things the right way.

The first of those was Alex Brown, a winger, who joined Hull KR. Alex began his career with a Super League club, Huddersfield Giants, but wasn't judged to be good enough and so dropped down a level to Batley. He played for the club under Karl Harrison and scored a couple of tries in the 2010 Northern Rail Cup final win over Widnes Vikings, but then switched codes to try his hand at union with Sale. That didn't work out and I snapped him up when I discovered he wanted to come back. I think Alex initially didn't realise how good he was and lost his way a bit. When he came back for his second stint with Batley his attitude and application was first class, because he had learned his lessons.

Alex Walmsley was an even greater success story. He's a young prop who we signed from the Dewsbury Celtic community club and who had done very well in the student game, with Leeds Metropolitan University. He was still green as grass when we got hold of him, but you could see his raw potential. I saw him as an uncut diamond and when we initially took him on trial I remember telling the club chief executive, Paul Harrison, he would probably play half a dozen games in his first season.

Once he had played two or three he was the first name on my team sheet as an interchange front-rower. He altered the whole flow of the game when he came on and he did that in every match he played. With, I would like to think, some better coaching and the experience of playing at a higher level he came on in leaps and bounds, so much so that St Helens snapped him up on a three-year deal at the end of the season. He is a good 'un and he is one to watch out for at Super League level, mark my words. I will be surprised if he isn't pushing for international honours by the end of his initial Super League contract.

Both Alexes have a big future in the game, but I am not sure about the competition they are leaving behind. It is no secret that the Championship is the poor relation of Super League and it's regarded as a bit of a backwater. Though Premier Sports do a good job with their coverage, it isn't widely seen on TV and gets very little press, away from the local papers. That upsets me because clubs like Batley are as old as the game itself and they are traditional breeding grounds of top players. The RFL, and the Super League clubs, should do more to help clubs like the Bulldogs. There's an old saying, you don't realise how much you need something until it's not there. The game as a whole would suffer massive, irreparable damage if some of its traditional clubs went to the wall.

As for my own future, I hope and believe this isn't the end of the story. I reckon I have still got something to offer to the game, both as a coach and a pundit and if I am being really honest, I haven't given up hope of one day getting back into Super League for one last shot at the big time.

Batley has re-energised me and I will continue to give the club everything I have got, but I am also keeping an eye on what is happening in the full-time game and if an opportunity comes along, I'll think seriously about taking it. There are one or two jobs in Super League which I haven't done yet, that still appeal to me.

I have never made any secret of the fact I would like to coach Castleford Tigers and I think that would be the perfect way to end my career, bringing things full circle. At the moment they have got a good coach, Ian Millward, to whom I genuinely wish all the best. I would never do anything to undermine a fellow coach and I am definitely not after Ian's job. But if a vacancy at Cas ever does arise, then you never say never.

I will continue coaching, at some level, until I don't enjoy it any more. Come that day, then I will pack in, but at the moment I am having as much fun as I've ever had. I am still hungry, still enthusiastic and still enjoying it. There isn't the same pressure at Batley as there is in the full-time game, but the rewards - though maybe not financially - are just as great. There is a fantastic camaraderie among the players and coaching staff and I feel as if I am contributing and making a difference.

I enjoy going to work and what more could anybody want? I can't say there are no regrets when I look back on my coaching career; I still have at least one unfilled ambition which is to win the Challenge Cup with a third different club. Nobody has ever done that and at the moment it looks like I'm not going to get that opportunity, but twice isn't bad and that disappointment is something I can live with.

I have had ups and down; I would have liked to have achieved a bit more as a player - though I accept I was never good enough to go any higher than I did - and if I could go back and change things I would alter the way my time at Hull ended.

But overall I feel very lucky to have spent a lifetime in the sport I love and to have been paid for doing something which - please don't tell the Batley chairman Kevin Nicholas this - I would happily have done for nothing. When the day eventually does come and I call time on my coaching career, that won't be the end of my life in rugby league. The sport is in my blood and it is part of what I am. I could never turn my back on it, nor on my first love Castleford Tigers.

So when I'm not coaching any more I'll be back there as a supporter. At the time I am writing this Cas are struggling on and off the field and there are suggestions they may abandon plans to move to a new ground and instead redevelop Wheldon Road. What effect that will have on their Super League future I don't know, but I won't be totally sorry. It means I might still get the opportunity to buy a season ticket for seat E5 in the main stand, the one occupied by my dad for more than 20 years.

Then whether they are in Super League, the Championship or whatever I'll be back at Cas as a fan, going out the way I came in.

If you enjoyed this, you'll love these from Scratching Shed Publishing Ltd...

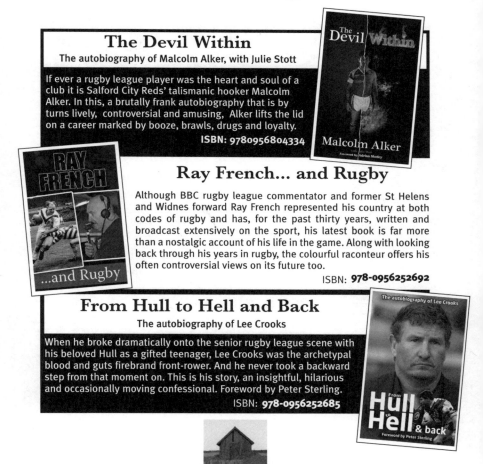
Scratching Shed Publishing Ltd

Scratching Shed Publishing Ltd is an independent publishing company founded in May 2008. We aim to produce high-quality books covering a wide range of subjects - including sport, travel and popular culture - of worldwide interest yet with the distinctive flavour of the North of England.

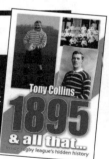

THE STORY OF FOOTBALL:

via the Moors, Dales and Wolds of England's largest and proudest county

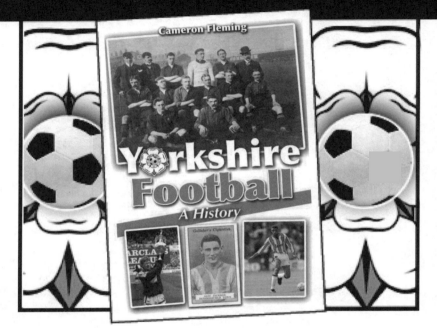

YORKSHIRE FOOTBALL - A HISTORY

Cameron Fleming

ISBN: 978-0956252654

Scratching Shed Publishing Ltd

Scratching Shed Publishing Ltd - Bringing history to life

Border City Blues
The History of Carlisle Rugby League - Alan Tucker

The previously untold story of rugby league football in the proud Cumbrian city of Carlisle. Author Alan Tucker – a former chairman of the club – shares his inside view of the highs and lows and ups and downs of life in English league's most northerly outpost. Foreword by Dean Bell.

ISBN: 9780956478771

Tries & Prejudice
The Autobiography of Ikram Butt

The revealing, hard-hitting and often amusing autobiography of former Featherstone, Leeds and London rugby star Ikram Butt. Born and bred in Leeds and, these days, the driving force behind BARA - the British Asian Rugby Association - England's first muslim rugby international tells his unique life story, whilst also offering an insight into the muslim experience of British sport.

ISBN: 9780956007537

A Lawyer for all Seasons
Tales of celebrated trials and famous sporting personalities

Ronnie Teeman - the longest-serving solicitor in Leeds and former President of the Rugby Football League - has represented or been involved with some of the highest profile sportsmen in the UK. This is his long-anticipated memoir. An inside view of astonishing dramatic events? An entertaining and informative read? Guilty on both counts!

ISBN: **978-0956478788**

Scratching Shed Publishing Ltd

Scratching Shed Publishing Ltd is an independent publishing company founded in May 2008. We aim to produce high-quality books covering a wide range of subjects - including sport, travel and popular culture - of worldwide interest yet with the distinctive flavour of the North of England.

Stay up to date with all our latest releases at
www.scratchingshedpublishing.co.uk